CONSTRUCTING QUESTIONS FOR INTERVIEWS AND QUESTIONNAIRES

CONSTRUCTING QUESTIONS FOR INTERVIEWS AND QUESTIONNAIRES

THEORY AND PRACTICE IN SOCIAL RESEARCH

William Foddy

Department of Anthropology and Sociology, Monash University

CAMBRIDGE
UNIVERSITY PRESS

Published by the Press Syndicate of the University of Cambridge
The Pitt Building, Trumpington Street, Cambridge CB2 1RP, UK
40 West 20th Street, New York, NY 10011–4211, USA
10 Stamford Road, Oakleigh, Melbourne 3166, Australia

First published 1993
Published in paperback 1994
Reprinted 1995

Printed in Hong Kong by Colorcraft

National Library of Australia cataloguing-in-publication data

Foddy, William H. (William Henry).
Constructing questions for interviews and questionnaires:
theory and practice in social research.
Includes bibliographical references and index.
1. Questioning. 2. Questionnaires. 3. Interviewing. I. Title.
302.22

Library of Congress cataloguing-in-publication data

Foddy, William, 1942–
Constructing questions for interviews and questionnaires: theory
and practice in social research / William Foddy.
Includes bibliographical references and index.
1. Sociology – Research – Methodology. 2. Interviewing in
sociology. 3. Questionnaires. 4. Social surveys.
HM48.F57   1992
301'.072–dc20   92–11109
                                                                CIP

A catalogue record for this book is available from the British Library.

ISBN 0 521 46733 0 Paperback

Contents

List of tables

List of figures

Preface

More than forty years ago, George Gallup (1947:385), the director of the American Institute of Public Opinion, observed that:

> students of public opinion are fast coming to the realization that, relatively speaking, too much attention has been directed toward sample design, and too little toward question design . . . differences in question design often bring results which show far greater variation than those normally found by different sampling techniques . . .

Thirty years later, Gallup felt the need to repeat these views in a foreword to a reprinting of Stanley Payne's classic work, *The Art of Asking Questions* (1951):

> While great strides have been made in improved sampling design and technique — and electronic data processing has given us almost immediate access to the survey findings themselves — there has not been a comparable amount of progress in perfecting question or questionnaire design.

About the same time similar comments were made by Belson (1981:11) in his introduction to a report of a major investigation that he and his colleagues had conducted on the way respondents interpret survey questions:

> At the time this study was designed, relatively few reports of empirically based research into the understanding of survey questions had been published. Since the appearance of the present report in mimeograph form, very little else has appeared. It is to nobody's credit that anything so important to survey research should have been so neglected.

Today, another ten years on, it would still have to be said that the theory of question wording has not been as far advanced as one might wish. Although a number of studies have been carried out to increase our understanding of question–answer processes, there are few signs that social researchers have made major improvements in their ways. In his foreword to Payne's book, Gallup suggests that two factors explain this lack of progress. First, the acceptance and growth of survey research in business and the increased dependence of the media and industry on information derived from marketing and opinion polls have spawned a demand for instant results which does not lend itself to concern about how questions should be worded. Second, the growth of the allied social research professions has inevitably drawn many people into the field who have little interest in the methodological issues underlying the collection of verbal data. In the main, social researchers have been content to rely on common sense and a few rules based on past, collective experience. Few attempts have been made to integrate the methodological issues that have been discussed in the literature and little effort has been directed toward applying the conclusions that have been advanced.

Stanley Payne's book, first published in 1951, is still one of the most widely read and cited texts on the methodology of question formulation. Most writers of survey methodology texts have devoted little more than a few pages to the problems associated with the construction of questions to be used in interviews and questionnaires. For instance, the authors of the widely used and respected text, *Research Methods in Social Relations* (Kidder and Judd, 1986, 5th edn), devote fewer than twenty pages to these problems. In similar fashion Converse and Presser (1986) allot less than half of their eighty-page monograph, *Survey Questions: Handcrafting the Standardized Questionnaire*, to them. The other half of their text is spent discussing pre-testing procedures. There have, in fact, been more books devoted to the problems associated with actually conducting interviews than there have to the prior task of formulating questions. There have also been numerous texts on sampling procedures for selecting respondents and on statistical techniques for analysing data once they have been collected. But these books do not allow us to escape the simple truth that questions are the foundation stones upon which most contemporary social science rests. If our ability to ask questions that are understood as intended has not been as good as we might have wished it to be (and there is lots of evidence that this is the case), social science will continue to suffer until something is done about it. As computer buffs are fond of muttering, it is a case of 'garbage in, garbage out'.

Of course the remarks that have just been made should not be construed as suggesting that procedures for collecting verbal data are worse than procedures that produce other kinds of data for the social sciences (e.g. observational procedures, unobtrusive measures and procedures for the content analysis of documentary material). Indeed they are not likely to be. My remarks are meant, however, to suggest that it is high time to press for improvements in the procedures we use to collect verbal data.

This book, then, attempts both to integrate past insights into how questions should be formulated and to develop these insights further. Successive chapters are aimed at reinforcing a number of fundamental but related principles that are assumed to underlie question–answer behaviour. It does not deal with such problems as: how to go about drawing representative samples, how to lay out questionnaires, how to go about actually conducting interviews, or how to go about analysing data once they have been collected. It is not that I do not recognise the importance of these topics, it is simply that I recognise that they have been handled well by others. There are many good books on sampling and applied statistics. In addition, there are books such as Dillman's (1978) book, *Mail and Telephone Surveys: The Total Design Method*, that give a thorough account of how questionnaires and interview schedules should be laid out. Books such as *Contemporary Field Research*, edited by Emerson (1983), and *Standardised Survey Interviewing* by Fowler and Mangione (1990), deal extremely well with the human relations side of unstructured and structured interviews. This book is directed, instead, toward the task of increasing the general level of understanding of the nature of verbal data with the ultimate goal of increasing the validity of the questions we use. It represents an attempt to take interviews and questionnaires seriously, 'in much the same way as physicists take particle accelerators seriously' — one of the recommendations made by the Panel on Survey Measures of Subjective Phenomena of the National Academy of Sciences (Smith, 1984b:228–229).

It should be emphasised that taking questioning procedures seriously does not mean that they are seen as mechanical procedures which can be improved without regard to either the properties of the interactants or the contexts in which they are used. I am sympathetic to the view which has been forcefully expressed by Douglas (1985):

> *Creative interviewing is purposefully situated* interviewing. Rather than denying or failing to see the situation of the interview as a determinant of what goes on in the questioning and answering processes, creative interviewing embraces the immediate, concrete situation; tries to understand how it is affecting what is communicated; and, by understanding these effects, changes the interviewer's communication processes to increase the discovery of the truth about human beings. The structured interviewer is like the ignorant swimmer who fights against a powerful rip tide and finally succumbs to the tide because of exhaustion. Creative interviewers try to divine the flow of the rip and to swim with it in order to eventually gain control of the outcome — saving themselves. You can't beat the reality of human nature and the communication processes that flow from that nature, so you might as well understand them and then work with them to triumph over ignorance and falsehood. (Douglas, 1985:22) [my emphasis]

A basic assumption behind most of the arguments in this text is that question–answer behaviour involves complex interrelationships between sociological, psychological and linguistic variables.

A major issue that is addressed is the question of the degree to which the *kinds* of answers respondents are required to give must be specified if successful communication is to occur between interviewers and respondents. This issue has been at the centre of many past methodological discussions and I have accorded it central significance here. Indeed, the principal thesis advanced in this book is that most of the problems associated with the construction of questions are either avoided or lessened in importance by a clear specification of the kind of answers that respondents should give. I hasten to add that by using the phrase 'kind of answers' I do not want to suggest that respondents should be pressured into giving this or that substantive response. The concept of 'kind of answer' is explained at length in chapters 3–6.

Finally, I would like to stress that, because this book is an attempt to deal with fundamental aspects of question–answer behaviour, it is directed at all those who use questions in social research. Although many of the examples I have used to illustrate particular issues have been taken from the survey research literature, the matters that they raise have a wider relevance. Certainly I had in mind social science in general, and not just social surveys, as I worked on each of the chapters. My hope is that sociologists, anthropologists, political scientists, psychologists, social psychologists, social policy researchers, social workers, pollsters and market researchers will all find the contents of this text useful.

William Foddy

Chapter 1

AN INITIAL
STATEMENT OF THE PROBLEM

There is no doubt that the use of verbal data has come to dominate the social sciences. Asking questions is widely accepted as a cost-efficient (and sometimes the only) way, of gathering information about past behaviour and experiences, private actions and motives, and beliefs, values and attitudes (i.e. subjective variables that cannot be measured directly). A review of practices adopted in the 1960s revealed that:

> the sociologist today limits himself rather generally to the construction and conduct of questionnaires and interviews. In 1940–41, 25 per cent of the 85 empirical studies depended on interviews and questionnaires for their data; in 1965–66, 48 per cent did. However, if we consider studies based on secondary data that, in turn, derived from interviews, then 64 per cent of the 136 research papers in the latter two years were based on such verbal reports.
>
> Increasingly, these verbal reports are limited to expressions of attitudes, feelings, and opinions rather than to factual accounts of past behaviour and interactions. In 1940–41, 8 of the 22 studies using questionnaires and interviews obtained statements about opinions or feelings, 6 focused on actual behaviour and 8 gathered information about both past behaviour and attitudes. In 1965–66, 49 of 66 studies in which interviews were collected dealt only with opinions and sentiment, 6 with behaviour and 8 with both behaviour and attitudes. It would seem that our colleagues tend to ignore actual behavioural patterns and also fail to come to grips with the fundamental problem of the relation of attitudes and sentiment to behaviour. To an even greater extent, sociology is becoming the study of verbally expressed sentiments and feelings, rather than an analysis of human performance. (Brown and Gilmartin, 1969:288)

1

This was the situation in the sixties but there is no reason to believe that the pattern would be any different today — if anything, it is likely to be stronger.

Such an entrenched interest in the use of verbal data would not, in itself, be a bad thing if it could be shown that it always, or even usually, leads to valid conclusions in social research. Unfortunately, it must be admitted that our ability to construct questions which produce data that are reliable and lead to valid conclusions has not been very impressive to date. What is more, recognition of the prevailing situation is far from new. In a report of a survey of expert opinions, Hovde (1936) noted that 74 per cent of the experts who responded mentioned improperly worded questions as a principal defect in commercial social research. The next most frequently mentioned complaint concerned the related issue of faulty interpretations (58 per cent). These figures contrast with 52 per cent mentioning improper statistical methods. The lack of progress since Hovde reported his findings is indicated by Belson's (1986:36) conclusions that the principal causes of error in the gathering of data through survey procedures are:

(a)   respondents' failure to understand questions as intended;

(b)   a lack of effort, or interest, on the part of respondents;

(c)   respondents' unwillingness to admit to certain attitudes or behaviours;

(d)   the failure of respondents' memory or comprehension processes in the stressed conditions of the interview; and,

(e)   interviewer failures of various kinds (e.g. the tendency to change wording, failures in presentation procedures and the adoption of faulty recording procedures).

Examples that illustrate the inadequacy of many of the questions that have been used in social research in the past

It is not difficult to find examples to reinforce the claim that there is a great deal of scope for improving the quality of the data we collect for social research. All ten problems discussed in the next few pages demonstrate this.

Factual questions sometimes elicit invalid answers

Palmer (cited by Deming, 1944) found that, when respondents in a Philadelphia study were re-interviewed eight to ten days after an initial interview, 10 per cent of the reported ages differed by one or more years between the interviews. Likewise, Parry and Crossley (1950) reported that objective checks revealed that 5–17 per cent of a random sample of over 900 Denver residents gave incorrect answers to a series of factual questions. The questions included whether or not respondents had registered and voted in various elections, had contributed to the community chest; and possessed library cards and driving licences, as well as details of car ownership.

If questions concerning such simple and apparently objective matters as 'age' elicit inaccurate data, one must wonder about the validity problems that might be associated with more threatening, more complex, or less well known issues. A summary of the findings of a number of health surveys published by Marquis (1970) indicates how serious the problem might be. Typically 12–17 per cent of known hospital episodes, 23–26 per cent of recorded visits to physicians, and at least 50 per cent of the chronic and acute conditions listed in medical records were not disclosed by respondents.

The relationship between what respondents say they do and what they actually do is not always very strong

Social scientists have long been tempted to assume that respondents' behaviour is congruent with their attitudes. Yet the evidence for this link has never been very strong. This issue was first given salience by LaPiere (1934/35) in a paper which has subsequently been discussed by a number of writers (e.g. Deutscher, 1966 and 1973; Phillips, 1971; Schuman and Johnson, 1976). LaPiere spent some weeks during the 1930s travelling around the United States with a Chinese couple. He kept a record of the way in which they were treated at sixty-six hotels and motels in which they had wanted to stay and 184 restaurants and cafes in which they had wanted to eat — only one establishment had refused them service. Six months later, LaPiere wrote to the places in which they had either been given accommodation or meals, asking the proprietors of each establishment if they would accept members of the Chinese race as guests. Fifty per cent replied to his letters and, of these, 90 per cent said 'No'! This finding focused the spotlight on the apparent fact that respondents do not always do what they say they do.

Findings like those reported by LaPiere have led a number of methodologists (e.g. Cicourel, 1964, 1982; Deutscher, 1966, 1973; Phillips, 1971; Douglas, 1985; Briggs, 1986) to argue that social and social psychological factors which operate in the interview situation invalidate most, if not all, attempts to predict behaviour on the basis of verbally expressed attitudes. The general argument is perhaps extreme; nevertheless, the evidence for a relationship between attitudes and behaviours has always been weak. While this observation might reflect the true nature of the relationship between the concepts, it is also possible that it reflects either a lack of clear conceptualisation of what is being measured and an inadequate theoretical explication of the assumed link between the concepts (see e.g. Weigel and Newman, 1976), or the use of inadequate questions to test hypotheses — this last possibility is discussed in chapter 11.

Respondents' attitudes, beliefs, opinions, habits, interests often seem to be extraordinarily unstable

Twentieth-century social science has predominantly been directed by behaviourist, reductionist and naturalist premises — namely that the objects of inquiry (i.e 'the stuff out there') has two primary properties: stability and accessibility. And yet available evidence suggests that many sorts of respondents' answers are strikingly variable over time. Converse (1964), for example, reports very low correlations between attitudes expressed by the same respondents over a two-year period. In another study, Bishop *et al*. (1984) found that respondents were less likely to claim that they follow what is going on in public affairs if they had first responded to a set of difficult questions about a congressman's record than if they had to answer the questions about the congressman's record after they had reported their own interest in public affairs. In a third study, Gritching (1986) asked respondents the same question (designed to measure their attitudes toward the setting up of a gambling casino in their community) at the start and at the end of an interview schedule. Gritching reports that 17.6 per cent of the respondents changed their position during the course of the interview.

The results of the studies that have just been reviewed leave us in the position of not knowing whether the observed variation is due to: true variability in the respondents' memory processes (a topic that we will return to in chapter 7), inadequacies or instability in the interpretation of the questions themselves, the impact of cognitions that have been stimulated by earlier questions, the impact of social-psychological variables (e.g. interviewer–respondent status differences — discussed in chapter 9); or the tendency for respondents to spontaneously ask interviewers for their views during interviews (discussed by Oakley, 1981).

Small changes in wording sometimes produce major changes in the distribution of responses

This problem is nicely illustrated by results from Butler and Kitzinger's study of the response distributions for different questions that were formulated by National Opinion Polls to gauge the British people's attitudes toward entering the European Common Market in 1975 (Butler and Kitzinger, 1976:60). On the one hand, the difference between the percentages of 'pro' and 'anti' responses for the question: 'Do you accept the government's recommendation that the

United Kingdom should *come out of* the Common Market?', was 0.2 per cent in favour of the 'pro' Market position. On the other hand, for the question: 'Do you accept the government's recommendation that the United Kingdom should *stay in* the Common Market?' the difference between the percentages of 'pro' and 'anti' responses was 18.2 per cent in favour of the 'pro' Market position.

A second example that demonstrates the impact that supposedly innocent changes in question wording can have is provided by Bishop *et al.* (1978), who conclude that apparent 'trends' in attitudes over the last thirty years in the United States are likely to be due to changes in the format of the questions that have been used in surveys. Before 1964, the Michigan Survey Research Center asked respondents if they had an opinion about an issue before asking them to rate the issues on a 7-point scale ('No opinion — Agree strongly, Agree but not very strongly, Not sure . . . it depends, Disagree but not very strongly, Disagree strongly, — Don't know'). Between 1964 and 1972, a dichotomised format was used: 'Some people feel X while others feel Y; have you been interested enough to side with X or Y?' After 1972, respondents were told that, 'Some people feel X while others think Y and of course some people have opinions somewhere between', before being asked where they would place themselves on a 7-point numeric scale (with alternative X being paired with 1 and alternative Y being paired with 7). The post-1972 scale does not include either a 'No opinion' or a 'Don't know' response option. Whereas the format used prior to 1964 eliminated one-third of the respondents and the format used from 1964 to 1972 eliminated less that one-sixth of the respondents, the format used after 1972 hardly eliminated any respondents. In other words, after 1972, all respondents were forced to give answers to the questions whether or not they had preformed opinions to give, or had been interested in the topic in the past. Bishop *et al.* suggest that differences between the filtering power of each of the formats used (i.e. their ability to eliminate respondents for whom the topic is not relevant) are great enough to account for the apparent changes in public opinion in the United States since the fifties.

A third example that illustrates the effects of what, on the surface, appear to be harmless differences in wording comes from an Australian newspaper (the Melbourne *Age* 6/7/85:3). It was reported that when respondents in a national survey had been asked to rate the performance of the two main federal parliamentary parties on a scale of 'Very good' to 'Very bad', 39 per cent thought the prime minister was doing a good job and 27 per cent thought the same of the leader of the opposition. It was also noted in the same report, however, that two other national polls which had been conducted about the same time had found that 47 per cent approved of the prime minister while 48 per cent approved of his opponent; and 56 per cent saw the incumbent as making the better prime minister, compared with 27 per cent thinking the same for the leader of the opposition. Since the differences between the percentages are too large to be ascribed to sampling differences, it has to be concluded that 'doing a good job', being 'approved of' and being seen as 'making the better prime minister' must be quite different matters — even though there would have been little reason to suspect this before the polls were conducted.

Last, lest it be thought that only opinion or attitude questions are susceptible to the effects of small differences in wording, it is worth noting that even questions about supposedly simple matters of fact can be vulnerable. Peterson (1984) has reported the results of a study that was designed to compare the non-response rates associated with different ways of asking respondents for their age. Whereas only 3.2 per cent of a random sample of registered voters failed to answer the question 'What is your age?', the question 'How old are you?', put to a similar sample, produced a 9.7 per cent non-response rate. Again, a researcher would have had no reason to anticipate this outcome before the experiment was carried out.

Respondents commonly misinterpret questions

A number of writers have discussed this problem at length (e.g. Cantril and Fried, 1944; Nuckols, 1953; Cannell, 1977; Belson, 1981, 1986; Hunt *et al.*, 1982). Nuckols (1953) discusses the results of an experiment in which nine questions that had been used by a national polling organisation were re-presented to a sample of respondents who were asked to repeat in their own words their interpretations of them. In all, 17 per cent of the interpretations given were judged to be either partially or wholly incorrect. Belson (1981) investigated respondents' interpretation of a number of common words including 'usually', 'generally', 'people', 'children' and 'weekday', and concludes that even these words elicit a wide range of different interpretations. Cannell (1977:44) presents similar data. It would appear that variation in the way respondents interpret everyday words is a common feature of questions used in social research.

Answers to earlier questions can affect respondents' answers to later questions

Available evidence suggests that 'contrast' and 'consistency' effects can be generated by prior questions. Rugg and Cantril (1944:28) found that the proportions of respondents agreeing with the idea that Americans should be allowed to enlist in: (a) the French army and (b) the German army, were affected by the order in which the questions concerning the two armies were presented. And Noelle-Neumann (1970) found that, when German respondents were asked to rate various foods in terms of how 'German' they were, potatoes were seen as being particularly 'German' by more respondents if that item followed rather than preceded rice.

No doubt it is because of the perceived likelihood of the occurrence of order effects that most methodologists advocate asking general questions about a topic before going on to more specific questions about it. Certainly, answers to prior specific questions often seem to influence answers to later, more general questions, although the nature of this influence is not always the same. Sometimes a consistency effect seems to operate and sometimes a redundancy effect seems to operate. For example, a consistency effect occurs when respondents are asked to indicate how often they pray before being asked to indicate how religious they think they are — that is, respondents who have just reported that they pray a lot are more likely to say that they are very religious (McFarland, 1981). A redundancy effect appears to occur, however, when respondents are asked about how happy they are with their work before being asked about how happy they are in general — that is, respondents seem to exclude consideration of work when answering the second question (see Strack and Martin, 1987; McClendon and O'Brien, 1988; note: we will return to these issues on pages 61–66 of chapter 5).

Changing the order in which response options are presented sometimes affects respondents' answers

The order in which response options are presented sometimes affects the probabilities of respondents selecting particular options. More specifically, it appears that respondents are more likely to endorse the options that they see first when they are able to read the items for themselves, and more likely to endorse items that they hear last when the items are read out aloud to them (e.g. Krosnick and Alwin, 1987). Notwithstanding these findings, it also appears to be the case that the first response option in a list has a greater impact on evaluative judgements than the last. Thus respondents who are asked to indicate which income category they fall into tend, if the categories are arranged in ascending order, to endorse lower categories than they would if they were arranged in descending order (Locander and Burton, 1976).

Respondents' answers are sometimes affected by the question format per se

Open ended questions (i.e. questions that allow respondents to supply their own answers) often produce quite different results from closed ended versions of the same questions (i.e. questions that force respondents to select a response from a pre-set list of alternatives). Two issues seem to differentiate the two formats. In the first place, respondents are more likely to endorse a particular option if it has been explicitly listed than they are if they have to spontaneously think of it for themselves. In the second place, it has been found that respondents often give very different types of answers to open questions than they do to congruent closed questions.

The following two examples demonstrate the fact that respondents are more likely to endorse an answer if it has been explicitly listed for them than if it has not. The first is provided by Belson and Duncan (1962:160), who found that a checklist question yielded higher periodical and newspaper readership rates than a comparable open question — for one periodical (the *Radio Times*) the percentage of respondents who checked it on the checklist was over five times the percentage who mentioned it when answering the open version of the question (38% : 7%). The second example comes from Schuman and Presser (1981:86). They report that, whereas 22 per cent of a sample of respondents who had been presented with an open question about what they thought was the most important problem facing the country mentioned the energy shortage, less than 1 per cent of a sample presented with a comparable closed question, which did not specifically include this issue as an option, mentioned it.

That respondents often give quite different kinds of answers to equivalent questions is illustrated by results reported by Schuman and Presser (1981). Some of the respondents, who gave the answer 'the pay' to an open question about what they would most prefer in a job, were subsequently found to have meant 'high pay' while others had meant 'steady pay'.

Respondents often answer questions even when it appears that they know very little about the topic

Respondents frequently answer questions that appear to be marginally relevant to them or about which they have thought little.

It has been found, for instance, that up to 25 per cent of respondents will check substantive options when a 'Don't know' is not offered but check a 'Don't know' option when it is offered (Schuman and Presser, 1981:186). And Ferber (1956) notes that in a random sample of 600 residents of Champaign Urbana, between 14 and 62 per cent of the 50 per cent of respondents who did not know about particular items in an array of topics, still volunteered opinions about them. Similarly, Gallup (1978:1176, cited by Smith, 1984a:221) found that, while 96 per cent of a national sample offered opinions about the importance of a balanced Federal budget, 25 per cent did not know whether the budget was balanced or not, 8 per cent wrongly thought that the budget was balanced, 40 per cent thought that it was unbalanced but did not know by how much, and 25 per cent thought that it was not balanced but either underestimated or over-estimated the amount it was out of balance by more than 15 per cent. In all, Gallup estimates that a mere 3 per cent of the respondents offered an answer that was based on accurate information. Other evidence that relates to respondents' willingness to offer answers that are not well grounded in knowledge comes from studies in which respondents have been asked about either fictitious or extremely obscure topics. Typically, these studies have disclosed that up to 30 per cent of the respondents have been prepared to answer the questions as if they dealt with topics that were real and familiar to them. (See Smith [1984a:223] for a review of the literature.)

The cultural context in which a question is presented often has an impact on the way respondents interpret and answer questions

An example that illustrates the importance of the context in which a question is asked is provided by Briggs (1986), who discusses an ethnic survey that was designed to assess the way a neighbourhood facility could best meet the demands of the residents in the area. He notes that it almost failed because a key question was interpreted quite differently by Navajo respondents, as compared to Zuni, Mexican-American and Anglo-American respondents. The level of demand for services indicated by the Navajo was much lower than that for each of the other groups. While this could have been interpreted as meaning that the Navajo were much less interested than the others in using the services, Briggs realised that the Navajo had not answered the question in the same manner as the other ethnic groups because of their cultural beliefs. Apparently the Navajo deem it highly inappropriate to speculate about the beliefs held by others. In their culture, such talk is seen as a usurpation of others' decision-making powers.

> Speculating on the preferences of one's spouse and children would accordingly be deemed extremely rude. Rather than doing so, Navajo respondents would estimate which services they themselves would be likely to use. The use of a probe to obtain data on the family members generally yielded statements such as 'no, I don't think so . . .'. (Briggs, 1986:97)

Critiques of past practices

Perhaps because of the sorts of problems discussed above, several trenchant critiques of the use of questionnaires and interviews in social research have been published over the last two decades (see, e.g., Deutscher, 1966, 1973; Phillips,

1971; Cicourel, 1964, 1982; Douglas, 1985; Mishler, 1986; Briggs, 1986; Pawson, 1989). Cicourel sums up the situation in the following way:

> Despite the fact that virtually all social science data are derived from some kind of discourse or textual materials, sociologists have devoted little time to establishing explicit theoretical foundations for the use of such instruments as interviews and surveys. A key problem has been the lack of clear theoretical concepts about the interpretation of interview and survey question and answer frames. We lack a theory of comprehension and communication that can provide a foundation for the way question–answer systems function . . . (Cicourel, 1982:Abstract)

Yet for all the criticism, reliance on verbal data does not appear to be in any danger of waning. Indeed many critics (e.g. Phillips, 1971; Cicourel, 1982; Briggs, 1986 and Pawson, 1989) have implicitly recognised this and have directed their analyses toward improving rather than demolishing current methodological practices. Cicourel acknowledges the value of interviews for many 'theoretical purposes' and takes for granted that a number of old issues have been generally resolved. He assumes, for example, that it is generally accepted that qualitative interviews should normally precede the construction of formalised questions. He also assumes that it is necessary to pre-test the resulting questions to ensure both that respondents understand them and that answer categories reflect respondents' thinking. Briggs continues in the same vein by suggesting several procedures which, if followed, might help to sensitise the researcher to the communicative norms that prevail in the respondents' community. He advocates, for instance, that the researcher undertake preliminary pilot work to discover who talks to whom; who listens when individuals talk and when they remain silent; the ways in which individuals communicate with one another; how questions are asked; and what sort of questions are seen as legitimate. He suggests, too, employing other procedures — for example, video tapes — to help discover how, and what, individuals communicate; to allow the researcher to look at the same interactions several times to identify underlying assumptions or perspectives adopted by interactants, and to allow respondents to reflect and comment upon the researcher's interpretations of their interactions. And Phillips stresses both that social psychological factors (e.g. interviewer–respondent social status differences) have to be taken into account and that interview behaviour is a form of social interaction and should be analysed accordingly.

Thus, Cicourel, Briggs and Phillips all imply that question–answer situations are more complex than have generally been appreciated. Their arguments suggest that questions and answers should be understood in relation not only to one another but also to the social contexts in which they operate. The important implication of these arguments is that it is not enough to arbitrarily limit attention to aspects of questions themselves; to the way properties of questions interact with the cognitions and motivations of the interviewers and respondents, or to the properties of the relationship between interviewers and respondents. We must come to grips with the idea that all of these elements somehow constitute a dynamic, interrelated set of elements.

Summary

The use of verbal data has been made the keystone of contemporary social science and there is no sign of this situation changing. There is much evidence, nevertheless, to support the conclusion that the verbal data we collect are very often of dubious validity and reliability. It is also clear that we have lacked a proper understanding of the causes of these shortcomings. This is not to say that other kinds of data used in the social sciences suffer from less severe validity and reliability problems. Rather, attention has been directed at the problems associated with verbal data simply because the use of verbal data plays such a major part in contemporary social research.

Up to now the most influential attempts to provide a basis for improving interview or question–answer methodology have been based on efforts to summarise a huge number of diverse, *ad hoc* research findings (see, e.g., Sudman and Bradburn, 1974; Van der Zouwen and Dijkstra, 1982). Efforts to provide a more sophisticated basis for the formulation of question wording have been hampered by the lack of an encompassing theoretical framework, although a number of methodologists have made suggestions about the possible directions that might be taken. Phillips (1971), for instance, has stressed the social interactional nature of question–answer situations. Cicourel (1982) has stressed the relevance of cognitive and linguistic processes and the idea that question–answer behaviour should be treated as a form of communication. And Douglas (1985) and Briggs (1986) have stressed the impact of contextual variables on the way respondents interpret questions. The suggestions made by these writers should be taken on board, if for no other reason than the fact that no great improvements have been made over the last fifty years to our techniques for collecting verbal data.

Chapter 2

A THEORETICAL FRAMEWORK

In this chapter we address the need for a theoretical framework within which the methodological assumptions underlying the use of verbal data in social research can be discussed. A theoretical analysis of these assumptions is necessary because they inevitably influence the way we go about collecting data about the social worlds in which we are interested. If we want to improve our ability to formulate questions which work in the way we want them to work, we must understand the methodological implications of the assumptions underlying the procedures we use.

Leaving aside the reasons for the current state of affairs, for most of this century the social sciences have been characterised by two broad approaches to collecting verbal data. On one side we have had the increasingly dominant survey researchers who have tended to go about their work in a way that might be compared to the way physical scientists go about theirs. They have typically proceeded with the positivistic orientation that they are either discovering or describing an 'objective', 'real' world 'out there' and that their measures have 'true' values. To this end, they have typically employed a stimulus–response model which assumes that each question is understood in the same way by all respondents. Because the stimulus–response model implies both that each stimulus must be carefully standardised and that each respondent will only give one response to each stimulus, survey researchers have favoured the use of forced choice questions (otherwise referred to as closed questions). Here respondents are required to choose one response from a pre-set array of response options. The fact that questions are carefully standardised, coupled with the fact that each respondent is required to give one and only one standardised response to each question, leads survey researchers to assume that different respondents' responses to each question can be meaningfully compared.

More specifically, the approach adopted by the survey researchers is defined by a number of assumptions that have been identified and discussed (usually critically, but not always so) by a number of writers (e.g. Dijkstra and Van der Zouwen, 1977; Oakley, 1981; Davies, 1982; Cicourel 1982; Van der Zouwen, 1982 and Brenner 1985). The most important of these are listed below.

The principal assumptions that have defined the general orientation adopted by survey researchers in the past

1 The researcher has clearly defined the topic about which information is required.
2 Respondents have the information that the researcher requires.
3 Respondents are able to access the required information under the conditions of the research situation.
4 Respondents can understand each question as the researcher intends it to be understood.
5 Respondents are willing (or, at least, can be motivated) to give the required information to the researcher.
6 The answers that respondents give to a particular question are more valid if they have not been told why the researcher is asking the question.
7 The answers that respondents give to a particular question are more valid if the researcher has not suggested them to the respondents.
8 The research situation *per se* does not influence the nature of the answers given by respondents.
9 The process of answering questions *per se* does not change the respondents' beliefs, opinions, habits, etc.
10 The answers that different respondents give to a particular question can be meaningfully compared with one another.

In Pawson's words, the survey researcher's goal

> of creating common meaning in the exchange of questions and answers is attacked by what one might refer to as the 'lowest common denominator' approach. Questions are asked in the simplest possible form which will nevertheless remain faithful to the conceptual intentions of the researcher. To these ends, the major effort of this school can be summarized in the oft-stated goals that the interview schedule should be clear, precise, unambiguous, intelligible, etc., and not leading, hypothetical, embarrassing, memory defeating and so forth. Great care is also taken over question form, dealing with such matters as whether to phrase questions negatively or positively, whether to include don't know categories, how to arrange the sequence of questions and so forth. Since the stimulus is compound and includes both the interviewers and their questions, equivalent care is taken to neutralise and standardise social and personal factors which might affect the nature of the response . . .

> [A]ttention paid to question and situation management is in aid of gaining knowledge of the respondent's 'true opinion' or a 'true record' of the activities . . . (Pawson, 1989:291–292)

The essence of the traditional survey model is expressed schematically in figure 2.1 (below).

The important point to notice about the model set out in the figure is that responsibility for controlling the question–answer process is entirely exercised by the researcher. Not only does the researcher try to formulate questions that have standardised meanings for all respondents but the researcher tries to prescribe the ways in which the questions can be answered.

Turning to the other side, we have a group of researchers representing a variety of different theoretical persuasions who can nevertheless all be subsumed under the label 'qualitative field researchers'. This group includes cultural anthropologists, ethnographers and ethnomethodologists. The members of this group accept the phenomenological or subjectivist point of view that social science should be interested in how human beings 'experience' their worlds rather than how physical events impact upon one another. They favour the use of data collecting procedures that they hold to be sensitive to the actors' meanings — for example, procedures that are based on prolonged, intimate immersion in the social interaction in question or the use of non-directive, open questions that respondents answer in their own words rather than in terms of pre-set response categories. As Collins (1983:71) puts it:

> The method is the same as is used by members absorbing a new system of categories, or language, or way of seeing. This method consists of interacting with the native

Figure 2.1   *The traditional survey model*

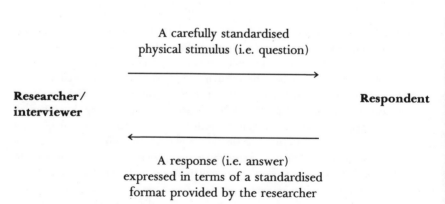

members as much as possible, until their way of life has been absorbed. Competence is indicated when the new member can act in new situations with confidence and without making mistakes.

To a person, the qualitative researchers are scathing in their denunciation of the survey researchers' failure to attend seriously to the commonplace observations that different respondents often give quite different interpretations to the same question, and that the answer given by a particular respondent to a question in one social situation is often quite different to the answer given by the same respondent in another situation. Qualitative researchers take as axiomatic the principle that the behaviour exhibited by actors in any social situation depends upon the way they have defined that situation. They accept the dictum first expressed by W. I. Thomas and discussed at length by Robert Merton (1957:chapter 11) that: 'If men define a situation as real then it is real in its consequences'. Because they believe that, in order to understand the way human beings behave in a given situation, one must understand how the actors define that situation, they also believe that any explanation of social behaviour must be formulated in terms of the concepts the actors themselves use to make sense of the situation in which they find themselves.

Pawson (1989:292–293) sums up the qualitative researchers' position in the following way. They are:

> committed to understanding the respondent's 'meaning' and so regard data collection as a task for inducing everyday talk within unstructured interviews in near-to-naturalistic settings ... [They] ... have no truck with ... any notion of the interview as a stimulus–response system. They assume that even identical, plain words, identically and plainly delivered by identical and plain interviewers can still mean quite different things to different people ...
>
> What is distinctive about sociological inquiry is that human behaviour is intentional and that our subjects are meaning creators. Since it is assumed that the basis of action lies in the intelligibility of the social world to the subjects, steps must be taken to ensure that the research act is intelligible to them. In order to penetrate the meaningful world of the subject it is thus necessary for the researcher to engage in a process of joint construction of meaning ...
>
> Such principles demand a rather different kind of practice. Ideally the joint construction of meaning takes place over many months of ethnographic study, although it is sometimes allowed that the informal unstructured interview can act as an imperfect substitute for this. In terms of interview language, apart from the topic of inquiry, no frame of reference is imposed upon the subject. There are no dilemmas over question wording and question sequence because the nature of the interview is conversational. Data thus emerge as a narrative and not in the form of ticks in pre-coded boxes ...

Criticisms of both approaches

The most common criticism of the survey researchers is that their pre-set response categories determine the way the respondents can answer a question, making it impossible to evaluate the validity of their answers. Put another way, it is argued that the provision of sets of response options may cause respondents to give answers which they would not think of if they had to supply answers themselves.

The survey researchers, however, are not alone in being criticised. The qualitative field researchers also run into their share of criticism. Katz (1983:127), for example, points out that four questions are repeatedly raised about qualitative field research. These concern the probability that observations are selectively reported so that it is impossible to gauge the extent to which they are typical; the probability that the very act of conducting the research influences the respondents' behaviour; the fact that interpretations typically have very low levels of reliability because of the low level of control over the selection of data for analysis; and the difficulty of replicating findings. Katz notes:

> Qualitative field studies appear especially vulnerable to criticism because they do not proceed from fixed designs. They do not use formats for sampling that could produce statistics on the representativeness of data. They abjure coding books that might enhance reliability by spelling out in advance the criteria for analysing data. They fail to give detailed instructions for interviews — the questions to ask, their order, when to give cues and when to probe — that might give the reader faith that differences in subjects' responses were not due to variations in the researchers' behaviour. Because of their emphasis on informal and flexible methods, qualitative field studies seem to make replication impossible. (Katz, 1983:128)

It should be added that, even if qualitative field researchers honestly strive to 'absorb' the culture (i.e. the organising concepts and rules which govern the perceptions and behaviour) of the members of a social group, in the final analysis they have either to infer or to guess the nature of the cultural elements. For this reason, it can be argued that qualitative researchers are little better placed to claim that they have properly understood their subjects' behaviour than are researchers who adopt a more positivistic approach. Qualitative researchers cannot directly ask subjects to confirm the validity of their inferences without exposing themselves to all of the criticisms (e.g. of suggesting answers to respondents) that they themselves make of the way the survey researchers work. At best they have to rely upon subjective impressions of their ability to properly understand their subjects' behaviour — for example, they have to rely upon such things as their confidence that they can reliably appreciate, understand and even anticipate, the reactions to disturbances, jokes and moral judgements that their subjects might make (Collins, 1983).

The key issue: the comparability of answers

It would seem reasonable to assume that, if a question–answer sequence is to make sense, the question must be understood by the respondent in the way intended by the researcher and the answer given by the respondent must be understood by the researcher in the way intended by the respondent. Although these two statements may appear, on the surface, to be straightforward, they slip over a host of complexities. Minimally, one might argue that four steps must occur in a successful question–answer sequence:

(a)   the researcher must be clear about the nature of the information required and encode a request for this information;

(b)   the respondent must decode this request in the way the researcher intends it to be decoded;

(c)   the respondent must encode an answer that contains the information the researcher has requested; and,

(d)   the researcher must decode the answer as the respondent intended it to be decoded.

Each of these steps must go smoothly if a question is to 'work' properly. Unfortunately, there is a great deal of scope, at each step, for the sequence to break down. While survey researchers usually try to ensure that question–answer sequences will be successful by defining key terms for respondents and providing sets of response options, qualitative researchers try to achieve the same end by accepting the principles that key terms should be both provided and defined by the respondents themselves and by giving the respondents the freedom to formulate their own answers. Presumably, either approach would work if the necessary total control could be exercised by the researcher in the first instance and by the respondent in the second. It has never been demonstrated, however, that total control has been established by one of the parties in a question–answer situation. Many of the examples cited in chapter 1 demonstrate how apparently small changes in the wording of closed questions have had major, unanticipated, effects upon the resultant response distributions. This is surely evidence that survey researchers all too often fail to control the way respondents interpret their questions. In the case of qualitative research, it is clear that open-ended questions often elicit extraordinarily diverse kinds of responses, which suggests that they have received an equally wide range of interpretations (see Campbell, 1945; Schuman and Presser, 1979a). It is significant, too, that respondents presented with open ended questions often appear to look to the interviewer for guidance. This phenomenon is caught by Mishler (1986) who observes that if a researcher

> remains silent after the initial response, neither explicitly acknowledging or commenting on the answer nor proceeding immediately to the next question, respondents tend to hesitate, show signs of searching for something else to say, and usually

continue with additional content. Sometimes they look for a sign that the interviewer understands or try to elicit a direct assessment with a query like 'you know?'. Their 'answers' are as responsive to his assessments as to the original questions. They display the respondents' effort to arrive at a shared understanding of the meanings of both questions and answers. (Mishler, 1986:57)

Mishler goes on to provide an excerpt from the transcript of an unstructured interview which neatly captures the joint struggle made by a researcher and respondent to disambiguate a question about the 'high' and 'low' points in the respondent's life.

I.   [What] I'd like are times that were high points or low points in the marriage . . . as you reflect back on it what would be the best time for your marriage?

R.   Well the best times were the years that the children were growing up . . . If you want a literal interpretation of a high point I can't seem to make too much differentiation between the two. We went through a period where you know we didn't have any money . . . [R. continues]

I.   You wouldn't call those times troubling times? Low points in that sense?

R.   Well they . . . weren't troubles in the sense of real troubles . . . but they were . . . enforced lean times . . . [R. continues with extended account of the cost of medical care for a sick child to demonstrate how he succeeded in coping with adversity.]

I.   Part of the question is what would you count as high or low points . . . Not every year has to be a high or a low point.

R.   No I Know. I — I can't make a tangible construction out of this in terms of definite high points and low points . . .

I.   Well let me ask you the question a little bit differently . . . If you think back maybe five or six years ago . . . you might think of . . . a good year or some stretch of time, that you might think of as being what I'm calling a high point.

R.   Oh well there was . . . a time I started my own business . . . and . . . as you might expect there were very trying times . . .

I.   That would be what you call a low point? (Mishler, 1986:60–62. Transcript shortened, new format by the author.)

This excerpt is also of interest because it indicates how different interviewer–respondent pairs are likely to negotiate quite different definitions for the central concepts that govern the conversations in which they take part. It is not uncommon for conversations between different interviewers and respondents that are supposedly about the same topics to follow quite different trajectories. Indeed, earlier in his text, Mishler provides transcript material that perfectly demonstrates this (Mishler, 1986:38–45).

The main point, again is that it is probably not possible for one of the parties in a question–answer interaction to exert perfect control over either the definition of the situation or the interpretation of a question. It happens that this conclusion is congruent with the general view of social behaviour advanced by symbolic interactionists, a school of sociological theorists. The fact is, the basic tenets of symbolic interactionism throw a great deal of light upon the processes underlying question–answer behaviour. For this reason, it is worth taking a more detailed look at them.

Symbolic interactionist theory

The term 'symbolic interactionism' was coined by the sociologist Herbert Blumer, who has been a lifelong advocate of a set of ideas first put forward by the social philosopher George Herbert Mead. Blumer (1967, 1969) concisely lists the key ideas that define the way symbolic interactionists view social interaction. Symbolic interactionists would argue that these ideas go a long way toward capturing the fundamental characteristics of human behaviour — including question–answer behaviour.

The following is a list of the tenets identified by Blumer:

1 Human beings interpret and define each other's actions. They do not merely react to each other in a simple stimulus–response fashion. Responses are not made to acts but rather to 'interpreted' acts — that is, to the meaning social actors ascribe to one another's acts.
2 Human beings can be the objects of their own attention. In other words, they can act toward themselves as they act toward others. Mead used the concept of 'self' to refer to this phenomenon. Social actors have selves to the extent that they can orient to themselves as objects, as others orient to them as objects. That social actors have selves is indicated by the way they get angry with themselves, blame themselves, take pride in themselves, argue with themselves, and so on.
3 Conscious social behaviour is intentional behaviour. Human beings construct and rehearse different possible lines of action in their imagination before choosing how to act in a given social situation.
4 Interpreting, planning and acting are ongoing processes which begin anew at every stage of a social interaction. Further, both parties in a dyadic interaction engage in these processes. Basic to these processes is the fact that each actor takes not only his or her own view of the other into account but the other's views of him- or her- self, when constructing, and choosing, possible lines of action.
5 Mead referred to the general process of taking another into account when imaginatively constructing possible lines of action as 'taking-the-role' of the other. Along with the observation that social actors have selves, the observation that human intelligence is, in part, reflexive in character is especially important. Social interaction

  takes the form of a fitting together of individual lines of action. Each individual

> aligns his action to the action of others by ascertaining what they are doing or what they intend to do — that is, by getting the meaning of their acts. For Mead, this is done by the individual 'taking the role' of the others — either the role of a specific person or the role of a group (Mead's 'generalised other'). In taking such roles the individual seeks to ascertain the intention or direction of the acts of others. This is the fundamental way in which group action takes place. (Blumer, 1967:184)

(See Thomas *et al.* (1972) and Foddy (1978) for discussions of empirical investigations that provide clear support for Mead's ideas regarding role-taking in social interaction.)

6   Finally, Blumer takes pain to stress that these processes occur in all social situations — long established social situations as well as newly formed ones — although they will be most obvious in newly formed situations as the interactants struggle to align their behaviours with one another.

> Usually, most of the situations encountered by people in a given society are defined and 'structured' by them in the same way. Through previous interaction they develop and acquire common understandings or definitions of how to act in this or that situation. The common repetitive behaviour of people in such situations should not mislead the student into believing that no process of interpretation is in play; on the contrary, even though fixed, the actions of the participating people are constructed by them through a process of interpretation. Since ready-made and commonly accepted definitions are at hand, little strain is placed on people in guiding and organising their acts. However, many other situations may not be defined in a single way by the participating people. In this event, their lines of action do not fit together readily and collective action is blocked. Interpretations have to be developed and effective accommodation of the participants to one another has to be worked out . . . (Blumer, 1967:187–188)

In brief, symbolic interactionists claim that social actors in any social situation are constantly negotiating a shared definition of the situation; taking one another's viewpoints into account; and interpreting one another's behaviour as they imaginatively construct possible lines of interaction before selecting lines of action for implementation.

The implications of symbolic interaction theory for social research

The basic propositions of symbolic interaction theory have been listed above because they bear upon the limits of the assumptions which underpin both qualitative field research and quantitative survey research.

Neither survey researchers nor qualitative field researchers have paid much attention to how respondents take-the-role of the researcher when framing an answer. Nor have they paid much attention to the possibility that the respondents' perceptions of the researcher's purpose for asking a question will influence their answers. They have paid little attention to the possibility that respondents' perceptions of the way the researcher sees them will influence their answers. And they have almost totally ignored the possibility that the way the research situation is defined will influence the manner in which interactants interpret one another's acts (i.e., questions and answers).

The most basic implication of symbolic interaction theory for social researchers is the hypothesis that the meaning ascribed to social acts is a product of the relationship within which those acts take place. Symbolic interaction theory predicts that respondents will constantly try to reach a mutually shared definition of the situation with the researcher. If researchers fail to indicate how they define their research situations, respondents will search for clues (and even make guesses about the researchers' definitions of the situations), to help them interpret the researchers' acts. They will try to ascertain the researchers' reasons for asking the questions, determine what assumptions the researchers hold regarding them, and so on. If the researchers do not indicate precisely what kind of information is required, the respondents will search for clues about the kind of information the researchers require. If questions are not clearly expressed, respondents will do their best to clarify them for themselves so that they can answer them. A model of this portrait of question–answer behaviour is set out in figure 2.2 (page 22).

More to the point, if respondents typically search for contextual clues to help them interpret a question, different respondents may attend to different clues so that they end up with quite different interpretations of the question. When this happens, it makes little sense for the researcher to compare different respondents' answers with one another, since the different answers are, in essence, answers to different questions.

In passing, it should also be pointed out that if the hypothesis that researchers and respondents role-take with one another when they seek to formulate and interpret questions answers is taken seriously, several of the assumptions identified as underpinning survey research (at the start of this chapter) will be seen to be in need of modification. For instance, if respondents are left to guess about the researcher's purpose, different respondents may very well make quite different guesses and consequently interpret a question quite differently. Thus it has to be recognised that not telling respondents the reason for asking a particular question is quite likely to lead to a decrease rather than an increase in standardisation.

Before concluding this chapter, it should be noted too that the sources of variability in how respondents interpret questions that the symbolic interactionists have stressed are not the only ones about which the researcher has to worry. There are at least four additional sources of response variability that the researcher should keep in mind when formulating questions. It will suffice, for

Figure 2.2 *A model of the symbolic interactionist view of question–answer behaviour*

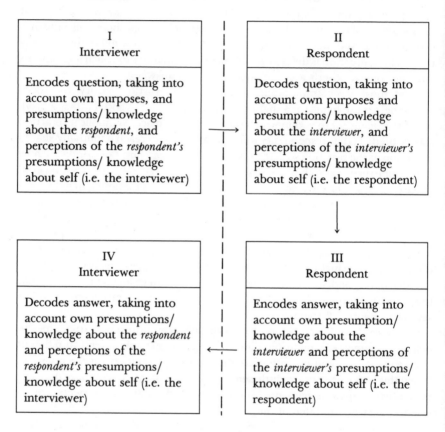

I Interviewer	II Respondent
Encodes question, taking into account own purposes, and presumptions/ knowledge about the *respondent*, and perceptions of the *respondent's* presumptions/ knowledge about self (i.e. the interviewer)	Decodes question, taking into account own purposes and presumptions/ knowledge about the *interviewer*, and perceptions of the *interviewer's* presumptions/ knowledge about self (i.e. the respondent)
IV Interviewer	III Respondent
Decodes answer, taking into account own presumptions/ knowledge about the *respondent* and perceptions of the *respondent's* presumptions/ knowledge about self (i.e. the interviewer)	Encodes answer, taking into account own presumption/ knowledge about the *interviewer* and perceptions of the *interviewer's* presumptions/ knowledge about self (i.e. the respondent)

the moment, to merely list them here. Each will be discussed in much greater depth in the next three chapters, along with the implications of the tenets of symbolic interactionism.

First, because any topic is multidimensional, any topic can be defined in terms of either a single dimension or a combination of dimensions. Second, utterances (including questions and answers) can be made on different levels of generality. One can orient to a topic in singular or pluralistic terms as well as give personal or normative responses. Third, utterances about a topic can also be made on a number of theoretical levels: one can make a statement about X or a statement about a statement about X. And fourth, utterances are always framed within a descriptive, explanatory or evaluative frame of reference.

These four sources of response variability, coupled with the complexities generated by the fact that social interactants role-take with one another as they try to coordinate their behaviours, ensures that different respondents can make *many different kinds* of interpretations of, and thus give different kinds of answers to, the same question.

Because each of the sources of variability that has just been mentioned involves at least two degrees of freedom, taken together they define a very large (perhaps infinite) number of different kinds of answers that can be given in response to a particular question. In turn, this means that the assumption that the answers given by different respondents to the same question are comparable will only hold true if each respondent has oriented to each of the sources of variability in the same way. It should be emphasised here that this conclusion constitutes one of the principal themes of the remaining chapters of this book.

Summary

Four important theoretical contributions have been presented in this chapter. At the start, the most important methodological assumptions underpinning past survey research were identified. Next, the major criticisms made of the stimulus–response model and the use of pre-set response categories were delineated, and the criticism that closed questions impose the researcher's concepts upon respondents was discussed at some length. Then, the major criticisms that have been directed at qualitative field research were listed. In particular, attention was drawn to the criticisms that qualitative researchers can never be sure that they have properly identified the concepts used by respondents and that because the steps involved in qualitative research projects are typically poorly specified they cannot be replicated. A theoretical model that incorporates these assumptions and criticisms (figure 2.2, p. 22) was included. This model depicts question–answer behaviour as involving complex four-step communication cycles. Central to this model is the assumption that before a successful communication cycle can occur, a question must be understood by the respondent in the way the researcher intended, and the answer must be understood by the researcher in the way the respondent intended. It was suggested that it is a mistake to view respondents as passive agents. Rather, they should be seen as being engaged in joint 'sense-making' activities with the researcher. It was also argued that both the researcher and the respondent exhibit a kind of reflexive intelligence as they negotiate the meaning of questions on the one hand, and the meaning of answers on the other. More specifically, it was argued that if the researcher fails to indicate how he or she defines the research situation, respondents will search for clues, and even make guesses, about the researcher's assumptions and purposes to help them interpret the researcher's acts and decide what information they should give. It was further suggested that, when each respondent is allowed to do this in his or her own way, each will, in essence, be answering a different question. Finally, it was noted that the problems associated with the respondents' freedom to arrive at different interpretations and then give different answers are exacerbated by the fact that topics are multi-dimensional, the fact that observations can be made in individual or collective terms, the fact that there are many different kinds of explanations, and the fact that evaluations can be made in terms of different standards of comparison.

Subsequent chapters will take up the task of assessing, within the symbolic interactionist framework, each of the assumptions that has been identified as underlying survey research, so that the conditions which must be satisfied before each can be seen to be valid can be specified. The overall aim is to understand the conditions that must be met if we are to increase our confidence that the questions we formulate for use in questionnaires and interviews will work as we intend them to work.

Chapter 3

*D*EFINING TOPICS PROPERLY

This chapter focuses upon the first three assumptions that were identified as underpinning survey research at the start of the last chapter. They were: that the researcher has clearly defined the required information; that the respondents have the required information; and that the respondents can access the required information under the conditions of the research situation. All three relate to the need for questions to be directed at properly defined, accessible information. And all three relate to the first step in a question–answer cycle (figure 3.1, page 26).

The researcher has clearly defined the required information

As with many assumptions that appear at first sight to be straightforward, this assumption is more complex than it first appears to be. To begin with, it implies that the researcher must begin with a clear definition of the topic to be investigated. It also implies that the researcher has a clear understanding of the kind of information about the topic that will satisfy the theoretical or practical reasons for carrying out the research. It is worth looking more closely at each of these implications in turn.

The researcher has clearly defined the topic

Some years ago the author acted as a methodological consultant for a community self-survey project. A small town had received a grant to carry out a survey of the residents' views about how their town should be developed. A committee of community leaders had been formed to plan the project and develop a questionnaire. One of the committee members wanted to include the question: 'Do you think . . . [our town] — has a drug problem?' Mindful of what the media might make of the finding that a number of the residents of a well known tourist centre thought that their town had a drug problem, the author advised against the inclusion of the question. The committee member, however, was adamant that it should be included. When asked what he thought they would find out if the question were included, he said that it would be valuable to find out what the residents thought should be done for student transients who camped on the shores of the lake beside the town each summer. Should the town build toilet facilities around the lake? Should a hostel be built in the town? It is not hard to see that the question that had been suggested would not elicit answers to these questions.

Figure 3.1   *The focus of chapter 3*

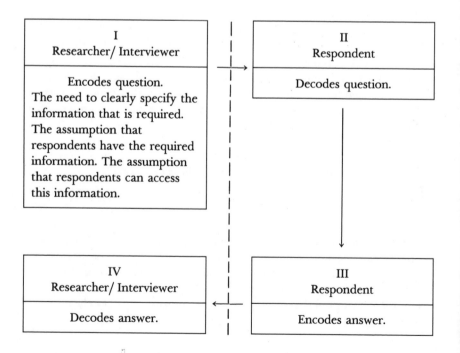

But lay people are not the only ones who run into problems when formulating questions because they have not defined the topic properly. It is not difficult to find examples in the professional research literature that suffer from the same shortcoming. For instance, almost every social researcher regularly collects data concerning respondents' occupations even though occupational status is a notoriously difficult topic to handle for reasons that the following discussion highlights.

The question sequence used by the National Opinion Research Center and the Michigan Survey Research Center to collect information about respondents' occupations (see Sudman and Bradburn, 1982:189–194) begins with a closed question designed to establish respondents' levels of education. Respondents are then asked whether or not they are 'presently employed, unemployed, retired, a student, a housewife, or what?' Respondents who are in employment are asked to classify themselves as working full-time or part-time, and those who indicate that they are working part-time may be asked how many hours per week they actually work. Respondents who say that they are unemployed are asked whether or not they are looking for paid work. People who work 15+ hours as unpaid workers in a family business or a family farm are regarded as 'working'; volunteer charity workers are classified as 'not working'.

Employed workers are then asked to provide a job description of their present occupation:

a: What kind of work do you do? . . . .
What is your main occupation called? . . . .
b: Tell me a little about what you actually do in that job? . . . .
What are some of your main duties? . . . .
c: What kind of business or industry is that in? . . . .
What do they do or make at the place where you work? . . . .
[If respondents have changed jobs, they are asked to focus on the jobs that they have done for the longest time (i.e. their 'usual' job)]

Finally, respondents are asked:

d: Are you (were you) an hourly wage worker, salaried, on commission, self employed, or what? [Farmers who cannot be considered hourly wage workers are considered 'self-employed'.]

Despite the amount of information collected and the level of detail involved, Sudman and Bradburn (1982:193) still make the comment that respondents' answers about their occupations are among the most difficult to code. And they add that, if this information is needed, *the responses that are collected should contain sufficient detail to allow them to be coded properly*. They then cite examples and instructions that the Survey Research Center gives its interviewers to try to ensure that they manage to get the required details — for example, interviewers are told:

— The name of the place the respondent works at is insufficient (e.g. 'Bank' — respondent may be a manager, teller or janitor).
— And vague job titles (e.g. engineer, teacher . . .) can cover a variety of occupations.

The sequence of questions that has just been presented was designed to make sure that respondents give an unambiguous description of what they do. Does it achieve this?

Occupations, like any other phenomenon, are multidimensional. They can be full-time/part-time, paid/unpaid, permanent/temporary, casual/contract/seasonal, legal/illegal, in the primary/secondary/tertiary sectors, government/private enterprise and so on. They can isolate incumbents from the products of their labour, involve being supervised by others or having to supervise others, involve being responsible for one's own work schedules or not, be skilled/semiskilled, be considered 'clean' or 'dirty', involve day-time or night-time shifts, allow one to spend a little or a lot of time with one's family, and so on. The work can be voluntary or forced. Respondents can have more than one job at the same time, which gives rise to the concept of 'usual' or 'main' jobs versus 'fill-in jobs', 'second jobs' and 'moonlighting jobs'. Respondents can nominally have jobs but not be working because they are on sick leave, maternity leave, holiday or strike. And respondents can be paid by piece-work, commission, wage rate, salary or honorarium.

The researcher must decide which of the many different dimensions should be focused upon. But this cannot be done without taking into account the reason for wanting the information in the first place. If, for instance, the researcher wants to estimate the portion of the labour force that is involved in the provision of social services, the dimensions focused upon might include: the number of hours worked, whether the work is permanent or temporary, paid or unpaid, private or public; and whether or not respondents are nominally employed, even if they are not actually working at the moment. If, on the other hand, the researcher wants to code respondents' answers according to level of occupational prestige, the emphasis will be placed on such dimensions as: the legality of the occupation; the required level of education and training; whether it involves clean or dirty work; whether respondents have control over their own work schedules; whether or not they are supervised; how they are paid; whether the work is temporary/permanent, or casual/seasonal/contract; and whether respondents are employed or self-employed.

Here is another example. Imagine that a soft drink manufacturer wants to find out whether or not respondents think that they would be likely to buy a drink based on a new recipe that the company has developed. But what is meant by the word 'buy'?

Consider an innocent appearing question such as, 'what brand of soft drink do you usually buy?' If the question is taken seriously, the respondent must first make a mental decision on the time period involved. A second decision is then necessary on which conditions to include. Are purchases at work, in restaurants, at sporting events, and at movies to be included; or are only purchases for home use to be counted? The respondent must decide on the meaning of the word 'you'. Does it refer only to the respondent or to the household of which the respondent is a member? How are purchases by one household member for other household members to be treated? A final question to be resolved mentally is the definition of a soft drink. Are lemonade, iced tea, fruit punch, and mineral water to be included or not? (Sudman and Bradburn, 1982:39)

The occupation and soft drink examples that have just been discussed serve to underscore the fact that all topics are multidimensional. That is, it is possible to think of any topic either in global terms or in terms of a specific number of dimensions. This problem bears on question–answer behaviour in at least three ways:

(a) It has to be appreciated that respondents' *answers in terms of specific dimensions will not always be congruent with their global judgements.*

Roslow *et al.* (1940) cite results from two surveys that demonstrate this fact. In the first study, respondents were asked: '*On the whole,* do you approve or disapprove of Roosevelt's international policy?' (August 1939). In the second, respondents were asked: 'Do you approve of Roosevelt's policies *with regard to the European situation up to now* (September 1939)?' Whereas 69.2 per cent approved of Roosevelt's policies in regard to the European situation, only 40.5 per cent approved when asked to react globally to Roosevelt's 'international policy'.

Another example that illustrates the same problem is provided by Cantril and Fried (1944:9–10) who report that whereas only four of forty respondents answered 'no' to the question: 'Are you in favour of Labour Unions?', the level of support as indicated by answers to six specific questions was more problematic. For instance, eighteen of the forty respondents believed that the government should have more control over the unions and twenty-five felt that the unions should be prohibited if they got into 'radical' hands.

A moment's reflection upon the examples that we have just looked at forces one to the view that the researcher must not only decide how respondents should orient to the topic — that is, whether they should orient to it in global terms or in terms of a number of specified dimensions — but also instruct respondents accordingly so that they will all orient to the topic in the same way. If the researcher does not do these things, different respondents can either answer in terms of different dimensions from one another, or answer in terms of different dimensions to those which the researcher has in mind. If either of these things happens, the researcher is likely to misunderstand the replies given by respondents and make invalid comparisons between the replies given by different respondents. The following anecdote indicates the sorts of things that can go wrong:

> The visiting teacher from the country town was giving her first demonstration to a class of nine-year-olds in an upland farm area . . . She had chosen as her subject: 'Wool', and started off by showing a large coloured picture of a sheep and remarking brightly: 'Now I am sure you all know what this is'. Much to her surprise, there was no response to her implied question. When she put it more pointedly, one sturdy boy asked if he could see the picture nearer at hand. On permission being given with much wonderment, he surveyed it carefully and hazarded: 'It's a two-year-old Border-Leicester, isn't it?' (Laing, 1957:24)

(b) It should also be appreciated that when respondents are required to answer in terms of specific dimensions, *the dimensions that they are to focus on must be properly defined.*

The next example indicates the kind of difficulties that arise when this is not done. In a study of the social changes and reforms that residents of the United States wanted to see once the Second World War had ended, Crutchfield and Gordon (1947) found that 41 per cent of the males and 54 per cent of the females who were interviewed wanted things to remain the same. Further analysis of the respondents' answers, however, revealed that while 80 per cent of the males had domestic changes or reforms in mind, only 53 per cent of the females had thought in terms of this dimension. Moreover, when the answers for the men and women who had domestic changes in mind were analysed separately, the percentages for the men and women who said that they would like things to remain the same were practically identical (60% and 59% respectively). It should also be noted that although most of respondents in the total sample interpreted the question in terms of the domestic changes or reforms dimension, a sizeable minority (43%) had a variety of other dimensions in mind — for example, social, economic, political or technical changes.

(c) The fact that any topic can be defined in terms of different dimensions has the important corollary: *how a topic is defined can dramatically affect the way the responses are distributed:*

> An example of the effect of increasing the specificity is seen in questions from a Gallup Poll of May–June 1945:
>
> Do you think the government should give money to workers who are unemployed for a length of time until they can find another job? (yes: 63 per cent; no: 32 per cent; don't know: 5 per cent).
>
> It has been proposed that unemployed workers with dependants be given up to $25 per week by the government for as many as twenty-six weeks during one

year while they are out of work and looking for a job. Do you favour or oppose this plan? (yes: 46 per cent; no: 42 per cent; don't know: 12 per cent).

Would you be willing to pay higher taxes to give unemployed persons up to $25 a week for twenty-six weeks if they fail to find satisfactory jobs? (yes: 34 per cent; no: 54 per cent; don't know: 12 per cent). (Bradburn, 1982:70)

Note that Link, 1943:267; Cantril and Fried, 1944:9–10; Payne, 1951:196–197; and Smith, 1984a discuss similar examples.

To recapitulate, researchers must decide whether global or specific responses are required, and then clearly indicate this to respondents. If specific dimensions are to be focused upon, they must be properly defined for respondents.

There may be times when a researcher wants to measure global responses: for example, questions about overall party preferences may be used as a general indicator of how respondents will vote in an election. All the same, it must be appreciated that, when respondents are left to define a topic in global terms for themselves, the researcher cannot be sure that all will do it in the same way. In addition, if respondents are free to select their own dimensions of focus, there is nothing to stop them from changing these over time as different dimensions occur to them. If global responses are required, the dimensions that respondents should focus upon should be clearly specified. Freed is undoubtedly correct in his view that:

> A common error is for a question to be so generally structured that neither the writer nor the reader understands what is being sought. This 'general fallacy' also invites a variety of interpretations so that the respondent must decide for himself what the researcher intended; thus, the researcher is often thwarted in his endeavour because the respondent misinterpreted the intent of the question. General and vague questions are usually indicative of a lack of clarity on the part of the writer, bewilder the reader, and produce unreliable results. Don't let questions that are too general be a subterfuge for inadequate preparation. A clear and pointed question elicits an effective and relevant response. (Freed, 1964:188)

More generally, it is difficult to reject the view that, unless all respondents focus upon the same topic and respond to it in terms of the same dimensions, the answers that they give cannot be meaningfully compared with one another.

The researcher has a clear idea of the kind of information that is required about the topic

Besides demonstrating the sort of problem that arises when the researcher fails to define the topic properly, the example of the local businessman wanting to ask residents whether or not they thought their town had a drug problem (alluded to at the start of the last section) illustrates what can happen when the researcher does not have a clear idea of the information that is required about the topic. Although it is obviously the case that defining the topic properly is a major step toward having different respondents give the same kind of answers, it should not be forgotten that the information collected should satisfy the reason for conducting the research in the first place. Three rules advocated by Sudman and Bradburn (1982:13) are pertinent to this issue. They are:

(a)   Do not formulate specific questions until you have thought through the research question.

(b)   Write the research question down and keep it handy while formulating specific questions.

(c)   Keep asking, 'Why do I want to know this?' ('It would be interesting to know' is not an acceptable answer.)

Adherence to these rules will go a long way to ensuring that the questions which are asked are relevant to the researcher's goals. Yet adherence to them is not enough to guarantee that the questions asked will cover all relevant aspects of the topic, so it is worth adding a fourth rule, which is advocated by both Kidder (1981) and Deming (1944):

> An excellent test . . . is the preparation of 'dummy tables' showing the relationships that are anticipated. By drawing up such tables in advance, the investigators force themselves to be definite about what data are required and how they will be used. They can even enter figures representing different possible findings in order to visualize the bearing each would have on alternative hypotheses and to see what new hypotheses they suggest. (Kidder, 1981:60)
>
> Without some pretty good idea of what the analysis is going to show it will be impossible to design the questionnaire so that any useful proportion of [its] . . . aims will be accomplished. An understanding of the subject is accordingly demanded as one of the qualifications for planning a survey. Likewise the tabulation program (which really should precede the questionnaire but usually does not) demands enough knowledge of the problem to see what tables are going to be needed and which ones will be significant. (Deming, 1944:364)

When researchers are not clear in their minds about the nature of the information they require, they cannot hope to ask questions that are relevant to their topics of interest. While this basic requirement might appear to be so obvious that it scarcely needs to be stressed, it is all too easily forgotten. Researchers are all too prone either to asking questions without bothering to clarify the meaning of key concepts or to letting initial formulations of the questions cause them to lose sight of their original goals. As Payne puts it:

> Many of the problems of wording result from our going off half cocked. Once the issue is posed in even the vaguest terms, we start trying to put it in words that are understandable to the public . . .

If we did but realize it, the first half of the battle consists of putting the issue in a form that we can understand ourselves. *We need to first and foremost define the issue precisely*, regardless of the general understandability of the words. The news reporter has the stock questions to ask himself about each issue: Who? Why? When? Where? How? . . . We can well ask the same questions of ourselves for each issue we intend to pose . . . (Payne, 1951:26) [my emphasis]

Lamentably, although clearly sensible, the advice offered by Sudman and Bradburn, Payne, Kidder and Deming, is seldom followed by the experts. And it is difficult to make novice researchers follow it. The author, for example, has found that it always requires concerted pressure to motivate students to systematically write the avowed purpose beside each question in the first drafts of questionnaires or interview schedules (i.e to write beside each question what information they think it will elicit and what they will do with that information). It is as if the reason for wanting to ask a question is so obvious before it is explicated that researchers see little merit in writing it down. Yet, typically, when these working procedures are adopted, the adequacy of most questions becomes far less certain. Explication of the purpose of each question and how resulting data will be used has an almost fiendish ability to force implicit assumptions out into the open and highlight any mismatches between the researcher's actual interests and the proposed questions.

Respondents have the required information

An assumption survey researchers commonly hold is that the respondents have the information they want:

> [The] structure and administration of the interview reflects an expectation of 'opinionatedness' characteristic of only a few levels of the social structure. (Manning, 1966/7:306)
>
> The typical survey question incorporates assumptions not only about the nature of what is to be measured, but also about its very existence. (Converse and Presser, 1986:35)

Most methodologists would agree that there is very little point in asking respondents hypothetical questions. In Converse and Presser's words:

> If we ask a hypothetical question, will we get a hypothetical answer — as some lighthearted critics have warned? Perhaps not, but the counsel of experience and research suggests that asking most people to imagine what if — what might have happened in their lives if things had been otherwise, or what they might do if — confronts them with a special task that is likely to be difficult . . .
>
> Hypothetical questions provide no guarantee that respondents will feel the full force of political or economic realities . . . (Converse and Presser, 1986:23)

Converse and Presser go on to suggest that if hypothetical questions are asked, at least one question pertaining to the respondents' actual experience should be included.

In spite of the general suspicion regarding the worth of hypothetical questions, questions are commonly presented to respondents without first checking their relevance to respondents (see Converse and Schuman, 1984, for an analysis of the types of questions used by polling organisations). This must be coupled with the unfortunate fact that respondents' willingness to answer questions cannot be taken as a sign of their relevance. Smith (1984a:215) reports, for example, that studies of the American electorate during the 1950s developed a picture that was startlingly at odds with the assumption of a rational citizenry. In extreme cases, it was found that up to 80 per cent of respondents answered attitude questions even though they had no real position on an issue. They appeared to randomly choose responses in order to come up with answers to the questions. In a similar vein, Belson (1981:371), after an intensive analysis of respondents' interpretations of a series of market survey questions, concludes that when respondents find it difficult to answer a question they are likely to modify it so that they can answer it more easily. They might eliminate difficult elements, overlook qualifying phrases and clauses, limit the question to things that they know about, and interpret the scope of the question more or less broadly than the researcher intended.

Such findings have led many survey methodologists (e.g. Smith, 1984a:245; Converse and Presser, 1986:35–38) to argue for the use of filter questions that gauge the level of respondents' knowledge about the topic, its salience to them, and the intensity of any opinions or beliefs that they may hold about it.

Cicourel (1982) has also suggested that it should not be simply assumed that respondents will hold opinions, attitudes and beliefs. He advances the view that ignorance should be treated as a variable:

> Why not assume that the actor's thoughts about social objects are loosely structured but are perceived as concrete until we begin to probe them with specific questions that put him on the spot about matters which he takes for granted and to which he seldom gives much time? Survey research procedures do not assign variable status to ignorance, much less acknowledge it as a critical factor in the structure of social action . . . (Cicourel, 1964:115)

Although the views put forward by methodologists (such as Smith, Converse and Presser, and Cicourel) touch on obviously important matters, it is interesting — if depressing — that similar views were expressed more than four decades ago. In the late forties, Riesman and Glazer (1948/49) proposed that an alternative model to the conventional survey researcher's model might divide a population into:

(a) Those who have grounds for their opinions and those who do not (see e.g. Katz, 1945/6, who criticises a study of Whites' perceptions about the way

Blacks were being treated on the grounds that respondents were not asked whether they knew any Blacks).

(b) Those who take their opinions seriously and feel that they are of consequence and those who do not. 'For most people in modern society, there is no . . . direct relation between responsibility for having an opinion and responsibility for action.' (Riesman and Glazer, 1948/49:635)

Further, it would seem reasonable to assume that those respondents with most responsibility for formulating decisions and planning courses of action will be most motivated to gather information and spend time thinking about the relevant issues. And it would seem reasonable to predict that such respondents will be most likely to have associated information, beliefs and opinions.

Notwithstanding the apparent reasonableness of the suggestions that have been made over the years, it has to be admitted that they have yet to have much impact on general practice.

Still relevant to the issue of whether or not respondents have the information required by the researcher, it must be kept in mind that, even if respondents have the information at one point in time, it is possible that they will forget it with the passing of time. It is also possible that individuals will not always be aware, or conscious, of stimuli that impinge upon them and influence their behaviour. These considerations simply mean that, even when respondents have in the past been exposed to experiences which are relevant to the topic being investigated, it cannot be taken for granted that they will have retained any information about them. (Note: these issues are dealt with more fully in chapter 7.)

The conclusion that one is forced to accept, then, is that it should not just be assumed that respondents have the information that is sought. In the case of each respondent, the relevance of a particular question must be independently established. Ways in which this can be done are discussed in chapter 8.

Respondents are capable of verbalising the information the researcher wants under the conditions of the research situation

There are a number of factors that relate to the assumption that respondents can access the information they do have. Training respondents in research techniques is enough to convince anyone that the single most serious failing of novice interviewers is the tendency to go too fast — not to give respondents time to answer fully. In everyday situations, interactants typically 'uhm' and 'ahh', scratch their heads, look into the distance, and so on. In other words, they take their time to give answers to questions. Standardised interviews, however, pressure respondents to work at the interviewer's pace and interviewers often proceed too quickly (see e.g. Cannell *et al.*, 1981).

Fowler and Mangione (1990) add to this problem another twist that stems from the fact that interactants constantly interpret each other's behaviour:

> Fowler (1966) found that the pace at which the interviewer conducts the interview is a significant correlate of the respondent's perception of the task. *If interviewers go fast, respondents conclude that accurate and complete answers are less important than quick answers.* To our knowledge, a direct link between pace and data quality has not been documented. However, we think it is likely that having interviewers speak slowly is one important and practical way in which researchers can increase the standardization across interviews ... (Fowler and Mangione, 1990:71) [my emphasis]

In addition to failures associated with interviewer speed, questions can fail because they fail to stimulate respondent recall. There is some evidence that questions must link up with cues associated with material in the respondent's memory if that material is to be successfully recalled (see Thompson and Tulving, 1970; Tulving, 1974; Martin, 1986). They can fail, too, because question tasks may be too difficult for respondents — especially when they are pressured by interviewers who are impatiently waiting for answers. A question may be so complex that respondents have trouble comprehending the individual words let alone the overall sense that is intended. And questions can be so long that respondents are not able to concentrate long enough to absorb them.

More practically, if questions require respondents to remember information, they must be worded in a way that helps respondents accurately retrieve the information from their memories. They must be short enough to fit within each respondent's attention span and simple enough to be fully comprehended. Techniques that can be used to achieve these goals are discussed in chapter 7.

Summary

A necessary precursor to a successful question–answer cycle is that both researcher and respondent have a shared understanding of the topic under investigation. Since all topics are multidimensional, respondents can orient to a topic in either a global or a more narrowly defined fashion. If different respondents define a topic in different ways and the researcher is not aware of this fact, the respondents' answers will neither be properly interpreted nor meaningfully comparable with one another.

The researcher can take one of two tacks to meet this problem of different respondents giving different kinds of answers. The researcher can try to identify the dimension(s) each respondent has focused upon. Alternatively the researcher can specify the dimensions(s) upon which all respondents should focus. The first of these solutions runs into a number of difficulties, such as the fact that respondents may not be aware of the dimensions that influence their answers when they define the topic for themselves and the fact that their definitions of a topic are likely to vary over time. While the second solution runs into other problems, such as the danger of imposing inappropriate response categories upon the respondents, it does ensure both that the topic is clearly defined for each respondent and that each answer will be relevant to it.

To maximise the likelihood that questions are relevant to the topic as well as to the reason for wanting to collect information about it, a researcher should continually ask him- or herself: 'Why do I need to know this? and 'What am I going to do with the answers respondents give? In addition to indicating how the topic should be defined and what kind of information is required, the researcher must establish the basis upon which it can be assumed that respondents are likely to actually have the information that they are asked to provide. The researcher should try to avoid putting respondents in the position of having to entirely invent or fabricate answers on the basis of little information. And, last but not least, it is important that respondents be given enough time to formulate appropriate answers.

Chapter 4

*F*ORMULATING INTELLIGIBLE REQUESTS FOR INFORMATION

The last chapter dealt with the need for the researcher to begin with a clear definition of the topic and a clear idea of the information that is required about the topic. In this chapter, the focus will still be on the first step in the question-answer communication cycle, as we consider some of the problems the researcher has to confront when trying to formulate a request for the required information which will be understood by the respondent (see figure 4.1, p. 39).

In the past, social researchers have typically assumed that their questions would be understood by respondents as they are intended to be understood. But, just as it is often doubtful that researchers always have a clear idea of the information that should be collected, it is doubtful that respondents always understand what information the researcher wants.

If respondents are to understand a question as intended by the researcher, they must minimally give the same meaning to individual words and attribute the same overall meaning to the structural elements (i.e. component phrases, clauses, etc.) that make up the question. Both of these requirements involve a host of complexities that need to be discussed at length.

The meanings of individual words

Before respondents can interpret a question as the researcher wants, they must understand each word in the same way as the researcher understands it. Unfortunately, one cannot safely assume that the meanings of ordinary words — let alone exotic or uncommon words — are necessarily shared even by respondents who have been socialised in the same general culture as the researcher.

> As men have known throughout the ages and as modern semantics has pointed out in detail, the meaning of even the simplest word can be slippery. When we add to the ordinary problem of verbal communication the additional problem of presenting a meaning to groups of people widely separated in background, experience, estimations and terminologies peculiar to interest or occupational groups, the difficulty confronting a public opinion investigator becomes clear. (Cantril and Fried, 1944:3)

The failure of respondents to give the same meaning to individual words is generally explained by reference to the following four factors: (a) the evolution of context-specific nuances of meaning; (b) their relative difficulty (defined either in terms of number of syllables or the frequency of occurrence in everyday life); (c) lack of clear empirical referents; and (d) the operation of related nuances of apparently similar words.

Figure 4.1   *The focus of chapter 4*

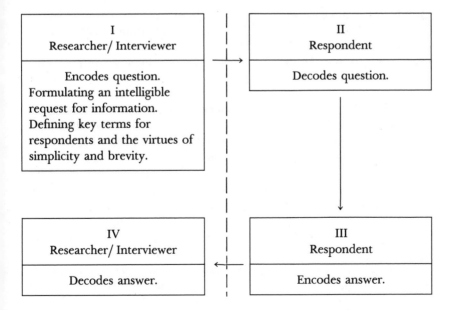

The evolution of context specific meanings

In chapter 2, attention was drawn to the symbolic interactionist hypothesis that human beings constantly negotiate the meanings of, and labels for, the social acts and events that affect them. This explains why acts and events, and the symbols that are used to represent them, can have different meanings at different times and in different places. For example, whereas the British use the word 'tea' to refer to an evening meal, Americans use this word to refer to a drink. Whereas Australians use the word 'backyard' to refer to the garden area behind a house, the British use it to refer to the small, concrete area that is typically found at the back of a low-cost house in a working class area — the area behind a middle-class home is called a 'garden'. Whereas older generations use the words 'obscene' or 'gross' to mean disgusting or degrading, contemporary Australian teenagers use these words as marks of approval, especially after a joke has been told. Whereas people in Australia use the word 'outside' to refer to the outdoors, residents in the Canadian North West Territories use it to mean 'out of the territories' (i.e. 'down South'). And, whereas businessmen in Australia interpret 'yes' in answer to the question: 'Do we have a deal?' to mean that the deal has been finalised, Japanese businessmen take it to mean that they will go away and think about it.

Even when words seem to carry shared meanings, unexpected difficulties can emerge. For instance, although 'age' is a concept that one might expect to have a shared meaning among all members of any Western society, different age groups may have different ways of thinking about age. Most teenagers, for example, define anyone over forty as old, while most people in their sixties tend to reserve this category for people over eighty. And income seems to be categorised according to locally current norms, so that the meanings associated with different income levels vary from region to region. An income which makes a person wealthy in one community may not make a person wealthy in another.

The above examples serve to highlight a fundamental issue. Minimally, researchers must be confident that they know how respondents will interpret key words. Such confidence might be based either on the fact that they have defined the key concepts for the respondents or the fact that they have taken time to investigate how the respondents interpret the key concepts when left to do so for themselves.

It should not be assumed, however, that it is easy to avoid problems arising from a lack of shared meaning. Even when words are understood as intended, it is possible that unintended nuances can interfere with communication. Sorensen (1972, cited in DeLamater, 1982:24), for example, used the word 'ball' to refer to sexual intercourse in a questionnaire used in an American survey because he assumed it was the word that the respondents would use themselves and that its use would enhance rapport. Certainly, Sorensen's reasoning is in line with Cicourel's (1964:10) view that question wording should reflect the concepts used by the actors. Nevertheless, it has to be recognised that the use of slang runs the risk of transgressing the norms of politeness and of violating respondents' expectations regarding proper 'professional' behaviour. If this happens, using the actors' own concepts might have a negative rather than a positive effect on rapport, and might introduce nuances that escape the researcher — for example, that the researcher is unprofessional and that the research project is not worth the respondents' time.

The choice of which words to stress can also change the meaning of questions. Lazarsfeld (1944, reprinted 1972a) discusses the way in which the meaning of the question, 'Why did you buy that book?' is dependent upon the word that is stressed. Stressing the word 'why' conveys surprise or disapproval; stressing 'buy' conveys a desire for an explanation of that course of action rather than other courses of action (e.g. borrowing it from the library); stressing 'that' implies a particular book rather any book; and stressing 'book' conveys a request for an explanation (e.g. for spending money in that particular way rather than in some other way).

The relative difficulty of words

The relative difficulty of words affects respondents in a number of ways. Sudman and Bradburn (1974:50) suggest that increasing the difficulty of the words in a question increases the degree to which the question threatens respondents and consequently the tendency for respondents to give 'Don't know' responses. And Payne (1951:chapter 8) presents results which suggest that vocabulary difficulty (measured in terms of either the average number of syllables per word or average number of prefixes and suffixes per word) relates to the tendency to endorse the last option mentioned.

Words that may seem simple enough to middle-class, well-educated researchers may not be intelligible to many respondents. Belson (1981), for instance, asked respondents: 'Do you think T.V. news programs are impartial about politics?' In follow-up probes put to fifty-six respondents, twenty-five interpreted the word *impartial* as the researchers intended; ten overlooked the word altogether; nine interpreted it as 'tending to spend too much time on politics; five gave an opposite meaning (e.g. unfair, biased); two interpreted it as 'giving too little time to information'; and the remaining seven had no idea what the word meant at all. Similar results were generated by the inclusion of the word *proposition* in a question. When potentially difficult words (e.g. words that are not commonly used or have a technical meaning) have to be included, it is clear that they should be defined for respondents.

Most survey researchers would subscribe to the rule that 'terms must be simple and comprehensible even to the least educated respondents' (Kidder and

Judd, 1986:245), even if this approach runs the risk of offending some respondents. Payne (1951:117) gives examples of how to do this without insulting the intelligence of better-educated respondents. He claims that it is better to ask: 'How do you feel about the amount you have to pay the government on the money you take in during the year — your income tax, that is?' than to phrase the question in the reverse order: 'How do you feel about your income tax — that is, the amount you have to pay the government on the money you take in during the year?' It is certainly possible that defining a term informally first might lessen any didactic overtones to a particular question formulation while allowing the interviewer two shots at communicating the intended meaning. It is also preferable because it minimises the likelihood that respondents will begin to answer the question before they have fully understood it.

The lack of empirical referents

> When more than one plausible interpretation exists, the respondent needs to consider the various possibilities and often must think up and answer an *internal* questionnaire to help decide which interpretation to accept. Take, for example, this question: 'How many times have you talked to a doctor about your health during the past month?' The respondent may wonder whether to include telephone consultations, whether visits to chiropractors should be included, whether immunisations are part of health, or whether 'past month' refers to the past four weeks or to a calendar month. Whether or not the respondent goes through this process explicitly, he or she must proceed on the basis of assumptions concerning the intended meaning of the question. (Cannell *et al.*, 1981:394)

Bradburn (1982:69) cites the results of an investigation of the interpretation of political symbols (Fee, 1981) which illustrates the point that is being made here. Fee found that the term 'Big Government' is associated with four distinct meanings:

- welfare, socialism and overspending
- government for big business and the wealthy
- federal control and diminished state rights
- bureaucracy and a lack of democratic process

More importantly, Fee found that each of these meanings correlated with quite different attitudes so that, without knowing which meaning respondents ascribe to the term 'Big Government', it is impossible to interpret with any confidence their responses to questions that incorporate this term.

Of course, general questions, by definition, are cast in abstract terms that have, at best, vague empirical referents. It is for this reason that Payne (1951:149) argues that words like 'art', 'business', 'government', and 'world affairs' should be avoided. He maintains that there is so little consensus over what they mean that we may just as well substitute the word 'blab' every time one of them occurs. The following is an example of what Payne calls 'blab-blab' questions: 'Should our country be more active in *world affairs?*' Such a question, he asserts, means little more than the question: 'Should our *blab* be more *blab in blab?*' He asks:

> What is conveyed by the word 'country' in this instance — our government as a whole, the State Department, our commercial firms, our industrialists, or what? 'More active?' In what way? How active is our country now?
> 'World affairs?' Oh brother!
> These are the kind of terms that have to be defined explicitly before philosophers can begin to discuss them. Let's not inflict them on the general public with no definitions whatever! That is, let's not do it unless we have some follow-up questions which enable us to realise the multitude of combinations or frames of reference such blab words bring up. (Payne, 1951:150)

There is little doubt, too, that Converse and Presser (1986:31) are correct in arguing that the more general the question, the wider the range of interpretation that will be given to it. To be more precise, words can lack clear meaning in two ways. First, a word may have several meanings associated with it. It is for this reason that Payne (1951) counsels the avoidance of words with multiple meanings — an issue that he says can be settled quickly by reference to a dictionary — on the grounds that the more meanings a word has, the more likely it is to be ambiguous in meaning. The fact that even simple words can have different meanings in different social situations, however, should be kept in mind. Different cultural or subgroup nuances are not likely to be listed in a dictionary. Secondly, a word may lack empirical referents. For example, Rugg and Cantril (1944:25) found that forty respondents gave a variety of interpretations to key words in a question taken from a 'Fortune Poll': 'After the war is over, do you think people will have to work harder, about the same, or not as hard as before?' Twenty-three respondents interpreted 'people' as people in all walks of life, while twelve interpreted 'people' as one class; ten interpreted 'would have to work harder' as produce higher quality work, while six interpreted it as 'work longer hours' and five as 'compete harder'.

Regrettably, there are many abstract words which provide potential pitfalls for the interviewer. Many are very common. The list includes frequency terms such as 'regularly', 'usually', 'often', 'frequently', 'seldom' and 'rarely', as well as evaluative words such as 'good', 'bad', 'approve', 'disapprove', 'agree', 'disagree', 'like', and 'dislike'. All of these words lack clear empirical referents. How many times a year is 'often'? And what is meant by 'usually'? Belson (1981:357) reports the results of investigating 445 interpretations of the word 'usually' where it had been meant to be interpreted as 'ordinarily', 'in the ordinary course of events', 'commonly', 'as a rule', 'generally', 'normally', 'habitually', 'as a routine', 'almost always', 'mostly', 'typically', and various other interpretations closely similar to these. Eighty-five of the respondents overlooked the word altogether and only 60 per cent of them interpreted it in one of the ways listed. To make matters more complex, the ways in which many of these words are to be interpreted are dependent upon the topics with which they are paired. Thus, 'once a day' may be 'very often' when one is talking about haircuts but not 'very often' when one is talking about brushing one's teeth.

Generally speaking, abstract words generate problems because they are:

(a) more likely to be affected by contextual influences since respondents are forced to search for interpretative clues;

(b) more likely to produce non-comparable responses from different respondents since respondents can focus upon different dimensions of the concept in question; and

(c) more likely to allow respondents room to change the intended scope of the words in order to answer the questions.

Relevant to the last point, Belson (1981) hypothesises that there is a strong tendency for respondents to interpret broad concepts less broadly as they limit interpretations to their own experience (e.g. 'programs' will become 'adult programs').

The important lesson to be drawn from the foregoing discussion is that *the words used by the researcher when formulating questions should be as specific and as concrete as possible*. Concepts should be defined in empirical terms. Relevant to this point, Bradburn and Sudman (1979) recommend that frequency questions should be worded in terms of numeric referents per specified time period. In other words, the researcher should ask, 'How many times did you go out to see a movie during the last month? (1,2,3, etc.)' rather than asking the question, 'Would you say that you go out to the movies: rarely, once in a while, quite often, often, etc.?' When possible, concrete examples should be given (e.g. following an illustration given by Payne, 1951: 'leafy vegetable' could become 'leafy vegetables like lettuce and cabbage, etc.').

Starting questions with short vignettes giving a little word picture of the situation, so as to clarify the meaning of a key concept, is an extension of the same principle (see Alexander and Becker, 1978). Lemkau and Crocetti (1962), for example, used vignettes to define categories of mental illness for respondents. The following is one that they used:

> Now I'd like to describe a certain kind of person and ask you a few questions about her. She is a young woman in her twenties — let's call her Betty Smith. She has never had a job, and she doesn't seem to want to look for one. She is a very quiet girl, she doesn't talk much to anyone — even her own family — and she acts as if she is afraid of people, especially young men her own age. She won't go out with anyone and whenever someone comes to visit the family, she stays in her own room until they leave. She just stays by herself and daydreams all the time and shows no interest in anything or anybody. (Lemkau and Crocetti, 1962:694)

Similarly, Mellinger *et al.* (1982) used vignettes to define ethical issues. The next vignette was used to define the ethical dilemma posed by the use of placebos in research.

An example of the use of placebos is this research on rheumatoid arthritis. This is a condition that does not kill people but it can be very painful. There's no cure for it but there's a new drug that researchers believe will relieve arthritis pain and keep the disease from getting worse.

In order to test the drug, researchers need to compare it over a long period of time with a placebo. They would give the new drug to one group of arthritis patients, and a placebo to another group. The test would last one year. If the new drug is as good as the researchers think, most of the people taking it would no longer be in pain, and their arthritis would not get worse. Most people taking the placebo would continue to have pain, and their arthritis would steadily get worse. The patients would not be told which they are getting — placebo or new drug.

In this study, then, the possible benefits of the new drug would be withheld from half the subjects for one year. But if the study is successful, a more effective drug would be available for all arthritis sufferers.

Do you think it is OK or not OK to do this study? (Mellinger *et al.*, 1982:109)

The operation of unintended nuances associated with apparently similar words

Occasionally it becomes apparent that words which on the surface appear to be very similar produce very different responses when used in parallel forms of the same question. A classic example of this which has been discussed by a number of writers (e.g. Rugg, 1941; Schuman and Presser, 1981, Hippler and Schwarz, 1986) is a survey experiment conducted by The Roper Public Opinion Research Center in 1940 in which respondents were asked either: 'Do you think the U.S. should *allow* public speeches against democracy?' or 'Do you think the U.S. should *forbid* public speeches against democracy?' Whereas 62 per cent said 'no' to the first question, only 46 per cent said 'yes' to the second. Rugg (1941) comments that 'evidently the forbid phrasing makes the implied threat to civil liberties more apparent'. One could also argue that 'allow' and 'forbid' are not exact opposites: that to allow is to permit but not necessarily to encourage while to forbid is not only to discourage but to try to prevent. But how we assess the strength of negatives versus positives is also a factor here. Jordan (1965) reports that negative response options for rating scales are perceived as being stronger than the countervailing positive response options, which explains why respondents' negative responses (e.g. forbid) tend to be less extreme than their positive responses (e.g. allow).

A second, similar, example of how unexpected nuances can differentiate apparently similar words is provided by Murray *et al.* (1974, cited by Bradburn, 1982:71). They compared the response distributions for two versions of a question aimed at measuring respondents' acceptance of daylight saving. The first version was phrased in terms of whether or not they *approved* of daylight saving.

The second was phrased in terms of whether or not they *liked* daylight saving. A cross-tabulation of results indicated that although the two response distributions were highly correlated, it was possible for some people to like daylight saving and not approve of it and vice versa. Of those who liked year round daylight saving very much, 68 per cent approved of it. Of those who disliked it very much, 10 per cent approved of it!

A third illustration of the problems of defining nuance was mentioned in chapter 1 (pp. 5–6), where it was concluded that the terms 'doing a good job', 'being approved of' and, 'making the better Prime Minister' appear to refer to quite different things.

The difficulty with all these examples is that the problem they embody is not obvious until after the fact. While much of the trouble is undoubtedly a consequence of the fact that terms such as 'approve', 'like', 'allow' and 'forbid' are ill defined, it is not clear how one could reliably predict either the positive or negative nuances that seem to be associated with them. The best course would seem to be to avoid using terms that have been found to have moral overtones. More generally, the best course would seem to be to avoid ill defined evaluative terms.

Again it seems appropriate to conclude that the problems associated with poorly defined words can be serious. Unfortunately, it must be acknowledged that the advice to use words that are concrete and specific (i.e. defined in empirical terms) is not enough to avoid all of the problems that underlie the construction of clearly interpretable questions. The sorts of problems that have just been looked at are only likely to be flushed out by the use of the in-depth question testing procedures that are discussed in chapter 12.

Structural complexities and the requirement that questions should be interpreted as intended

The overall meaning attributed to a question involves more than the sum of the meanings of the individual words. Interpretations of a question are influenced by its structural complexity. Structural features that have been found to create confusion in respondents include the sheer number of words, the number of grammatical parts and the use of negatives.

The sheer number of words used

Payne (1951) was perhaps the first to present data to support the hypothesis that the level of respondent confusion is related to the length of a question.

Payne concluded that respondents are more affected by the order of alternatives when questions are more that twenty words in length. More recently, Molenaar (1982:55), having reviewed the relevant literature, has concluded that short questions reduce the likelihood of a number of different response effects occurring. The response effects he considered were those which stem from grammatical complexities, task conflicts, and the tendency on the part of some respondents to give either socially desirable or acquiescing responses. Molenaar also concludes that: *the greater the number of substantive or informative words used, the more likely it is that the question will be interpreted wrongly.*

Grammatical complexities

Asking two or more questions at once

Most texts on question construction assert that questions should be as short and simple as possible. In practice this means that the researcher should avoid asking two or more questions at the same time, as well as avoid adding qualifying clauses, phrases and instructions.

Rather than asking: 'Did you see or hear anything?', it would be better to ask:

Q1 Did you see anything?

Q2 Did you hear anything?

Rather than asking: 'Can you give me some idea of the number, makes and sizes of each size that you have sold to date or have in stock at the moment?' (discussed by Belson, 1981:25), it would be better to ask:

Q1 How many of size X have you sold to date?

Q2 How many of size Y have you sold to date?

Q3 How many of size X have you currently got in stock?

Q4 How many of size Y have you currently got in stock?

and so on.

It should be said, however, that multiple questions are not always obvious. 'The question: How many of each sized packet have you bought?' (Belson, 1981:25), should be broken down into its implied parts:

Q1 How many size X packets have you bought?

Q2 How many size Y packets have you bought?

and so on.

And it is quite common for a second question to be implied by the way a question is worded. Fowler and Mangione (1990:84) discuss the problem of what they call 'hidden questions' — questions about whether other questions are actually relevant. For example, the question: 'For whom do you think you will vote in the next election?' is really two questions. The first — 'Will you vote in the election?' — is implied. And it would be better to ask it explicitly:

Q1 Will you vote in the next election?

and, if the answer is 'yes',

Q2 Who will you vote for?

Finally, an example discussed by Payne (1951:160) draws attention to the fact that the simple conjunction 'and' can imply a second question because it can be taken as either joining two subjects into one or adding a second subject. Thus the question: 'Is there much rivalry among the boys who sell the soda pop and crackerjack?' can be answered in terms of rivalry within a single group, rivalry between two groups, or rivalry within each of two groups. If the last possibility were intended, one would have to ask:

Q1 Is there rivalry among the boys who sell soda pop?

Q2 Is there rivalry among the boys who sell crackerjack?

Likewise, the question: 'Do you distrust banks and building societies?' can either be interpreted as a question about financial institutions in general or as two questions — one about banks and one about building societies.

The addition of clauses, phrases and instructions

Almost all survey methodologists advocate *brevity* in questions. It is a rule, nevertheless, that is often broken when researchers succumb to the temptation to add qualifying clauses, phrases or instructions. The problem is forcefully illustrated by the following question: 'Have you bought any in the last seven days not counting today?' (discussed by Belson, 1981:25). The trouble with such questions is that, because the first half makes sense by itself, respondents can begin to answer it before they have heard the second half. As Cannell (1977:27) comments: 'When questions are extremely long and complex, respondents often interrupt at the end of a clause to answer without allowing the interviewer to finish the question.'

Of course, the problem could be partly overcome by putting the qualifying component(s) first (as suggested by Kidder and Judd, 1986:246). It would be better to ask, for example: During the last seven days — not counting today, have you bought any X?

Although the general case for brevity in wording questions would be accepted by most methodologists, it should be pointed out that it is not regarded as a virtue in all quarters. In the last few years, it has been challenged by methodologists concerned with the problem of getting respondents to recall material and by methodologists concerned with the effects of question threat. Laurent (1972) found that questions that began with a repetitive or redundant introduction (e.g. 'The next question is about medicines. We want to know about this. What medicines, if any, did you take during the past four weeks?') induced respondents to give more information than briefer versions of the same questions. And Blair *et al.* (1977) and Sudman and Bradburn (1982) have reported that long, open questions worded in the respondents' own language increased the level of reporting for socially sensitive or threatening topics. While the results of these studies are provocative, they should not be over emphasised here. For one thing, it is not clear what is really going on in each case. In the use of the 'medicines studies', as Converse and Presser remark (1986:11–12), the additional words may have stimulated respondents to talk more (i.e. a modelling effect), aided recall, or just given respondents more time to formulate an answer. In the case of the studies of questions concerning threatening topics, it is not clear whether the extra words generated a modelling effect (i.e. if the interviewer can talk about the topic without embarrassment, so can I), desensitised respondents to the threat, or just gave respondents more time to formulate an answer. Alternatively, as Hippler and Schwarz (1987:106) suggest, respondents may take the length of the question to be an indication of the importance the researcher places upon the question. Whichever are the correct explanations, it may be better to deal with the implied factors directly — that is, to explicitly provide appropriate recall cues, make the threat as low as possible, make sure that respondents have plenty of time to think, and make sure that respondents know why the researcher wants the information. (Note: we will return to these issues in Chapters 7 and 9.) It is worth adding that none of the suggestions that have just been made actually conflict with the idea that questions should be as brief as possible without lessening the clarity of the definition of key concepts.

The use of negatives

Another structural complexity that has been associated with respondent confusion over the interpretation of questions is the use of negatives. Most writers counsel against the use of double negatives because they have to be translated into positives. For example, the question: 'What is your view about the statement that conservationists should not be so uncooperative with the government?' has to be translated into the question: 'What is your view about the statement that conservationists should cooperate with the government?'

Regrettably, double negatives can sneak into questions without being noticed. Converse and Presser (1986:13–14), for instance, point out that the rating response option 'Disagree' can lead to double negatives as happens with attitude scale items: 'Teachers should *not* be required to supervise students in the halls — Agree . . . *disagree*'.

But it is not only double negatives that cause confusion. Even single negatives can create difficulties. Akiyama *et al.* (1979) provide data that indicate that questions such as: 'Isn't a robin a bird?' or 'Aren't you going to do X?' are harder to answer than positively worded questions (e.g. 'Is a robin a bird?', or 'Are you going to do X?'). The underlying difficulty associated with single negatives seems to be due to the implied presupposition (e.g. A robin is not a bird) that has to be identified and corrected before an answer can be given. And when an answer is given, it is not clear whether it applies to the original presupposition or to the corrected presupposition.

Linguists (e.g. Kearsley, 1976) have also discussed how the structure of negative questions can imply the answers expected. 'Are you going to do X?' implies a neutral expectation. 'You are going to do X aren't you?' implies a positive expectation (i.e a 'yes' answer). 'Aren't you going to do X?' implies a negative expectation. And, 'You are going to do X, aren't you?' implies a doubtful expectation.

Summary

In this chapter we have looked at the issues that have to be confronted if we want to formulate intelligible requests for information. We saw that both difficult and abstract words are best avoided. If a difficult word has to be used, it is best to define it clearly for respondents. Further, it was recommended that any definition should precede the difficult word rather than follow it, since this course is less likely to insult the intelligence of respondents who already know what the word means. It was suggested that abstract words should be given empirical referents by either providing specific, concrete examples or by providing illustrative vignettes. And it was suggested that words with multiple meanings and words with moral overtones should be avoided. In sum, it was argued that the overriding principles should be brevity, simplicity and concreteness.

We saw that long questions are more likely to elicit biasing response effects. Complicating phrases and clauses are often ignored by respondents — especially when they are placed at the end of a question so that respondents can start to answer before they have heard the complete question. If qualifying phrases or clauses have to be used, they should be put first. For clarity's sake questions should be positively worded. Whenever possible, the use of negatives should be avoided because they make questions and answers more difficult to interpret correctly. Single negatives imply complicating implicit propositions that become confused with the intended question and double negatives have to be translated into positives.

As a way of reinforcing the conclusions that have been reached in this chapter, it is worth ending by referring to the results of a program of research carried out by Belson (1981). Belson and his colleagues began by analysing the questions from 2140 questionnaires developed by twenty-four researchers. Types of questions generally recognised to generate response problems were identified and listed in order of the frequency of their occurrence (see opposite).

Notice that all of the questions involved complexities that conflict with the principles of brevity, grammatical simplicity, specificity and concreteness. Belson and his colleagues then presented variants of the six most frequently occurring types of questions to respondents. All were misunderstood by at least 42 per cent of the respondents: more than half were misunderstood by over 70 per cent.

Belson's sixteen categories of difficult questions arranged in order of decreasing frequency of occurrence

1   Two questions presented as one (e.g. 'Which brand do you use or do you change brands frequently?').
2   Questions with a lot of meaningful words (e.g. 'How many of each sized packet have you bought?').
3   Questions which include qualifying phrases or clauses (e.g. 'Have you bought any chocolate in the last 7 days, not counting today?').
4   Questions with multiple ideas or subjects (e.g. 'Which have you heard of or shopped at?').
5   Questions that contain difficult or unfamiliar words.
6   Questions that contain one or more instructions (e.g. 'Do not include X in your answer').
7   Questions that start with words that are meant to soften them (e.g. 'Would you mind . . .').
8   Questions with difficult phrases.
9   Hypothetical questions.
10 Questions that are dependent upon prior questions for meaning (e.g. 'Q1/ Did you buy a copy of X?' Q2/ Where is it now?').
11 Questions with negative elements.
12 Inverted questions (e.g. 'The ones you bought last time — what were they?')
13 Questions including either 'if any' or 'if at all' (e.g. 'Which of these, if any, have you bought?')
14 Questions that are too long.
15 Questions that include both present and past tenses.
16 Questions in which singular and plural cases are used.
Source: Belson, 1981: table 6.1., pp. 24–27. Presented here in modified form.

Chapter 5

CONTEXTUAL INFLUENCES
ON RESPONDENTS' INTERPRETATION
OF QUESTIONS

Throughout this chapter, the focus will be on the second step in the question-answer communication cycle (figure 5.1, p. 53).

Chapters 2 and 3 were directed at the problems that have to be confronted when formulating a question. We saw that there is a great deal of scope for slippage in communication between the researcher and the respondents. Researchers may be unclear about the topic they want to investigate and thus about the nature of the information they want to collect. They may use words that are not understood by the respondents. They may construct questions that are too complex for the respondents to comprehend. We saw, too, that the fact respondents answer a question is not, in itself, proof that the question has worked as the researcher intended it to work. It appears that respondents do their level best to answer all questions that are put to them — even those they have trouble interpreting (Belson, 1981; Strack and Martin, 1987). Of course:

> In principle, any ambiguity the respondent is aware of could be resolved by asking for clarification. In surveys, however, further explanation is typically not available and . . . may even be discouraged for the sake of standardization . . . In this situation, the respondent may use other available information to infer what the researcher wants to know. (Strack and Martin, 1987:127)

Strack and Martin list three sources of information that respondents may use to infer the meaning of a question: the content of the question itself, the accompanying sets of response options, and preceding questions. There is, however, a fourth source of information that should be added to this list. In the last chapter, the point was made that people typically try to take into account

Figure 5.1   *The focus of chapter 5*

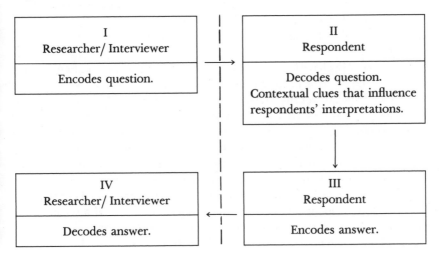

the researcher's purpose when answering. It is this fact that should be added to the list of sources of information that are available to respondents.

A closer look at each of the four kinds of clues that respondents can use to interpret questions will in turn cast additional light upon four of the assumptions that were identified as underlying the use of verbal data in social research (chapter 2) — namely that:

● answers are more valid if respondents have not been told why the question is being asked (assumption 6);

● answers are more valid if they have not been suggested to respondents (assumption 7);

● respondents' answers are not affected by the research situation *per se* (assumption 8); and

● the process of answering questions *per se* does not influence respondents' answers (assumption 9).

Clues afforded by either the question itself or its components

Clues associated with the question per se

It is almost impossible to ask a question without suggesting answers. The very fact that a question is asked implies that the researcher thinks the topic is of interest. Moreover, the way a question is asked inevitably reflects the researcher's *preconceptions*. Unstated presuppositions always underlie a question. For instance, Joshi (1983) notes that the question, 'How many students received the grade A in CIS 500 in the Fall of 1980?' presupposes both that the course CIS 500 was offered in the Fall of 1980 and that some students would have been given A grades.

Social scientists have long been aware that asking 'leading questions' of the sort 'When did you stop beating your wife?' can lead to biased answers because they indicate the answer that the questioner expects to be given. What has not been widely recognised is that all questions 'lead' respondents to some extent. If respondents are forced to accept incorrect preconceptions that are embodied in the way a researcher asks a question, they are likely to be pushed into giving answers that reflect the incorrect assumptions about the nature of their world that have been made by the researcher. Hiller (1973), draws attention to a particularly noteworthy instance of this. He argues that the closed ended questions requiring respondents to indicate membership of one of a set of social classes (e.g. working class, middle class, upper class) that many social stratification theorists had used in the past (e.g. Ray, 1971) presupposed both that the respondents lived in class-structured worlds and that these worlds were structured in the way implied by the questions. Such questions put pressure on respondents to put themselves into categories that had little meaning in their worlds as they defined them.

Another example (Briggs, 1986:55), this time an open question, is one in which an invalid assumption held by the researcher clashes with the culturally conditioned perceptions of a respondent, so that the researcher is in danger of misunderstanding the respondent's situation.

Briggs	How did the wealthiest local family make its money?
Respondent	There have always been wealthy persons all over.
Briggs	But how did the Xs get so rich when everyone else was so poor?
Respondent	Who knows?

While Briggs' initial question was based on the premise that a person becomes wealthy through a combination of will, hard work and fortuitous circumstances, his respondents believed that God bestows blessings on persons who work hard with a spirit of cooperation.

Clues provided by components of the question

Respondents use parts of the question to help them interpret other parts. For instance, Payne (1951:168) notes that the attempt to define abstract concepts by adding defining adjectival phrases ('like X' or 'such as X') has a strong tendency to make respondents equate the topic with the example given. For this reason, he claims, there would be a strong tendency to interpret the question:'Do you think that leafy vegetables like spinach should be part of the diet?' as asking 'Do you think that spinach should be part of the diet?' Similarly, he suggests that the question:'Do you approve or disapprove of women wearing slacks in public, such as while shopping?', is likely to be interpreted as: 'Do you approve or disapprove of women wearing slacks while shopping?'

Prestige names in a question also afford clues as to how the rest of the question should be answered. Smith and Squire (1990) have shown that the inclusion of a prestige name in a question (e.g 'President Reagan is asking Congress for . . . Do you agree or disagree?') had the effect of sharply reducing the percentage of 'no opinion' responses, because respondents used their knowledge of the prestige person's views and values to interpret the rest of the question. Smith and Squire conclude that:

> Adding prestige names does not simply shift all respondents in one direction. Instead, some become more favourable and others less so as partisanship and other factors begin to structure responses . . . (Smith and Squire, 1990:114)

Clues contained in accompanying sets of response options

In the past, most criticism about the tendency of questions to suggest answers has been directed at the presumed suggestive influence of pre-set response options. Certainly there is a great deal of evidence that pre-set response options are a source of interpretative clues.

At the most basic level, the ordering of pre-set options can be a source of information about how the options themselves should be interpreted. Holdaway (1971), for instance, reports that the percentage of respondents endorsing an 'undecided' category is much greater when it is put in the middle of a rating scale (i.e., 'Strongly agree, Agree, Undecided, Disagree, Strongly disagree') than when it is put at the end — for one item he investigated, the percentages endorsing the 'Undecided' response were 21.9 per cent vs. 0.8 per cent. Holdaway concludes that when the 'Undecided' category is placed in the middle position it is likely to be interpreted as 'Neutral' rather than as 'Undecided'. In other words, the position of the category suggests the meaning that should be ascribed to it.

More generally, pre-set response options may lead respondents into giving answers that they would not give if they had to provide the answers themselves — especially if the topic is very abstract or if the respondents have little knowledge upon which to base an opinion. This is demonstrated by the distribution of responses to two comparable questions used by the American Institute of Public Opinion before the US entered World War II (discussed by Rugg and Cantril, 1944:37). The first question was an open one which asked respondents, 'About how soon do you think we will be in the war?'. Twelve per cent said 'two months or less'. In response to a comparable closed question — 'Do you think we will be in the war within two months?' 'yes/no' — 25 per cent said, 'yes' (i.e. twice the percentage in response to the corresponding open question). In this case, it is hard to avoid the suspicion that the response categories that were part of the closed question had influenced the respondents' answers.

Critics have looked, too, at the effect of the 'incompleteness' of arrays of response options offered. Indeed, all methodologists have accepted the principle that any array of response options offered to respondents must be complete in the sense that all respondents feel that the options cover their 'true' positions. Molenaar (1982:52), for instance, states that a 'strong answer–suggestion, nearly an answer–coercion, emanates from closed questions whose alternatives are incomplete or unreal.'

The difficulty is that it is not always easy to detect 'incompleteness' in a response set both because, as has already been noted, respondents do their best to answer even those questions they have trouble with and because it is very easy to imply rather than fully list all the options. The corollary of the last problem is that it very easy to formulate sets of response options that fail to give equal weight or equal attention to all sides of an issue.

Another study reported by Rugg and Cantril (1944:32) demonstrates the suggestive effect that an 'imbalance' in the options can have. They prepared two versions of a question to elicit respondents' opinions about possible US policies. The first included four *isolationist* options, one borderline option and two *interventionist* options. The second included four interventionist options, one borderline option and two isolationist options. Whereas 24 per cent of the sample that responded to the first question endorsed an isolationist option, only 7 per cent responded thus to the second question.

It might be felt that the imbalance in the response options that accompanied the two questions used in the study discussed in the last paragraph would be obvious to most researchers. A failure to fully explicate options, however, is not always noticed. An example from Payne (1951:7–8) illustrates how easy it is to fail to explicate response options as well as the consequence of this failure. Sometimes the questioner assumes that the negative side of the question is so obvious that it need not be stated. He may simply ask:

Do you think most manufacturing companies that lay off workers during slack periods could arrange things to avoid layoffs and give steady work right through the year?

63% said companies could avoid layoffs,

22% said they couldn't, and

15% had no opinion

The alternative here seems to be so explicit in the question that it need not be stated. Either companies could avoid layoffs — or they couldn't. . . . But what happens when we take the trouble to state an alternative to another carefully matched cross section of respondents? '. . . or do you think layoffs are unavoidable?

35% said companies could avoid layoffs,

41% said layoffs are unavoidable, and

24% expressed no choice

In this example, an explicit statement on the other side of the picture resulted in a 28 per cent fall in support for the affirmative response option!

Another example, this time from Kalton et al. (1978:150–151), also demonstrates the effect of failing to fully explicate alternative response options. Kalton and his colleagues compared the response distributions for the question: 'Do you think that side streets should be closed to through traffic?' with the response distribution for the same question to which the following additional words had been added 'or should through traffic be free to use whatever route it likes?' Whereas 60 per cent of those responding to the first version agreed with the idea that side streets should be closed, 55 per cent agreed with this idea when it was presented with an alternative option.

More formally, the question: 'Do you approve or disapprove of P? — Approve, Disapprove', is clearly more balanced than the question: 'Do you approve of P? — Yes, No'. It is scarcely surprising, then, that Molenaar, in a review of the literature (1982:58), reports that the format: 'Is P better than Q? — Yes, No' produces a higher endorsement rate for P than does the question:'Which is best P, or Q? — P, Q'. Molenaar concludes that: 'each contrasting alternative tends to take responses from a specified alternative'. In sum, balanced formats produce lower response rates for a particular alternative than is the case if the weight of that alternative has not been offset by competing options.

Molenaar also reviewed the results of investigations into the effect of adding a 'pro' argument to one, but not both, possible answers to a question and concludes that such an imbalance results in an increase in support for the alternative with the 'pro' argument. He adds, though, that the inclusion of a 'counter' argument to the other alternative is not enough to balance the question. This observation leads him to conclude that arguments for alternatives should not be included in questions at all.

The failure to give equal weight to all alternative response options is not the only way that answers can be suggested to respondents — there are at least three general features of sets of response options that can influence, if not determine, the answers given by respondents. The first of these is simply the fact that *pre-set answer options act as memory cues* that help respondents remember answers that they might otherwise forget. The second is that *the range covered by a set of options is itself a source of information for respondents*. And the third is that *the number of options* per se *is associated with response bias*. The impact of each of these general features of sets of response options is discussed below.

Pre-set response options as a source of memory cues

It is a well-established psychological principle that people can more easily recognise stimuli to which they have previously been exposed than they can freely recall them. Applied to survey questions, this observation means that respondents will find closed questions that require them to recall specific information easier to answer than equivalent open questions. Selecting an answer from an array of pre-set options is easier than formulating an answer for oneself because it involves recognition rather than a full mental search for the information. For this reason respondents are more likely to be able to answer closed questions than open questions. But this raises a methodological problem for the researcher. Is the greater likelihood of respondents endorsing a particular option, when it has been explicitly listed, a consequence of memory cueing or a consequence of its having been suggested to respondents? It is true that adding contrasting alternatives to a closed question reduces the level of support each alternative receives (Molenaar, 1982, cited above), but this says nothing either for or against the 'cueing effects' hypothesis. The problem is that while suggestive processes would have to be seen as a source of invalidity in responses, cueing effects would have to be seen as a source of greater validity.

Information contained in the range covered by the options

The range a set of response options covers is another factor that has been found to affect the answers given by respondents to closed questions. Work done by Schwarz *et al.* (1985) produced evidence for this. In one study, 83.3 per cent of their respondents said they watched less than two and a half hours of television a day when they had responded in terms of categories which increased in half hour jumps, from 'Less than one half hour' to 'More than two and one half hours'. When respondents had to respond in terms of categories increasing in half hour jumps from 'Less than two and a half hours' to 'More than four and one half hours', however, the percentage saying that they watched 'Less than two and one half hours a day' dropped to 62.5 per cent. Schwarz *et al.* hypothesise that, in each condition, the respondents assume that the range of response options reflects the researcher's normative knowledge of the behaviour in question and hence the researcher's expectations concerning the respondent's likely answer. It follows that respondents should be reluctant to report behaviours that would seem 'unusual' in the context of the range of responses that have been offered to them. Schwarz *et al.* conclude that such 'response range' effects are most likely to occur when:

- It is difficult for respondents to either retrieve from memory or construct the required information — e.g. 'average' values for mundane, daily behaviours (like TV watching) — because respondents have never bothered to attend to it.
- The main concept is abstract, and respondents do not have direct knowledge of the normative levels for the behaviour in question.

The situation is summed up by Schwarz and Hippler:

> How strongly the scale biases respondents' reports will depend upon how much the scale deviates from respondents' actual behavioural frequencies . . . a precoded scale that matches respondents' behaviour may . . . be expected to increase the validity of the obtained reports. (Schwarz and Hippler, 1987:175)

On the basis of this reasoning, Schwarz and Hippler suggest that open questions may be more appropriate than closed questions for obtaining behavioural frequency data, especially about levels of behaviour that might be normatively deviant — for example, information about respondents' levels of alcohol consumption. Not every methodologist, however, would accept the idea of using open rather than closed questions even when inquiring about the frequency of normatively deviant behaviour. One alternative would be to make sure that the range of response options that is offered generously encompasses all likely levels of respondent behaviour. Of course, this can only be done if the deviant levels are 'high'. If they are 'low', they will appear more deviant if very high categories are included. This is a problem that researchers often run into when deciding upon an appropriate range of 'income' categories. The broader the range of categories that is offered, the more respondents with very low levels of income are likely to feel deviant.

Response biases associated with the number of options

The sheer number of response options offered is another factor which affects respondents' answers. Questions that include long lists of response options are prone to format effects that relate to the order in which the options are presented to respondents (see e.g. Krosnick and Alwin, 1987). When response options are presented on 'show cards' so that respondents can read them for themselves, respondents tend to select options early in the list (i.e. a primacy effect that is perhaps the result of a tendency for respondents to seize upon the first option that *satisfies* their interpretation of the question). When the options are read aloud, respondents tend to favour the last option they hear (i.e. a recency effect that may be due to interference to the memory traces for the early-presented options by the presentation of subsequent stimuli). Most methodologists have taken the view that the best way to control these biases is to vary the order in which the options are presented to respondents. The point of interest here, however, is that the likelihood of the occurrence of these biases has been found to be associated with the generality of the topic and the directness of its relevance to the respondents. It should be noted that both of these factors bear upon the general intelligibility of a question from the respondent's point of view.

Reviewing the situation, then, it is clear that pre-set response options can influence respondents' answers in a number of ways that can potentially lessen their validity. Several suggestions have been put forward to avoid some of these. Most importantly, the lesson is that the more clearly respondents understand the question, and the more adequate the array of pre-set options, the lower the potential for bias will be.

Beyond doubt, many of the problems that arise in question–answer situations do so because of the pressure put on respondents to respond. The conventional approach to this problem has been to include 'other' and 'don't know' categories as a means of reducing respondents' sense that they have been forced to endorse response options with which they are not comfortable. But another approach is implied by the theoretical framework set out in chapter 2. If respondents are seen as peers, they can be invited to correct questions that they feel are inadequate. The researcher, for instance, might instruct respondents to the effect that:

> It may be that you feel that you do not fit into any of the categories. If you feel that this is the case, I would be grateful if you would tell me — after all you are the expert on this topic and I would rather that you tell me that you have a problem with a question than that you feel forced to choose a response you are not happy with.

The impact of preceding questions

Researchers rarely ask single questions about a topic. A number of questions are usually asked, and this introduces the possibility that the answers given to later question can be affected both by earlier questions and by the respondent's own answers to them.

In fact, earlier questions are likely to influence respondents' answers in a number of ways, all of which challenge the validity of the assumption that the process of being interviewed does not change respondents' beliefs, opinions, attitudes and so on. First, prior questions about specific aspects of a topic can generate either a 'priming' or an 'avoidance of redundancy' effect that modifies the interpretation of subsequent, more general questions about the topic. These effects most commonly occur when a general question is preceded by one or more specific questions about the same topic. Second, a need to appear consistent can cause respondents to attend to the way they have answered previous questions. And third, the very act of answering earlier questions can make respondents think about their positions vis-à-vis the topic so that they are stimulated to formulate answers to later questions about the topic that they would not have given if they had not already been made to think about it.

Influences associated with prior specific questions

Most researchers follow the rule that, if a number of questions are to be asked about the same topic, they should be sequenced in terms of their levels of generality, with the most general question being asked first. Although the origins of this rule are far from clear, it is well ingrained in the literature on survey research. Over forty years ago, Gallup (1947) described a sequencing plan format that had been developed and used by the American Institute of Public Opinion since 1938. This format, which Gallup calls the 'quintamensional plan' (set out on page 62), is essentially structured around the idea of asking the most general questions first. The first and second questions are designed to establish (a) whether or not the respondent has ever heard of the topic, and (b) whether the respondent has ever thought about it. The third question is designed to focus respondents' attention on a specific aspect of the topic and the fourth and fifth questions refer to the aspect of the topic that has been specified in the third question.

According to Gallup, the quintamensional sequence was designed to overcome a number of common criticisms of opinion surveys, the first three of these being:

(a)   The charge that questions are often put to people who have no knowledge whatever of the issue being investigated.

(b)   The criticism that usually little or no effort is made to distinguish between respondents who have given little thought to the subject and those who have carefully weighed up the pros and cons.

(c)   The criticism that researchers usually ignore the fact that questions are often interpreted differently by different respondents.

It should be noted that the second question in a quintamensional sequence is always an open question because it is assumed that answers to open questions are more likely to reveal the respondents' frames of reference, which can then be taken into account when interpreting their answers about the specific aspect of the topic dealt with in questions 3, 4 and 5. The validity of this assumption is discussed in chapter 10.

The quintamensional plan for formulating questions pertaining to the same topic

1 A general question to establish whether respondents have the required information concerning the topic.	e.g. Have you heard of X? yes __ no __
2 An open question to get at respondents' general perceptions or feelings about the topic.	e.g. What are your views about X?
3 A dichotomous question to elicit perceptions or feelings about a specific aspect of the topic.	e.g. Do you favour or not favour Xi? favour __ not favour __
4 An open question to get at reasons for responses toward the aspect of the topic specified in step 3.	e.g. Why do you favour (not favour) Xi?
5 A rating question to allow respondents to indicate the strength of their responses toward the aspect of the topic specified in step 3.	e.g. How strongly do you feel about this?: Very strongly, Fairly strongly, Not at all strongly.

Other writers, too, have explicated the general-to-specific rule. Kornhauser and Sheatsley (1965, in Appendix C of Selliz *et al.*'s classic text) assert that application of the rule prevents specific questions from generating, in the minds of the respondents, mental sets that determine responses to later questions. For instance, they state that questions about strikes and union troubles should follow, rather than proceed, more general attitude questions about unions. In their well known text *The Dynamics of Interviewing*, Kahn and Cannell (1957:159) put forward a very similar argument to justify the general-to-specific rule (a practice that they refer to as the 'funnel sequence'). They also add that:

> [The] funnel sequence . . . assists the interviewer in maintaining a good relationship with the respondent and motivating full communication. It permits the respondent . . . in the early stages of the sequence to verbalize, as he will, those things which are salient for him. A sequence that begins with highly specific closed questions might force the respondent to postpone or refrain completely from talking about any of his salient attitudes.

And they go on to argue that, because general questions are the most easily justified in terms of their relevance to the avowed purpose of the study, they serve as natural leads for more specific questions.

Returning to the issue of whether or not previous, specific, related questions influence the answers respondents give: the evidence suggests that they do, although it has been proposed that several different processes can be involved.

It seems that prior questions sometimes have the effect of directly suggesting what should be said in answer to a question — in other words, they have a 'priming' effect. In other cases, prior questions seem to suggest what should not be said — that is, they have an 'anti-priming' or 'discounting' effect.

The following studies demonstrate the occurrence of 'priming' effects. McFarland (1981) found that respondents were more likely to evaluate the current energy crisis as 'severe' when they had been asked a series of specific energy-related questions before being asked for their general evaluations. Similarly, their evaluation of the 'future health' of the economy was more positive when it followed a set of specific questions. Likewise, their reported levels of interest in both politics and religion were greater after they had first answered a series of specific questions on each topic. McFarland advances the hypothesis that the general questions concerning interest in politics and religion were most sensitive to 'priming' because the specific questions were actually behavioural indices of the general concepts. That is, he suggests that such items as: 'How often do you pray?', or '. . . attend church?', are direct behavioural indicators of the general concept (interest in religion). He goes on to speculate that the less specific and the less concrete the general concept, the more likely it is that the content of specific questions will determine (i.e. 'prime') the respondents' interpretations of the (main concepts in the) general question.

Congruently, Bishop (1987) reports that respondents were much less likely to say that they follow political affairs if they had first been asked a number of difficult questions about their congressman's record. And they were much less likely to claim to be interested in politics after they had been asked an initial series of specific questions about the 1980 presidential elections. Such 'priming' effects were not lessened by intervening, unrelated 'buffer' questions (a result replicated by McClendon and O'Brien, 1988). Bishop concludes that respondents think about the general question only for as long as it takes for something to come to mind that allows them to formulate a relevant answer. The prior specific questions provide salient cues that allow them to do this. An alternative, but quite similar, explanation for the same results is offered by Bishop et al. (1984). Following Bem's theory of 'self-perception' (see e.g. Bem, 1978), they suggest that respondents use information from their responses to the first question when formulating responses to the second question.

> In effect, they ask themselves: What must my interest in politics be if I just told you that I don't know what my congressman has done for the district or how he has voted on any legislation . . . (Bishop et al., 1984:516)

But not all specific–general question sequences generate 'priming' effects. Some seem to generate what might be described as 'anti-priming' or 'discounting' effects. Kalton et al. (1978) set out to replicate the 'priming' effects demonstrated by a 1937 American Marketing Association survey of women's attitudes toward advertising. Apparently, in that survey, when a general question about advertising had been asked first, respondents had answered in terms of a wide range of products; when a number of specific questions about dresses preceded the general question, however, respondents tended to think in terms of dress advertisements. Kalton *et al.* used the following two questions relating to perceptions of the prevailing driving standards. The general question was: 'Do you think that driving standards generally are lower than they used to be, or higher than they used to be, or about the same?' The specific question was: 'Do you think that driving standards among the youngest drivers are . . .?' When the general question was asked first, 34 per cent of the respondents claimed that driving standards were lower than they used to be. When the specific question was asked first, 27 per cent thought they were lower. Further analysis indicated that this reduction occurred because the respondents who were over forty-five years old had excluded consideration of young drivers in their definition of drivers in general, when they had been asked the specific question first. Kalton *et al.* report similar results for another set of questions concerning traffic noise. Respondents who had first been asked about noise associated with truck traffic rated prevailing levels of traffic noise as less severe than respondents who had not been first asked about truck noise.

A second study that failed to generate an expected 'priming' effect is reported by Schuman *et al.* (1981). They begin by discussing the response distributions to questions on abortion that had been used in two National Opinion Research Center general social surveys in 1978 and 1979. In the 1978 survey a general question on attitude towards abortion had been preceded by a specific question on attitude towards abortion in cases showing evidence of foetal defect. In the 1979 survey, the specific question had been omitted. In the 1978 survey, 40.3 per cent of the respondents had agreed to the general idea that married women should be allowed to have abortions to limit the size of their families. The percentage of respondents agreeing with this item in the 1979 survey was 58.4 per cent. In 1979, Schuman and his colleagues replicated these results in a follow up split-half survey. Again, more respondents agreed with the general question when it was asked first. Since the specific–general sequence increased the difference between the response distributions, Schuman *et al.* describe the outcome as a 'contrast' effect. It would seem more descriptively accurate, however, to label such an outcome as an example of 'anti-priming' or 'discounting'. It should also be noted that Schuman *et al.* report that the effect in question was greatest for those respondents who were most uncertain about the general issue of abortion.

How are we to make sense of the discrepant findings that have just been discussed? When should one expect 'priming' effects and when should one expect 'discounting' effects? Tourangeau and Rasinski (1988) put forward a number of hypotheses that offer answers to these questions as well as sitting comfortably with the general thesis that underlies this chapter — namely that respondents who are asked about a vaguely defined issue are forced to search for clues in order to interpret it. Tourangeau and Rasinski argue that the context in which a question is asked affects the interpretation of questions in two ways: first, it provides clues as to what the question is about (i.e. how the key concepts should be interpreted), and second, it provides clues about what is worth saying. Following Grice (1975), they refer to the general norm of communication that holds that answers to questions should be informative. This means that respondents should understand that they are not expected to give information that they know the questioner already has. Hence, when prior specific questions (e.g. about marital happiness) can be seen to have already covered aspects of a wider matter (e.g. general happiness), the general question may be interpreted in a way that excludes consideration of the specific issues and 'discounting' will occur (Schuman *et al.* discuss this example). If, however, the specific questions are seen to be directly and logically related to the general question, they will tend to define the concepts in the general question and 'priming' will occur.

While the nature of the links between the specific issue and the general topic provide clues about how the general concept should be defined, the most direct indication of what is worth saying is the positioning of the specific questions. If a specific question immediately precedes a related general question, its content will be excluded from the content of the general question — on the grounds that the questioner has just been told about it. If, however, the specific question has been asked several questions earlier, it may still define the general context for the general question and generate a priming effect while being less likely to be discounted as something that has obviously just been said.

To complicate matters further, 'avoidance of redundancy' and 'priming effects' are not the only effects that can be triggered by previous questions. Ottati *et al.* (1989) distinguish between 'priming effects' and 'contrast effects' generated by prior specific questions. They report (1989:411) that the level of agreement with the proposition, 'People in general should receive a social benefit', increased with the favourableness of a related, prior question directed toward a specific group (i.e. a 'priming' effect occurred) providing the prior question came several questions earlier. They also note that these 'priming' effects were strongest when the priming episodes were subtle — when they were too obvious, respondents appeared to reject them to avoid appearing biased (Strack and Martin, 1987:139). When the related, prior question directed toward a specific group immediately preceded the general question (as opposed to coming several questions earlier), the level of agreement was lowered because 'comparison processes' appeared to be triggered off (i.e. a 'contrast' effect occurred). In addition, Strack and Martin (1987) hypothesise that the more information a respondent has about a topic (e.g. a particular politician), the more likely that prior thinking about a similar topic (i.e another politician) will produce such contrast effects.

More generally, the explanation for a number of different response effects which operate when a general question follows a related specific question lies, at least in part, in the fact that broadly defined topics, by definition, are poorly defined topics. Questions about vaguely defined issues inevitably put respondents in the position of having to search for clues about how they should be interpreted, and related, earlier, specific questions are often one of the few available sources of clues. The effects of such clues are eliminated by asking the general question before asking related, specific questions.

Although the general-to-specific rule would generally seem to be sound, it is worth asking whether there are any situations that call for the sequencing of questions in the reverse order. Kahn and Cannell (1957), for example, suggest that it makes sense to begin with specific questions, if the researcher wants to ensure that the respondents have considered certain points before making overall evaluations. Sudman and Bradburn (1982:208) take an almost identical stance in recommending that the researcher should:

> for personal interviews use funnelling procedures to minimise order effects. Start with the more general questions and move to more specific questions. For low salience topics, however, it may be necessary to ask questions on specific dimensions of the topic before asking for a summary view

Of course, one could take the view that, if the topic under investigation is properly defined in the first place, the use of such implicit stratagems will not be necessary. And given that there is no guarantee that all respondents would be influenced in the same way by the information implied by the content of the specific questions, the safer course must lie in beginning with a clear, explicit definition of the topic under investigation.

The psychological need to be consistent

We have just seen that the answers to prior, specific questions can affect interpretation of subsequent general questions. There are also other ways in which answers to prior questions can affect subsequent questions about the same topic. It has long been an axiom in social psychology that an individual's attitudes towards a particular topic have a tendency to become more consistent with one another over time — presumably because it is easier to operate socially if the attitudes one holds about any particular topic are consistent with one another. (See Hovland and Rosenberg, 1960; Feldman, 1966.)

The following (fictional?) excerpt from Lyn and Jay's *Yes, Prime Minister* (1986) indicates how the tendency to give consistent responses might operate in a social survey. The prime minister had seen the results of an opinion poll indicating that the majority of voters were in favour of national service, and had decided to announce in a television address to the nation that the government would bring national service back. Sir Humphrey was appalled that Bernard (the Prime Minister's private secretary) had failed to water down the planned speech. His solution was simple: have another poll done which would show that voters were really against bringing national service back. Bernard reports:

> I was somewhat naif in those days. I did not understand how voters could be both for and against it. Dear old Humphrey showed me how it was done . . . the market researcher asks questions designed to elicit consistent answers.
> Humphrey demonstrated the system to me. 'Mr. Woolley, are you worried about the rise in crime among teenagers?'
> 'Yes', I said.
> 'Do you think that there is a lack of discipline and vigorous training in our comprehensive schools?'
> 'Yes.'
> 'Do they respond to a challenge?'
> 'Yes.'
> 'Might you be in favour of reintroducing National Service?'
> 'Yes.'
> Well, naturally I said yes. One could hardly have said anything else without looking inconsistent . . .
> Humphrey suggested that we commission a new poll . . . He invented the questions there and then:
> 'Mr. Woolley, are you worried about the danger of war?'
> 'Yes', I said quite honestly.
> 'Do you think there is a danger of giving young people guns and teaching them how to kill?'
> 'Yes.'
> 'Do you think it is wrong to force people to take up arms against their will?'
> 'Yes.'
> 'Would you oppose the reintroduction of National Service?'
> I'd said 'Yes' before I had realised it . . . (Lyn and Jay (eds), 1986:106–107; extract reproduced from 'Yes Minister' with the permission of BBC Enterprises Ltd)

It should be noticed that this example rests upon the syllogistic principle of getting respondents to agree with a general, abstract statement before they are asked to agree with a related, less inclusive general statement. Although there have been few investigations of this principle reported in the literature, it is hard to imagine that it would not operate in an interview situation. One study that does provide empirical evidence for it, however, has been reported by McGuire (1960). McGuire's study demonstrated the effectiveness of syllogistic sequences for changing respondents' attitudes when the logical relationships between the questions have been made salient.

Even-handedness

We have looked at the way specific–general and general–specific question sequences generate distinctive order effects; in this section, we will look at the way the order of two evaluative questions that are on the same level of generality but involve two competing parties generate another kind of consistency effect that is different from those described above.

Schuman and Ludwig (1983) cite the results of several studies that clearly indicate that when respondents answer a question that allows them to favour their own side before answering a similar question favouring another side, the proportions of respondents favouring both sides are very different. When the questions are presented in the reverse order, the proportions of respondents favouring both sides are much closer to one another. This pattern of results is obtained even when the two focal questions are separated by a number of unrelated 'buffer' items (see, Schuman, Kalton and Ludwig, 1983). Schuman and Ludwig (1983), hypothesise that the pressure on respondents to be consistent stems from a general societal norm that dictates that one should be even-handed when dealing with two competing parties. If, for example, respondents first agree that their country should be allowed to set trade restrictions on a trading partner, they would be more likely to agree that trading restrictions should also be placed on their own country. This appears to happen, as long as the respondents are asked about their own country first. The principal difficulty with the even-handedness explanation is that the pattern of even-handedness does not seem to hold when respondents are asked about their opponents first. Why, when one favours one's own side first, does one not then equally favour the other side? Again, when one begins by being mean to the other side, why is one not equally mean to one's own side? One possible reason for the different response distributions is that in the own-side–other-side sequence, a self interested response is made before the issue of fairness or even-handedness is invoked and since even-handed responses to the second question would go too much against the respondents' self interest, the respondents are unable to follow the norm of even-handedness. If this explanation is correct, respondents should feel uneasy when answering the second question in an own-side–other-side sequence and be more willing to go back and change their answer to the first question, if they are given the opportunity, so that the norm can be applied. To my knowledge researchers have never given respondents this opportunity and all that can be said at the present time is that this is one of those issues that requires further empirical testing.

The impact of previous answers upon the respondent

The actual act of answering questions causes some respondents to either change the beliefs and attitudes that they held before being required to answer a particular question or generate views for the first time. A nice illustration of this possibility is provided by Gross (1964) who found that positive interest in buying a product-concept decreased by some 21 per cent when the question designed to measure level of support for the product was preceded by an open question about the product's perceived disadvantages and a further 11 per cent when another question about the perceived advantages was included. Grichting's (1986) finding that more than one in six respondents changed their views during the course of an interview, too, points to the same possibility.

The impact of the definition of the overall situation

In *The Invisible Man*, G. K. Chesterton suggests that people generally answer what they think you mean rather than what you may have technically asked:

> 'Is anyone staying with you?' The lady does not answer: 'Yes, the butler, the three footmen, the parlour maid and so on' . . . she says: there is nobody staying with us, meaning nobody of the sort you mean . . .
>
> All language is like that . . . you never get a question answered literally, even when you get it answered truly . . . (Cited by Lazarsfeld, 1972a:195)

Schuman (1982:23) has made the same point by suggesting that one's views about a 'good restaurant' may vary depending upon who is asking the question. The answer you would give to a poor student would probably be quite different from the answer you would give to a high status, visiting professor. In like fashion, Bilmes (1975) argues that ethnographical accounts are typically affected not only by what the respondent wants to say but by what the respondent thinks the interviewer either is capable of understanding or wants to hear.

Respondents have trouble taking questions seriously if they think the researcher already knows the answers. Emerson (1983) discusses this conclusion at some length.

> Similar problems have hindered the efforts of various 'indigenous' or 'third world anthropologists' to develop alternatives to the 'outside' descriptions and analyses of Western anthropologists by doing field studies in their own cultures (Fahim and Helmer 1980:646). Exactly because they are involved in a set of relations with

important local implications, indigenous fieldworkers often encountered resistances that the 'powerless and neutral stranger' did not. For example: 'the local anthropologist may not be taken seriously by informants if he probes types of behaviour that informants view as commonly shared knowledge, such as marriage customs, or he may be considered intolerably crude in broaching other topics such as sexual practices' (Fahim and Helmer (1980:646–647) . . . [And] . . . Platt (1981) experienced . . . these sorts of problems in her efforts to interview sociologists about their own research projects: For example, her questions appeared incongruous when respondents knew that she knew many of the things she was asking about. (Emerson, 1983:182)

Respondents are influenced by their assumptions regarding what the questioner already knows. Interpretation of the question: 'Why did John cycle to the store', for example, will be influenced by the questioner's assumed knowledge of John. If the questioner is assumed to know that John's car has broken down, the focus will be placed on 'the store'; if not, the focus will be placed on 'cycle' (as opposed to 'drive' or 'walk').

All of this leads one to the conclusion that questions necessarily operate in contexts, which in turn suggests that when interviewers do not explicitly provide contextual information, respondents will be forced to make their own guesses about the researcher's level of information in order to help them interpret the researcher's questions. But if respondents have to guess at the researchers' purposes or requirements, different respondents may very well make quite different guesses and hence give very different kinds of answers. Cicourel (1982) adopts a very similar line of reasoning when he argues that respondents will formulate their own hypotheses about the researcher's purposes, if they are not explicitly informed about them and that these hypotheses will influence the answers that they give. This situation is unavoidable, since, as Pawson points out:

No description, however detailed, can exhaust the subject or state of affairs it seeks to describe, so we have a permanent problem in organising any account we wish to make. According to the students of this dilemma, we routinely solve it through the application of 'multiple reflexive interactions between descriptor and described and between descriptions and their contexts' . . . In other words, we don't just utter descriptions as they take our fancy, rather we continually monitor what we have said about any situation, taking into account what has already been said about it and the purpose of the people with whom we are engaged in conversation.

Taking seriously the problem of meaning variation requires that we treat descriptions as social performances to be understood in terms of the practical purposes for which they are produced. This invites us to treat social research as an activity in which the subject actively examines the cues generated in the research process for appropriate forms of response. Respondents' utterances are made with an eye on what the researcher is really after. (Pawson, 1989:82)

In the past, survey researchers have typically, deliberately told their respondents very little about their aims. The explanations that they have given have usually been very general and given in introductory letters designed to win the respondents' cooperation rather than tell them exactly why the research was being done. Indeed, it has commonly been assumed by survey researchers that the answers given by respondents are more valid if the respondents do not know why the researcher is asking the questions. Thus, one has to suspect that many respondents have had, at best, a hazy idea of the purpose of the surveys in which they have participated.

While there have been few empirical investigations of this problem, it seems reasonable to suppose that survey findings reported by Fowler and Mangione (1990:59–61) and Gordon (1963, cited by Belson, 1981:20–21) would apply to most surveys that have been done in the past. Fowler and Mangione discuss the results of two health surveys which had begun with the usual sending out of advance letters explaining the purpose of the study to respondents, and had ended with follow-up interviews designed to measure the impact of the information given. Follow-up interviews conducted after the main survey had been completed revealed that over 50 per cent of the respondents had either no idea, or at best a vague idea, of the purpose of the study in which they had participated. The study by Gordon paints a similar picture. Gordon took thirty respondents through an interview in the usual way and then reinterviewed them to get at their perceptions about why each question had been asked. He found that there were many misunderstandings and that many of these were of a defensive kind (e.g., 'You wanted to grade me', 'You wondered if I was looking for the cheapest thing', 'did I feel out of place in the shop?').

When respondents are given only the vaguest of information about the purposes of the studies in which they are asked to participate, they are put in the position of having to make guesses about the researchers' requirements.

In summary, it is difficult to justify the assumption that concealing the purpose of individual questions from respondents is likely to result in the collection of more valid data. Presumably, this assumption rests on the belief that explanations given to respondents are likely to suggest answers to them that they would not otherwise give, or to unleash invalidating factors such as a desire either to help or to hinder the researcher. But keeping respondents in relative ignorance is not likely to avoid these problems. If respondents have to formulate their own hypotheses about researchers' purposes, because they have not been explicitly informed of them, and these hypotheses influence the answers that they give, respondents will try to help or hinder the researcher irrespective of whether or not they have been explicitly informed about the researchers' goals. Assuming that Cicourel and Pawson are correct, it makes more sense to tell respondents about both the overall purpose of a study and the specific purpose of each question. At least this way all respondents will take the same contextual information into account when they answer each question.

Such a course will only create problems if respondents perceive a research project to be against their interests — in which case, they might either refuse to cooperate or give invalid answers. It should also be said that if an investigation is not likely to serve the interests of respondents one could (and perhaps should) take the view that it should not be undertaken at all.

Again we should not lose sight of where we are going. The most important point in all of this is clear. It is simply that *respondents who know why a question is being asked are in a better position to help a researcher than those who do not*: for example, by correcting any incorrect presuppositions that the researcher appears to have made.

A common way in which respondents do this, when they feel free to do so, is illustrated by a politician's answer to a question put to him by a newspaper reporter (the Melbourne *Age* 18/5/88:16):
Reporter:

> The Green Paper argues repeatedly for the essential role of tertiary education for Australia's economic future. Why then is the Government prepared to reduce its funding responsibility for the expansion required to meet its economic goals?

Politician:

> Quite simply, *the assertion contained in this question is wrong, and provocatively so.*
> The Government is not prepared to reduce its funding responsibility in this area. Just as the Green Paper argued the economic importance of higher education, I have stated the Government's commitment to, at least, maintaining spending on it in real terms.
> The proceeds of the tertiary tax would be placed in a special dedicated fund, to be spent only on the identified aims of enlarging and improving the student assistance scheme . . . and providing more places in colleges and universities. That is, the funds . . . will be in addition to the current real level of expenditure. [my emphasis]

In this case the respondent's social status relative to the questioner's made it easy for him to challenge the assumption underlying the question. It should be remembered, however, that in most survey situations the respondents have lower social status than the interviewers. This makes it less likely that they will presume the right to correct the interviewer unless they have been explicitly invited to do so.

The insight that respondents might, under some conditions, be willing to correct any wrong assumptions they think researchers hold, is of fundamental importance. In chapter 2 we discussed the need for the researcher and respondents to give the same meanings to key terms, and it was noted that, whereas survey researchers have typically tried to achieve this by defining key terms for respondents, ethnographers have typically taken the view that researchers should take up the meanings used by their respondents. Both approaches, however, run into difficulties. The first runs the risk of *imposing* the researchers' understandings upon respondents. The second puts researchers in the position of *losing control* of the foci of their research projects. Two diametrically opposed reactions have been made to these dangers, neither of which is entirely satisfactory. Pawson (1989:294), on the one hand, argues that the fact that it is the researchers' responsibility to select the topic under investigation means that they cannot help imposing their frames of reference upon their respondents. Given this, they must then *teach* the respondents the theoretical framework that they are employing and get them to respond in terms of this framework. On the other hand, Mishler (1986:chapter 5) argues that researchers should not impose their own purposes upon their respondents but should collaborate with them with the aim of helping them describe their own worlds in their own 'voices'. The researchers should focus upon the respondents' needs, and should serve as advocates of their interests.

But the researcher does not have to take either of these courses. There is a middle way. The researcher can take the responsibility for choosing the research topic and treat respondents as peers (i.e give them the power to challenge any assumptions which the researcher holds about them that they think are unsound). Even if respondents are trained to view their worlds in terms of the theoretical framework being employed by the researcher and to respond in terms of its constituent concepts, there is no reason why they shouldn't also be empowered to comment upon the appropriateness of this framework, given their knowledge of the researcher's goals and their own experiences. In other words there is nothing to prevent the researcher from seeking feedback from the respondents. If, however, respondents are asked to give feedback about the adequacy of the theoretical framework, they must be informed as fully and honestly as possible both of the reasons for doing the research and of any prior assumptions held by the researcher regarding the respondents. These things could be done in communications leading up to interviews (e.g., initial conversations, prior letters and introductory paragraphs to question schedules) and in explanations which immediately precede particular questions. Only when respondents have a proper understanding of why each question is being asked will they be in a position to consciously formulate answers that are directed at the researcher's needs. Of equal importance, only when all respondents define the situation in the same way, will they give answers that can be meaningfully compared.

An additional contextual complexity: respondents' willingness to impart information

Survey researchers usually take it for granted that respondents are, or can be, motivated to impart any information that they may consciously hold. In fact, it is dangerous to accept this assumption without question. At the very least, respondents must both define the request for information as legitimate and be able to trust the researcher not to use it against them. Put another way, any information concerning the researcher's goals that is either implicitly or explicitly given to respondents is likely to condition their willingness to co-operate.

As an extension of this discussion about contextual influences, it should also be recognised that normative rules of interaction often bear on respondents' willingness to define requests for information as legitimate. Cicourel (1982), for instance, notes that 'norms of politeness' determine what, and to whom, infor-mation is given. There are other rules as well. For example, rules of group loyalty or status barrier rules determine what the members of one group (e.g. an 'age' or 'gender' group — Benney *et al.*, 1956) will say to a member of another group. An experience recorded by Rosalie Wax when carrying out a participant-observation study (with her husband) in a Sioux Indian community is instructive:

> We also found ... that when either of us approached an older man and asked a question like, 'Is there anything that your children particularly like about the schools?' he invariably ignored our question and proceeded to deliver an oration on the general value of education. Though eloquent, these speeches did not tell us what we wanted to know. When we approached younger married men and asked similar questions they looked away bashfully and changed the subject. We soon discovered that only ignorant White People would put such questions to men. For among the traditional Sioux, all matters involving children or child-rearing — at home or in the school — were culturally defined as women's business. Young men simply did not talk about children. Old men were expected to take a general benevolent interest in the welfare of the young. (Wax, 1979:510)

The assumption that respondents will always be willing to give information relevant to the researcher's goals, also presupposes that the respondents do not have goals of their own that override any claim that the researcher tries to make. If respondents are to help the researcher, they must be willing to accept the 'role' of respondent. Briggs (1986:56–57) discusses the potential impact of respondents' own definitions of their role. He recounts a situation in which he was asking an elderly couple about the wealthy individuals in the community. Whereas he was trying to obtain information about the theological expla-nations of inequality, his respondents tried to use the interview to convince him of the prevalence of religiously motivated cooperation in bygone days and of the superiority of this 'weltanschauung' over secular individualism. That is, they were intent upon pursuing their own goal of instructing him about the best way to live.

To repeat the point, it is dangerous to assume that respondents will always be willing to help the researcher in the way the researcher wishes.

Whether or not respondents will be motivated to help the researcher ulti-mately depends upon how they define the research situation. Researchers have no option but to try to make sure that their respondents understand and accept the aims underlying their investigations

Summary

We have learnt that respondents do their best to answer all questions that are put to them — even those they have trouble interpreting. It seems that when respondents have difficulty interpreting a question they use all available clues that might help them. In general, there are four kinds of clues available to them. There are: clues afforded by the way the way the question is worded; clues generated by the accompanying sets of response options; clues contained both in previous related questions and in the answers the respondents have already given to these questions; and clues afforded by the overall definition of the situation. Unless all respondents attend to the same clues, different respondents are likely to interpret particular questions in quite different ways.

The problems that arise when different respondents are influenced by different clues as they attempt to interpret a question, can be lessened either by making sure that the interpretive clues that respondents should use are explicitly drawn to their attention or, perhaps better still, by clearly defining the topic in specific, concrete terms and clearly spelling out the reason for asking the question so that there is no need for respondents to fall back onto contextual clues in order to clarify the question for themselves. The researcher should also ensure that the respondents have accepted the researcher's goal in asking the question and that they are not motivated to pursue their own goals instead.

Chapter 6

*T*HE NEED TO
PROVIDE RESPONSE FRAMEWORKS

We turn now to explore both the nature and consequences of a number of decisions which respondents must make when they formulate answers to questions that have been put to them (see figure 6.1, p. 77).

The decisions the respondents make define the kinds of answers they give. The basic thesis is that answers are always formulated within response frameworks; this chapter deals with the problem of defining these response frameworks.

That different respondents often give quite different kinds of answers to the same question is a commonplace observation. Similarly, it is commonly observed that respondents often seem to have very different things in mind when they give objectively identical answers to the same question. Methodologists have used the concept of 'perspective' or 'frame of reference' to explain these observations (see, e.g., Lazarsfeld, 1944; Crutchfield and Gordon, 1947; Kahn and Cannell, 1957). Although the 'perspective' concept has never been properly defined, the basic insight is that it is possible for respondents to respond to a topic in a large (perhaps infinite) number of different ways when answering a question about it.

It should be said at the outset, however, that the 'perspective' concept is not a simple one. Differences in past experiences can cause respondents to respond to the same topic in different ways (e.g. in terms of how it relates to their economic, political, religious or domestic situations). It is also the case that logical differences in perspectives arise because responses can be made on different levels of social generality, different causal explanations for the same event can fall into logically different categories, and evaluations of the same item can be made in logically different ways. Each of these matters will be explicated in the following pages.

Descriptive accounts

Kahn and Cannell (1957:120) report that researchers working for the US Bureau of Census found that the question 'Did you do any work for pay or profit last week?' resulted in lower estimates of the number of people in the workforce than when respondents were asked to specify their 'major' activity before being asked whether or not they did any additional work for pay. They note that the second approach added more than one million workers to the total estimated workforce. Apparently respondents who were asked the first question had tended to answer in terms of their 'major' activity and ignored part-time employment. For example, college students had tended to see themselves as students and women had tended to see themselves as housewives despite being employed part-time. In other words, the respondents' situations had determined how they related to the topic.

Figure 6.1   *The focus of chapter 6*

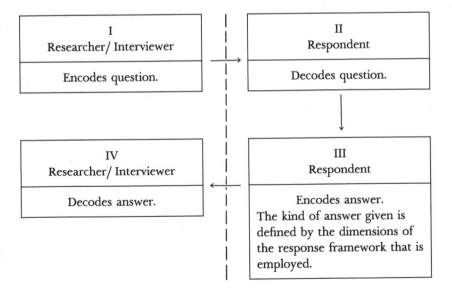

The fact is, respondents can look at any situation, and thus describe it, in many different ways. Payne (1951:175), makes the comments that respondents' answers to 'where?' questions vary greatly. In response to the question, 'Where did you read that?', one respondent might say, 'In the *New York Times*', another might say, 'At home in front of the fire', and a third, 'In an advertisement'. Yet another might answer in terms of a combination of the possible array of answers: 'In an ad. in the *New York Times* while I was at home sitting in front of the fire'. Moreover, all answers could be correct.

Kahn and Cannell (1957:116) use the following hypothetical example to draw attention to the same problem. They claim that if respondents were asked what they think about car production these days, and 50 per cent endorsed the view that production was too high, the respondents endorsing this view would not necessarily mean the same thing. Some might answer in economic terms (e.g. how the companies will have to cut back and how this will result in higher unemployment levels). Some might answer in terms of what they think the impact of cars has been upon people's morals (e.g. people don't go to church any more because they prefer to go driving on Sundays). Some may think in terms of the effect on traffic congestion, while others may think in terms of the social difficulty that new models create for them (e.g. I can't afford to trade in my car every year).

The problem that is being discussed here is not just of theoretical interest: it has practical consequences, as an example discussed by Crutchfield and Gordon (1947) indicates. In August 1943, Gallup Polls conducted a national poll in the United States in which respondents were asked: 'After the war, would you like to see many changes or reforms made in the US or would you rather have the country remain pretty much the way it was before the war?' Fifty-eight per cent said that they wanted things to remain the same. In September of the same year, the Division of Program Research in the US Agriculture Department carried out a small scale ($n = 114$) follow-up study in New York. Again, a similar percentage of respondents (49%) said that they wanted things to remain the same. But this time the investigators did not stop there. They probed the meanings that the respondents had given to the answer that they had endorsed. Respondents who wanted to see changes and reforms were asked:

(a) What sort of changes or reforms would you like to see?
(b) Are there any changes or reforms that you wouldn't like to see?
Those who wanted things to remain the same were asked:
(a) What sort of things wouldn't you like to see changed or reformed?
(b) Are there any changes or reforms you would like to see?

Crutchfield and Gordon note that the 114 respondents were found to have related to the topic in a wide range of ways. For example, 63 per cent had responded in terms of different domestic issues — a category that included education, unemployment, increased social security, making the political system more efficient, restricting immigration and eliminating hatred among people. Others had responded in terms of a range of technological changes, the political structure, foreign affairs, conditions that had prevailed before the war, or their own personal situation or ideals.

Yet another example illustrates the same general problem. Gilbert and Mulkay (1983) report how two groups of scientists gave conflicting accounts of the same event, because members of the first group focused on methodological issues while members of the second focused on political issues:

> Consider as an example the discovery of pulsars . . . The Cambridge research group who discovered them did not announce their finding either to other scientists or the public for some months. During that period they investigated the new phenomenon further. They later said that they did not make a public announcement of their important discovery immediately in order that they could make sure that they were correct in identifying the strange radio signals they had noticed as coming from pulsars, rather than from some more familiar source. However, a number of other scientists subsequently criticised the Cambridge group, saying that the delay in the announcement of the discovery was an inexcusable tactic designed to ensure that Cambridge had a headstart on other astronomers in further studies of pulsars. In short, they accused the Cambridge astronomers of engaging in a politically motivated stratagem. Thus we have two accounts of the same action, of which one asserts that the action was not political and the other, that it was. (Gilbert and Mulkay 1983:14–15)

The fact that different respondents can view the same topic in different ways raises two issues for the researcher. First, it gives rise to the danger that, if the researcher is not wary, answers that look the same on the surface (e.g. simple 'yes' answers), but that have been given from different perspectives, will be treated as if they have the same meaning. Second, unless the researcher knows what perspective a respondent has used, the researcher will not be able to interpret the respondent's answer with any confidence. The following anecdote demonstrates the potential for a failure of communication when interactants look at an issue from different perspectives:

> A judge, addressing a prisoner who had been found guilty of 'conning' an elderly couple out of their savings asked how it was possible that an obviously well educated man could take advantage of an elderly couple who had so plainly trusted him. 'With respect your honour', the convicted man said, 'I think you have missed the point — they would not have given me the money, if they had not trusted me'. (Told to the author by a colleague, source unknown)

If respondents adopt different perspectives when answering a question, it can be argued that they are not answering the same question. If this happens, the answers that they give cannot be meaningfully compared.

Given an unlimited number of possible perspectives that can be used to frame answers to any question, how should the researcher proceed? The traditional advice has been to look at answers to related open-ended questions in the hope that the various perspectives that different respondents have used can be identified. Comparisons between different respondents can then be limited to those who have employed the same perspective. But two difficulties beset this approach. First, it has to be kept in mind that the perspective that is salient to the respondent at the time of answering may very well be a matter of accident (unless it has been specified by the researcher). In other words, the perspective that is salient at one point in time is not necessarily salient at another. Second, it seems that respondents can shift from one perspective to another even as they are answering a question. Crutchfield and Gordon (1947), for instance, found that one quarter of the respondents who took part in a study spontaneously shifted from one dimension to another while explaining the answers they had given to the question about whether they would like to see changes or reforms after the war.

The two difficulties which have just been mentioned point to a more general problem that is discussed by Gilbert and Mulkay:

> Of course, disagreements, . . . in which the same action is characterised in apparently conflicting ways by different actors, are commonly found in sociological data. They are endemic to social life and therefore occur frequently in observers' field notes and in sociological interviews. But the usual method of treating such conflicts is to 'interpret' the available evidence in order to decide who is right, and what actually happened. This can be done . . . by assessing the reliability of the various items of evidence. This involves rejecting some accounts and favouring others on the basis of further data or the sociologist's own intuitive understandings. But this further data will consist of yet more accounts obtained from other participants or constructed by the observer. These additional sources are likely to raise more inconsistencies and conflicts. (Gilbert and Mulkay, 1983:15)

Given this view, Mulkay and his colleagues have opted for an alternative tack to that traditionally taken. Struck by the sheer diversity of accounts that scientists employ when talking about their work, Mulkay and his co-researchers have begun to look for patterns in the occurrence of different kinds of accounts:

> accounting systems tend to be deployed differentially from one social context to another. For instance, the standard utility account is rarely qualified or undermined in the formal research literature, whereas the contingent repertoire is hardly ever directly used in that literature. Thus, it is important to examine a variety of discursive products, both formal and informal, in order properly to elucidate the organisation of scientific accounting. Although interviews on their own will not fully elucidate this organisation, they provide a useful supplement to the formal literature

of science, with its narrowly constrained procedures for making scientific activity and belief accountable, and to the direct transcription of informal interaction, which for practical reasons is inevitably very incomplete in its coverage of the social life of science.

The crucial feature of our approach, then, is that we are not using interviews, or any other source of data, to build up an accurate picture of the actions and beliefs of participants in specific domains of social life. Rather, we are using interviews as a technique for generating interpretive work on the part of the participants, with the aim of identifying the kinds of interpretive repertoires and interpretive methods used by participants and with the goal of understanding how their interpretive practices vary in accordance with changes in interactional context. (Potter and Mulkay, 1985:268–269)

The principal criticism that can be directed at the tack adopted by Mulkay and his colleagues is that it comes close to throwing out the baby with the bathwater. Few researchers would be happy with having to give up the idea that respondents' answers contain substantive information about their worlds in favour of the idea that the answers merely contain information about the kinds of accounting schemata respondents use to make sense of their worlds both to themselves and to others.

As has been argued in previous chapters, there is yet another possible approach to the problem of the diversity of kinds of answers respondents give, besides the traditional tack and that adopted by researchers such as Mulkay and his colleagues. The researcher can assume the responsibility of clearly specifying the perspective that respondents should have in mind — be it moral, instrumental, political or other. In effect:

the respondent is instructed, as part of the question, with respect to the frame of reference which he is to employ. For example, 'How have you people been getting along this year? Financially I mean . . .' (Kahn and Cannell, 1957:118)

By doing this the researcher can be more confident that respondents will all give the same kinds of answers. While this course can be adopted with most topics, it is possible that it will not work if respondents are under emotional tension in respect to the topic, as Kahn and Cannell (1957:119) suggest. When that is the case, their emotional reactions are likely to overwhelm any attempts to specify the perspective that should be used. For example, an overweight male executive who has just been told by his doctor that he will have a heart attack if he continues to work so hard would, when asked about his job, probably find it impossible to think about anything other than the stresses associated it. The only hope in such a situation is that the respondent's emotional state would be obvious enough for the interviewer to be aware of it and to take it into account when interpreting the respondent's answers.

Levels of social generality of responses

In this section we will discuss the fact that the perspectives respondents adopt can vary according to their level of social generality. Respondents can answer in terms of their own points of view or from a broader group or community point of view. The consequence of this is that response distributions for personalised questions can differ markedly from response distributions for impersonal questions. The results of an experiment reported by Payne (1951:196) will serve to indicate the significance of this possibility:

> The personalised question read:
> If you could get some insurance for which you paid a certain amount each month to cover hospital care you might need in the future, would you rather do that or would you rather pay the hospital what it charges each time?
> The impersonal question read:
> Some people have a kind of insurance for which they pay a certain amount each month to cover any hospital care they or their families have in the future. Do you think this is a good idea or a bad idea?
> The response distributions for the two questions were as follows:

Personalised		**Impersonal**	
Prefer insurance	66%	Good idea	92%
Pay each time	28	Bad idea	4
No opinion	6	No opinion	4

> [By] ... changing from the personalized speak-for-yourself-John question to a general one which allows respondents to answer more altruistically or with less consideration of personal consequences, approval of prepayment hospital insurance increased by 26 percentage points. (Payne, 1951:197)

Because the word *'you'* can be either a personal or a generalised pronoun, there is room for miscommunication every time it is used. This conclusion is reinforced by the results of a program of research carried out by Belson and his colleagues who analysed the interpretations given to the word 'you' in the context of a question about TV watching: 'On an average evening, how often do you switch from one channel to another?' They found that twelve of fifty-three respondents interpreted 'you' to include family members. These and similar results for other questions led Belson (1981:386) to hypothesise that *the word 'you' is prone to being interpreted collectively when it is used in conjunction with behaviour which the respondent does with others.*

To take another example, a question of the sort: 'What proportion of your income should you give to charity?' is deficient as it stands because the level of generality has not been specified. The respondent can either give a personal answer or an answer in terms of general community norms and it would not be clear from the answer *per se* into which category it falls. Another example from Payne (1951:159) will serve as a final warning:

> 'How many radio sets did you repair last month?' — this question seemed to work all right until one repairman in a large shop countered with, 'Who do you mean, me or the shop as a whole?' . . .
> Sometimes 'you' needs the emphasis of 'you yourself' and sometimes it just isn't the word to use, as in the above situation where the entire shop was meant.

As with the problem of the accounting schemata respondents adopt, one practical solution is for the researcher to explicitly indicate what kind of answer is required:

e.g. (a) What is *your own view* about X?

vs. (b) What do you think *most people in your village* would think about X?

The potential for confusion between levels of social generality is again illustrated by data collected by Prendergast and Prout (1983:520–521). In a study of fifteen-year-old girls' views of motherhood, they found that although most of the girls responded in positive stereotypic or cultural terms, when asked to respond to the assertion that 'It's a good life for mothers at home with a young child', many expressed a more realistic view when they talked of their own experiences. The following is a typical response based on stereotypic cultural knowledge: 'Most women get pleasure looking after a child. Got someone to look after, most women have mothering instincts and want to look after people'. The next is typical of views based on personal knowledge: 'well, when you first of all have a baby you think how it's going to be bringing them up, but when you get to toddlers you wonder why you had it for in the first place, most mothers do'.

Before concluding this section, it is worth adding that the generalised pronoun 'one' is likely to generate the same ambiguity of meaning as 'you'. And the singular and plural pronoun 'who' is similarly ambiguous. Payne (1951:176), for example, notes that the question, 'Who is to blame?' can either be interpreted to mean 'which single person is to blame?' or 'which group is to blame?' (Note: one could add 'Which individuals are to blame?' and 'Which groups are to blame?')

The researcher's problem, then, lies in the fact that respondents can answer the same question in different ways, depending upon the level of social generality that they think is required. Further, it is not always possible to tell, just by looking at an answer, which level of social generality it has been pitched at. One way around this difficulty is for the researcher to clearly specify the kind of answer that is required — the kind of answer the researcher requires being determined by reference to theoretical or practical considerations. If the aim is to correlate individuals' views regarding a particular topic with their answers concerning other topics, personal answers would be appropriate. If the aim is to have respondents act as anthropological informants, or to measure the respondents' perception of the prevailing level of consensus, questions aimed at their perceptions of the social norms *per se* would be in order. And if the aim is to measure the degree to which respondents are integrated into their communities — that is, to measure the closeness of their personal views to the prevailing normative views, both types of questions would be called for so that answers to the two types of questions can be compared.

Explanations

We have just seen that respondents can honestly answer any question in more than one way because they can relate to the topic in different ways. For a similar reason, respondents can give any number of explanations for the same behaviour. As Menzel (1978) argues, a man mowing his lawn might be: beautifying his lawn, taking exercise, avoiding his wife, conforming to his neighbours' expectations, protecting the value of his property, and so on. It is also possible that he might give more than one of these reasons, or even all of them in any explanation of his behaviour.

It is no wonder, then, that researchers have proposed a number of different schemata for making sense of an apparently infinite number of possible kinds of explanations. Lazarsfeld (1972b), for example, has suggested that answers to open questions used in market research to determine why respondents buy a particular product can reflect internal motivational states (e.g. 'I like trying new products'); properties of the product *per se* (e.g. 'I like its rich flavour'); and external factors (e.g. 'it was all the grocer had'). Making the matter even more complicated, Zeisel (1958: chapters 4 and 7) extends this list by suggesting that explanations can focus on push–pull factors and social structural factors (e.g. focalising processes, crystallisers and precipitants).

The simple fact is that a respondent can frame an explanation in many different ways. Lehnert's (1978) work on causal explanations reinforces this conclusion, as do several other methodological discussions that can be found in the social scientific literature. Lehnert (1978) identifies five different kinds of answers to the question 'Why did you do X?' These are defined in terms of whether the respondent focuses upon:

(a) causal antecedents — what caused the respondent to do X;

(b) goal antecedents — the respondent's purpose in doing X;

(c) enablement factors — how it was possible for the respondent to do X;

(d) causal consequences — what happened after the respondent had done X; or

(e) the researcher's expectations — why the respondent had done X when the researcher had expected the respondent to do Y.

The following fictional case illustrates how actual answers can vary depending upon the explanatory focus adopted by the respondent. Imagine a situation in which an agricultural expert is interviewing a farmer and comes to the question, 'Why did you plant wheat this year?' Depending upon the explanatory factors focused upon, the answer might be:

(a) The rain came too late to plant potatoes.
(causal antecedent)

(b) I wanted time off about the time potatoes would need to be harvested.
(goal antecedent)

(c) I was able to borrow a wheat seeder this year.
(enablement)

(d) I didn't know that it would lead to an outbreak of grasshoppers.
(causal consequences)

(e) After you saw me last time, I had a call from the Wheat Board and they suggested that I plant wheat.

Lehnert's classification does not exhaust the possible range of causal perspectives respondents can adopt. Lazarsfeld and Barton (1962), for example, discussing the problem of how to code the diverse range of explanations that women typically give for buying this or that cosmetic item, suggest another set of perspectives:

> Women make a great many comments on their reasons which are hard to group if one takes them at face value. But visualise a woman buying and using cosmetics. She gets advice from people she knows, from advertising, and from articles in mass media; in addition she has her own past experiences to go on. She has her motives and requirements: she uses cosmetics in order to achieve various appearance values so as to impress others — one might even find out whom — and perhaps to impress herself. The cosmetics have various technical qualities which relate to these desired results. She may also worry about possible bad effects on health or appearance. There are the problems of applying the cosmetics. And finally there is the expense. All of the woman's comments might be related to the following scheme: 'Channels of information', 'desired appearance values', 'prospective audience', 'bad consequences', 'technical qualities', 'application problems', and 'cost'. (Lazarsfeld and Barton, 1962:88–89)

Another accounting schema is suggested by Campbell (1945), who notes that respondents can take different 'time' perspectives. Thus the question: 'Why do you think Germany is at war?' can elicit answers grounded in the past (e.g. 'The Germans want revenge for . . .'), answers grounded in the present (e.g. 'They are afraid to resist the Nazis'), or answers oriented to the future (e.g. 'The Nazis want to establish a master race').

Again, all of the coding schemata that have been advanced force one to the same conclusion. Different respondents can give quite different kinds of explanations for similar events depending upon how they orient to the events in question. Further, each respondent can honestly give more than one kind of answer. Thus, as in the last two sections, if different answers are to be meaningfully compared, the researcher either has to try to identify the perspective that each respondent has adopted or specify the perspective that all respondents should use.

Evaluations

Evaluative judgements are always relative. They are never absolute statements. Evaluations always involve comparisons with standards. When we use a metric measuring tape to judge the length of something, for instance, we are using an instrument that has been calibrated by reference to a 'standard metre' as have all other metric measuring tapes that we might buy. In other words, the length of the object we are measuring is being measured in terms of a defined objective standard. The same principle holds when a social issue is measured. For example, the question, 'Are you a generous person?', cannot be meaningfully answered in an absolute way. One can meaningfully answer it only by comparing oneself with another whom one knows is 'seen to be' a generous person.

But the standards that are associated with questions used in social research are typically poorly specified. Worse, there are different kinds of standards that respondents can use. Social standards can be either explicit or implicit as well as being either internal or external to the question. Hence, it is possible for different respondents to be influenced by different standards. When this happens — and the researcher does not know that it has happened — the answers cannot meaningfully be compared with one another. It is also possible for respondents to refer to a different standard, or standards, to that which the researcher has in mind so that the researcher is unable to properly interpret the respondents' answers.

Evaluative standards that are external to the question

> The New Yorker and the rural Arkansan are likely to disagree on whether Little Rock is a big city; the Alaskan and the Texan will have different ideas of what constitutes a hot summer; the airline pilot and the timid passenger will have different answers when asked if a trip was pleasant and uneventful. (Kahn and Cannell, 1957:115)

These comments from Kahn and Cannell draw attention to the way in which contextual standards can serve as evaluative standards. The same principle is evidenced by the results of an experiment reported by Charters and Newcomb (1968). They had Catholic subjects respond to seventy-two rating scale items that were directed at attitudes towards religion, feminism and political pro-gressiveness, under conditions which heightened their awareness of being Catholic. They also had a control group of Catholic subjects respond to the same items under conditions that did not emphasise their religious affiliation. They found that the answers given by the experimental group were closer to 'nor-mative' Catholic answers than were those given by the control group. Another finding reported by DeLamater (1973:54–55) illustrates the same principle. Female college students reported greater levels of sexual permissiveness if they reported their sexual behaviour before, as opposed to after, answering ques-tions about the sexual behaviour of their five best friends.

Although the examples that have just been discussed strongly suggest the importance of the 'reference group' principle, it should be admitted that there has been very little empirical investigation of it. Even so, it would seem prudent for the researcher to keep in mind that personal answers are likely to be affected by 'reference group' effects when: (a) they have been evoked by previous ques-tions, and (b) the researcher has neglected to clearly specify the standards that should be used.

Another cautionary note is perhaps in order at this point. It is not always obvious when contextual standards are likely to intrude into a question. In the last chapter we saw how implicit contextual standards can be introduced by the range covered by a set of response options. Work done by Schwarz and his colleagues (e.g. Schwarz and Hippler, 1987) clearly suggests that respondents interpreted the range a set of response options covered as an indication of how the researcher saw the situation — that is, as a clue to normative standards. This is also a plausible explanation for experimental results reported by Loftus (1982). When respondents were asked, 'How many products have you tried: 1? 2? 3? . . .' vs. 'How many products have you tried: 1? 5? 10? . . .', the average was 3.3 vs. 5.5.

A similar, and probably related, phenomenon to the 'reference group' effect is the phenomenon that Payne (1951:159) refers to as 'dead give-away' words. These are words in response options that are too extreme, such as 'all', 'always', 'each', 'every', 'never', 'nobody', 'only', 'none', and so on. Payne gives the following hypothetical examples to spell out the problem:

Q. Is the mayor doing *all* he can for the city?
A. I'm sure he could do more if he wanted to.
Q. Is your boss *always* friendly?
A. Well, he is sometimes not very friendly.
Q. Have you *ever* listened to X . . .?
A. I suppose I must have at some time or other.
Q. Have you been to *each* (in the sense of every) show?
A. Well, I've gone to most of them.

The problem with 'dead give-away words' is that *people learn that there are exceptions to most rules and consequently avoid selecting answers that include them.* Similarly, one might suspect that most respondents have learnt that extreme options such as 'agree very strongly' rarely reflect the normative standards of a group and for this reason will be less likely to endorse them.

Evaluative standards that are built into the question

Evaluative standards can be explicitly built into a question. This is the case when respondents are asked to assess each stimulus in a range of stimuli by comparing each with a defined standard. If this can be done properly, the researcher knows both what evaluative standard has been used and that all respondents have made their judgements in the same way. As desirable as these outcomes may seem to be, it is difficult to find convincing examples of their achievement in the research literature. Evaluative standards are usually either implicit or poorly defined. It is not difficult to find examples that require respondents to orient to the vaguest of standards. Consider the following question, for example: 'Compared with a year ago, are you more or less happy with your job?' (discussed by Payne, 1951:167).

The common rating scale, too, epitomises the failure to use properly defined standards of comparison in social research. Response options such as 'Strongly Agree', 'Agree' etc. (i.e. the evaluative standards provided for respondents) lack consensual meaning simply because they lack empirical referents. What one respondent means by endorsing a particular option (e.g. 'Agree') is not necessarily what another means when endorsing the same option. Further, the implied evaluative standards of many rating tasks are often biased or imbalanced. Loftus (1982) cites a number of examples which illustrate the effect of an asymmetric specification of anchor points. When respondents were asked 'how tall', as opposed to 'how short', a basketball player was, the average estimate was 79 inches vs. 69 inches. Presumably this effect would disappear if respondents had been asked 'What height do you think the basketball player is?' When respondents were asked 'how long', as opposed to, 'how short' a film was, the average estimate was 130 minutes vs. 100 minutes. When respondents were asked whether they got headaches 'frequently', as opposed to 'occasionally', and if so how often, the average number of headaches reported was 2.2 vs. 0.7 headaches per week. Similarly, estimates of the speed of a car in a film of an accident were influenced by whether respondents were asked how fast a car was going before it 'smashed' into another car, as opposed to 'collided' with it.

The failure to properly define evaluative standards for respondents is a very common failing in social research. It is such an important issue that we will return when discussing the measuring of attitudes in chapter 11.

Summary

Different respondents often give different *kinds* of answers to the same question. This happens because the general perspective that characterises an answer has a number of degrees of freedom. If the researcher does not specify the position that respondents should take on each of the key dimensions, respondents are forced to choose their own positions and they may or may not choose the same combination of positions. This inevitably leads to a diversity of kinds of answers.

The inherent danger presented by a diversity of kinds of answers is that the researcher will fall into the trap of trying to compare the answers that different respondents give — a bit like trying to compare apples and oranges. One approach to this problem is to try to classify respondents according to the kinds of responses that they have given and then to analyse separately the answers for the respondents who fall into each category. In the terminology of applied statistics, the researcher tries to 'control' for the kinds of answers given. This approach might be acceptable if the same respondents always gave the same kind of answer to the same question. Unfortunately, given no guidelines about the answers they should give, respondents often change the kinds of answers they give when allowed to answer a question a second time.

Any attempt to get respondents themselves to specify the positions they have taken in regard to each dimension when answering a question inevitably runs into a host of intractable problems that are associated with the use of open questions. These problems are discussed in chapter 10.

A more viable alternative is for the researcher to actually specify the kinds of answers that are required. In Briggs' words:

> Respondents can address a given subject from many different points of view and provide more or less detail. The provision of a referential frame by the question (or preceding discourse) assists the respondent in assessing the quality and type of information sought. (Briggs, 1986:54)

Following this line of thought, the researcher might elect to stipulate the kinds of answers that are required. That is, the researcher can decide to indicate to the respondents whether they should take a moral, instrumental, domestic or political point of view; whether they should give personal or cultural answers; what sort of explanation should be given — if an explanation is called for; and what standards of evaluation should be used — if evaluations are called for. In sum, the researcher can elect to specify a response framework for respondents.

Chapter 7

*T*HE LIMITATIONS
OF HUMAN MEMORY

In the past, many survey researchers have exhibited a tendency to assume that respondents have the information they want. Yet, even when respondents have been exposed to a particular event, there is no guarantee that they will have taken in much information about it or, if they have, that they will have remembered it. It is, therefore, important that researchers understand what can reasonably be expected of respondents' memories so that this understanding can be incorporated into the design of questions requiring respondents to report information about past events in their lives.

Relevant research suggests that respondents are often not aware of many of the immediate influences on their behaviour. Laird (1932) was one of the earliest researchers to reach this conclusion. He found that respondents would choose the 'best' stockings from an array of identical pairs of stockings on the basis of scent, without being aware that this was what they were doing. Henry (1971) presents the results of a number of similar experiments that have produced comparable results. In one experiment, knowledge of price advantage appears to have been the main factor underlying respondents' preference although few respondents mentioned this factor. In another experiment, respondents' taste preferences were influenced by the colour of the wrapping used and again they indicated little awareness of this fact.

The whole question of respondents' awareness of the factors or processes that appear to underlie their behaviour, evaluations and preferences gained wider recognition with the publication of two papers by Nisbett and Wilson (1977) and Wilson and Nisbett (1978). These papers triggered a wider debate about what kinds of stimuli are likely to enter into a respondent's awareness (e.g. Smith and Miller, 1978; Rich, 1979; White, 1980; Morris, 1981). The outcome has been a clarification of issues that relate to the types of information which a respondent might be expected to have in her or his memory.

Morris (1981) cites Smith and Miller's view that tasks that are novel and engaging for subjects, such as choosing a college or solving a challenging problem, often seem to evoke accurate introspection. He goes on to argue for a distinction between intentional and non-intentional behaviour, noting that all of the examples discussed by Nisbett and Wilson involve subjects' levels of insight into the determinants or processes underlying non-intentional behaviour after it has occurred.

> While Nisbett and Wilson's studies extend the evidence that many non-intentional processes are unavailable to introspection, they do not produce convincing evidence that people make inaccurate reports on their reasons for carrying out intentional actions. It is these actions for which explanations are usually requested and for these actions that explanations are confidently offered. (Morris, 1981:194)

The conclusion that is relevant here is that it is sensible to ask people only about their past intentional behaviour. Because respondents are unlikely to be aware of the causes of past unintentional behaviours, it makes little sense to assume that they will be able to recall such processes.

Problems associated with the recall of information in long-term memory

Besides the problem created by the failure of stimuli to impinge upon respondents' mental processes in the first place, there is at least one more reason to expect that respondents will not always be able to provide information that we might want. Memory and recall processes — even for factual material — naturally fail with the passing of time.

The results of a study carried out by the National Center for Health Statistics in the United States show how the non-reporting of hospitalisation events increases with time — see table 7.1, page 92.

Similarly, the results of a study of victimisation carried out by the US Census Bureau illustrates how recall of victimisation events decreases over time — see table 7.2, page 92.

Another study that suggests that the rate of forgetting increases over time has been reported by Bachman and O'Malley (1981). They calculated that estimates of annual student drug use based on reports of the use of drugs over the last month were three times the estimates based on reports of drug use over the last year.

On the basis of a review of studies like the three that have just been mentioned Sudman and Bradburn (1974) conclude:

> a substantial literature in experimental psychology suggests that, at least, short-term and intermediate memory decays exponentially with time. Although the same kinds of results are not available for long periods, it seems reasonable to begin with a simple exponential model to explain the relative rates of omissions . . . (Sudman and Bradburn, 1974:68)

The implication of this conclusion is that events that have occurred too far back in time will be seriously under-reported.

Table 7.1 *Effect of elapsed time on reports of hospitalisation*

Time elapsed since discharge (weeks)	Recorded discharges	Per cent not reported
1–10	114	3
11–20	426	6
21–30	459	9
31–40	339	11
41–50	364	16
51–53	131	42

Source: National Center for Health Statistics 1965, PHS Pub. No. 1000, series 2, No. 8, Public Health Service, Washington US, Government Printing Office, July 1965. Cited by Cannell, 1977:5.

Table 7.2 *Elapsed time and recall of victimisation*

Months between interview and recorded victimisation	Per cent of respondents not reporting events
1–3	32 (n=101)
4–6	50 (n=100)
7–9	54 (n=103)
10–12	70 (n= 90)

Source: Turner, A.G. (1972) 'The San Jose Methods Test of Known Crime Victims', Washington DC National Criminal Justice Information and Statistics Service, Law Enforcement Assistance Administration, US Department of Justice, p. 8.

Besides the complexity that forgetting that occurs over time follows some sort of exponential function, the ability to recall an event appears to be related to its salience. Cannell *et al.* (1981), for example, report that the ability to remember hospitalisation episodes is related to such factors as the length of stay in hospital and whether or not operations had been involved. While admitting that research on salience has been limited, Sudman and Bradburn (1982:42–47) conclude that three dimensions appear to define the 'salience' of events: *unusualness* (e.g. 'one off' purchases, illness, etc.), *associated high economic and social costs or rewards* (e.g. buying a house), and *continuing consequences* (e.g. a resulting disability). Of course some events will be salient on all three dimensions.

The complexities, however, do not end here. Experimental work indicates that the social researcher needs to recognise more than the effects of 'elapsed time' and 'salience' on the spontaneous decay of memory traces. Baddeley (1979) draws attention to the experimental investigations that indicate forgetting is also a consequence of retroactive interference (i.e. recent memory traces interfere with older traces). Baddeley reaches the conclusion that:

> forgetting will be maximal when asking for details of one out of many similar incidents, since the various incidents will inevitably be confused with each other. Obviously, such a situation will often occur in a survey, in which case *the most reliable strategy is to ask about only the last occurrence of any given event.* (Baddeley, 1979:23). [my emphasis]

Baddeley goes on to say that:

> People tend to remember in terms of their previous assumptions and beliefs. Memory is essentially a reconstructive process, and subjects will try to make sense of a given incident, often recalling their interpretation rather than what they actually literally observed. Bearing this in mind, it is particularly important to avoid leading questions. (Baddeley, 1979:23)

The basic principles to keep in mind, then, are that forgetting is related to elapsed time, salience and the number of events that compete with the particular event(s) that the respondent is asked to remember.

Generally, memory for salient events has been found to be satisfactory for up to one year. For low salience events, periods of less than one month appear to be more appropriate. Unfortunately, the researcher cannot solve the recall problem by merely shortening the recall period because it has been found that shorter periods of time run into another problem. Since people forget dates before they forget the events associated with them, respondents are prone to include events that occurred before the time specified if the recall period is too short — Sudman and Bradburn refer to this tendency as 'telescoping' and they argue that:

> If the behaviour is highly salient, so that the percentage of omissions is small, substantial overstatements will occur if the time period is too short. In this case the

researcher's desire for a longer time period to obtain more data coincides with the selection of a time period to get the most accurate recall. (Sudburn and Bradburn, 1982:44)

This phenomenon of telescoping creates a dilemma for the researcher, but Sudman and Bradburn claim that:

Since both telescoping and omission are occurring simultaneously, and since the effects of time work in the opposite directions for these two forms of forgetting, there is some period at which the opposite biases cancel and the overall levels of reported behaviour are about right. For many kinds of behaviour — such as grocery shopping, leisure activities and routine medical care — this period appears to be about between two weeks and a month . . . (Sudman and Bradburn, 1982:44–45)

Sudman and Bradburn also go on to suggest that the effects of telescoping can be lessened by using *bounded recall* techniques, which involve interviewing respondents twice so that the first interviews act as time markers that define the period specified and sensitise respondents toward issues so that they can remember them more accurately during the second interviews. For example, the researcher would ask: 'Since I saw you last time, how many times have you. . .?' A comparable procedure is discussed by Loftus and Marburger (1983) who phrased questions concerning criminal events of which respondents had been victims (e.g. theft) in terms of *landmark events* (e.g. 'Since the eruption of Mt. St. Helen, how many times . . .?'). More recently, Loftus *et al.* (1990) have shown that over-reporting of the use of medical services (e.g. blood pressure readings, colon tests, pap smears, vision tests) is reduced by asking patients about their use of such services during the last six months, before asking them about their use of such services during the last two months. It should be added, however, that we do not as yet have an adequate explanation for the effectiveness of this dual-time-frame questioning procedure. Loftus *et al.* reason that it may be due to an inherent message that the researcher wants more accurate data than a single question implies. But it is also possible that the effectiveness of the procedure lies both in the fact that it allows respondents more time to recall the required information and the fact that asking about the longer period first locks events which occurred prior to the two-month period into their proper time frame.

A different approach altogether to the problem of telescoping is Sudman and Bradburn's (1982:22) suggestion that the researcher can either have respondents keep diaries or encourage them to refer to any records that they may have kept.

Another feature of respondents' memories that needs to be taken into account is the fact that respondents recall pleasant events more easily than negative ones (see Edwards, 1942, for a review of relevant studies). This means that negative events are likely to be under-reported in comparison with positive events, which in turn means that some sort of adjustment to the data is called for when respondents are asked to recall negative events.

Despite the fact that our understanding of memory processes is at best fragmented and incomplete, Loftus (1982) asserts that recent theorists agree that humans do not simply record events in the manner of videotape machines. It appears that a three-stage model has generally been accepted as constituting a more satisfactory view. First, there is the *acquisition stage*, when information is encoded and laid down or entered into memory. Second, there is the *retention stage*, when information resides in memory but can be altered by any new information that becomes available. Last, there is the *retrieval stage*.

Loftus gives examples to show how memory traces can be altered after they have been laid down, by questions which suggest wrong information to respondents. In one experiment, respondents were shown a film and then asked, 'How fast was the white sports car going when it passed the brown barn while travelling down the country road?' Even though the car had not passed a brown barn, over 17 per cent of the respondents said that they had seen it when they were later asked about it.

That forgetting naturally occurs over time has already been commented upon. It should be pointed out, however, that two competing hypotheses have been advanced to explain why forgetting occurs (see, e.g., Thompson and Tulving, 1970: Tulving 1974). The first hypothesis is based on the simple idea that memory traces fade over time; the second is based on the idea that 'cues' that have been associated with the 'to-be-remembered' material, and would normally trigger its recall, have failed for some reason:

> No cue however strongly associated with the to-be-remembered item can be effective unless the to-be-remembered item is specifically encoded with respect to that cue at the time of its storage . . . (Thompson and Tulving, 1970:255)

Blum *et al.* (1971:131), using hypnotised subjects, tested this principle and report that indeed: 'recall is a function of the completeness of reinstatement of the original stimulating conditions'.

Godden and Baddeley (1975) also report confirming evidence for the cue-failure hypothesis. In a free recall experiment, underwater divers learnt lists of words on dry land and under water — the lists learnt under water were best recalled under water (i.e. in the presence of the original associated cues) and the lists learnt on dry land were best recalled on dry land.

Thus, it is reasonable to conclude, as Morris (1981) does, that the accuracy of recall depends upon the type and amount of processing at the time the learning takes place and the availability, at the recall stage, of cues associated with the memory trace. Norman (1973) adds that a question may not evoke appropriate recall if it is phrased differently from the storage format. Both Norman and Morris suggest that *researchers should get as familiar as possible with the events that they are investigating so that they can refer to key events in the same terms that the respondents would have used when they were encoded.* Likewise, it is probably helpful to ask respondents if they have any possessions (clothing, photos, letters, household records, reports, etc.) that relate to the event and can serve to 'jog their memories' (Gordon, 1984).

Sudman and Bradburn (1982:222) have also argued that it is useful, when collecting residential, job, or other personal data, to get respondents to work in chronological order either forwards or backwards — if the starting date is salient, they suggest that going forward might be more 'natural' for respondents. In this way any gaps in the record will become apparent and respondents will be forced to account for them. In fact, it is probably better to always have respondents work backwards. Whitten and Leonard (1981), for instance, have investigated the efficacy of 'ordered' recall and report that university students are much better at recalling their pre-university teachers' names when they are instructed to work backwards rather than to work either randomly or forwards from Grade 1. The investigators conclude that the relative superiority of having respondents work backwards through time is best explained by the fact that the successful recall of an item is primarily a function of recency. On the basis of our discussion about 'cues', we can add that once an item has been recalled it will act as a 'cue' for the next item in the ordered list. Working forwards is less likely to be as effective as working backwards because respondents are more likely to find themselves in the position of having to confront memory failures and hence 'cue' failures early in the task.

Work carried out by Cannell and his colleagues demonstrates the practical utility of a number of the principles that have been discussed so far. Marquis (1970) sets the scene with a precise summary of the findings of health surveys undertaken before 1970. Typically, 23 to 32 per cent of the chronic and acute conditions listed in the medical records were not reported. Marquis says that these studies all demonstrate that under-reporting correlates with variables associated with established principles of memory concerning, for example, 'recency', 'salience', and 'personal implications of the events'. These findings led Cannell and his co-workers to carry out research that was specifically designed to test the hypothesis that *providing multiple frames of reference or cues would increase the overall number of reported health problems.* They reasoned that respondents' failure to recall events is the result of questions not triggering associations in their memories.

> [What] is a simple, single-dimension variable for the researcher may not be a simple item for the respondent. The dental visit the researcher sees as a simple item of information may be organized in one of several frames of reference by the respondent. The respondent may think of the visit in terms of cost, pain, or loss of time from work. From this point of view the single question about the occurrence of the dental visit may be ineffective, it may fail as a stimulus to recall the event . . . (Cannell, 1977:53)

Cannell continues:

> Memory can process an illness in such a way that it gets transformed in storage and becomes organized around concepts such as pain, incapacity, cost, visits to doctors, hospitalizations, medication or treatment, symptoms, or more generally around other causal, circumstantial, or consequential events. The initial perceptions may be distorted in an association with another perception in order to fit into some structure. If one asks a broad question such as, 'Tell me about your illness', the respondent has to make the effort to review a multitude of cognitive structures in order to recall it properly. He has to create his own cues to reactivate traces of possibly weak salience. Altogether, the task is enormous and complex and the motivation to invest substantial effort in it cannot be expected to be spontaneously high, especially in the context of an information-getting household interview that has no immediate benefit for the respondent. Within this framework, underreporting is predictable; the broad question is not an adequate stimulus to the relevant frame of reference and the respondent is not going to work hard to recall information. (Cannell, 1977:55)

Given the results of the work done by Cannell and his colleagues, researchers should not just ask whether a respondent has been ill during the last month but should ask a series of cross-cutting questions. For example, whether the respondent has had any pain episodes, taken time off work; been hospitalised; needed to take any medication of any sort; and so on.

> Instead of asking one standard question essentially traced from a simple conceptualization of the event to be recalled, several questions may be asked that are traced from hypothesized states of information after memory processing. In other words, instead of requesting from the respondent the difficult task of building up his own cues and frames of reference, the researcher should attempt to create these recall aids and to build them into the questionnaire. If the researcher can be successful in predicting and designing the relevant cues and frames of reference, then the respondent's recall process should be significantly facilitated and the availability of information correspondingly increased. (Cannell, 1977:55)

Cannell and his colleagues' work provides clear evidence of the importance that associations play in aiding recall and for the superiority of procedures that provide a framework of associations. This conclusion is similar to that advanced by Strube (1987:94–97). Discussing the tendency on the part of respondents to underestimate frequencies of mundane events and to overestimate frequencies of rare or sensational events (both of which he sees as reflections of a regression to the mean phenomenon), Strube suggests the use of a decomposition procedure. Instead of asking: 'How often do you drink beer?', he suggests that the researcher should firstly assess how often the respondent watches TV, visits friends, etc., and secondly ask about the respondent's drinking patterns in each of these circumstances.

In addition to arguing for the need to provide respondents with recall cues, Cannell *et al.* (1981) draw attention to how traditional research practice encourages quick, shallow responses since interviews almost invariably proceed too quickly. They report the results of studies which support the hypothesis that more accurate recall on the part of respondents is achieved if:

(a)   Respondents are explicitly instructed to recall accurately and told to take their time in answering.

> A study of health reporting by Okenberg, Vinokar, and Cannell provides an example of the global instruction. After introducing the topic of the interview, interviewers told respondents:
>
> In order for your answers to be most helpful to us, it is important that you try to be as accurate as you can. Since we need complete and accurate information from this research, we hope you will think hard to provide the information we need. (Cannell *et al.*, 1981:407–8)

(b)   Respondents are given encouragement (e.g. 'That's the sort of thing we are interested in', or 'You are really a good respondent and I appreciate the effort you are taking to get this right') and encouraged to give more information if they do give quick, shallow answers. A study conducted by Marquis (1970), for example, showed that the use of such social encouragements produced an average of 25 per cent more symptoms of ill-health mentioned by respondents.

(c)   The interviewer tries to get the subject to make an explicit agreement to respond accurately and completely.

The data which Cannell and his colleagues collected indicate that each of these techniques increases the accuracy of recall by itself, while combinations of two at a time or all three together produce even better results.

Problems associated with short-term memory

Up to this point, we have been discussing problems associated with long-term memory processes, but attention should also be directed toward the short-term memory processes that are involved in the comprehension of questions.

If questions are to be comprehended properly they must be encompassed by the span of the respondent's short term memory. Respondents will not properly decode a question if they have forgotten the start before they reach the end. It is worth addressing the problem, then, of how questions should be presented so that they are least likely to overstretch respondents' short-term memories. While the results of the research that is relevant to this problem are far from clearcut, it does appear that respondents better assimilate structurally simple questions when they are able to listen to them. *When questions are complex in structure, it appears that it is better if respondents can read, and perhaps reread, them for themselves* (See Corey, 1934; Carver, 1935; Haugh, 1951/2; Beighley, 1952; Williams *et al.*, 1957; Hampleman, 1958; Kibler, 1962; Chaiken and Eagly, 1976).

The possibility of presenting questions in a multidimensional fashion — for example, of allowing respondents to read complex questions at the same time as they can hear them being read aloud by the interviewer — should also be considered. Although the author is not aware of any published studies that have looked at this possibility, he conducted a series of experiments in 1972 that relate to it. Subjects in these experiments either heard, read, or simultaneously heard and read the instructions for a replication of a classic social psychological experiment (Asch's 'warm–cold' personality impression formation experiment, Ward, 1970). Recall scores ranged from 0–15 and the results obtained suggest that simultaneously reading and listening had a marginally greater impact — see table 7.3, below. This problem is important enough, however, to warrant further research.

One way of allowing respondents to read complex questions for themselves in an interview situation is to give each of them a copy of the interview schedule to look at while the interviewer reads the questions aloud. This can be done by saying to the respondent, 'If I give you a copy of the questionnaire to look at, you'll be able to see what I'm doing while I record your answers on my copy so that I can make sure that we don't miss any questions and that we'll be able to read your answers later'.

The author has found that this procedure has the added benefit of making respondents more comfortable (perhaps because it gives them something to do). It also eliminates the need for 'show' cards, etc. While traditionalists might object to this procedure on the grounds that some respondents are likely to skip ahead and think about questions before the interviewer gets to them, the author has never found this to be a problem. It is fair to add that it does not allow any more freedom for respondents to look ahead than do questionnaires that respondents have to fill out for themselves. It might also be argued that, because the interviewer can control the pace of a face-to-face interview, the amount of time that respondents have to look ahead is limited.

Table 7.3 *Average recall scores by mode of presentation*

	Average score	s.d.	n
Read and listen	10.50	2.03	32
Listen only	10.26	2.03	27
Read only	8.67	1.65	30

Summary

Even when the researcher is sure that respondents have been exposed to an event, it is dangerous to assume that they will be able to remember information about it. First, there is evidence that human beings do not attend to, and thus are not able to remember, every stimulus that impinges upon them. Second, respondents are often not consciously aware of all the causes and motives associated with their behaviour. Third, memory traces of events and the cues associated with these fade with time.

Even when it can safely be assumed that respondents would have once had the required information stored in their memories, it makes little sense to ask them to recall it if it was entered into their memories a long time ago. Current thinking is that it makes little sense to ask respondents to recall fine details about either highly salient events that occurred more than a year ago or events of low salience that occurred more than thirty days ago.

Besides taking into account the time that the information has supposedly been stored in memory, the researcher should take steps to facilitate accurate recall. Questions about past events need to be worded in ways that help respondents access the required information. Preliminary questions to elicit answers that in turn cue answers to subsequent questions are useful. Asking respondents to recall sequences of events by starting with the most recent events and working their way back is one application of this principle. Cross-cutting questions that help respondents restructure past events in their minds are also valuable. The use of 'bounded' recall procedures should be considered. And instructions that exhort respondents 'to take their time' and 'to try hard to remember accurately' have been found to increase the validity of the data respondents retrieve from their memories.

Without backing away from the general view that much can be done to help respondents recall material accurately from their memories, it must always be kept in mind that sometimes respondents may be motivated to not cooperate with the researcher. This is especially likely to be the case when respondents feel threatened within the question–answer situation. But we will return to this problem in chapter 9.

Last, but just as important as the other issues that have been raised, is the fact that short term memory failures can cause comprehension failures in respondents. Some comprehension problems occur when questions are delivered too quickly. Others occur because of the way questions — especially complex questions — are presented to respondents. Effort needs to be directed toward the problem of determining the most effective way of presenting complex questions to respondents so that short-term memory problems are avoided. One possibility that should be entertained is that of letting respondents read them for themselves at the same time as the interviewer reads to them aloud.

Chapter 8

FILTERS:
ESTABLISHING THE RELEVANCE OF
QUESTIONS TO RESPONDENTS

Social researchers tend to assume high levels of opinionatedness on the part of respondents, so that little attention is paid to establishing whether or not respondents actually have had the necessary experience upon which an assumed opinion or belief could be based. This is a problem because it has been found that one cannot rely on respondents to indicate when questions are of marginal relevance to them. Respondents typically do their best to answer every question put to them — even questions that they have difficulty under-standing or relating to — either by cognitively adjusting the question so they can answer it or by falling back on contextual clues and general attitudes to formulate an appropriate answer (see, e.g., Schuman and Presser, 1980; Bishop *et al.*, 1980; Belson, 1981; Strack and Martin, 1987).

A question or question component that is explicitly offered to a respondent, either to establish the relevance of the question to the respondent, or to emphasise that it is acceptable for the respondent to not answer the question, is generally referred to as a 'filter'. A variety of filters have been invented ranging from the simple 'Don't know', 'Can't recall' and 'No opinion' response options, through the 'Undecided', 'Not sure', 'It depends' and 'Neutral' alternatives, to sets of questions that attempt to establish the extent to which an opinion or belief is based on experience of or knowledge about the topic.

In the process of developing a scale to measure attitudes towards unions, Dunnette *et al.* (1956) found that twenty-one of the 121 initial items generated rates of 'undecided' responses which varied between 20 and 30 per cent. In order to interpret these responses, they presented the twenty-one items with accompanying five-point rating scales (which included a middle 'Undecided' response option) to another sample of respondents. A third sample of respondents was exposed to the same items, but this time a sixth response option, 'I don't know enough about this to answer', was added to the rating scales. On the basis of the differences between the response distributions for the three samples, the researchers inferred that almost all of the respondents who indicated that they did not know enough to answer an item, would have endorsed the 'Undecided' category if the sixth response option had not been provided. In other words, in the absence of the knowledge filter, the 'Undecided' responses meant either that respondents were neutral or ambivalent, or that respondents didn't have opinions because they lacked the information upon which to base them.

This problem was again highlighted when Converse (1964) published an analysis of the attitudes held by American voters. Analysing responses from a sample of respondents who were interviewed three times for the Michigan Survey Research Center during 1956, 1958 and 1960, Converse discovered a high rate (sometimes as high as 80 per cent) of response inconsistency between successive surveys. Converse rejected the hypothesis that true social changes had affected the respondents who changed their opinions over time, because the number of respondents who had changed one way was balanced by the number who had changed the other way. In addition, the correlations between the responses to different questions were as high after four years as they had been after two. Converse discovered, too, that inconsistency was negatively related to education, to political involvement and to the simplicity and concreteness of the questions. These findings led Converse to invent the term 'non-attitudes' to refer to responses that, in his view, were essentially random responses which respondents had arrived at hastily to satisfy the demands of the interview situation.

The problem of 'non-attitudes' received further attention when Schuman and Presser (1980, 1981) reported that between 20 and 30 per cent of respondents who had been asked about an obscure bill before Congress, gave a 'Don't know' response when that option was explicitly available, whereas only 10 per cent of respondents volunteered a 'Don't know' response when provision for this was not explicitly made. They concluded that some 10 to 20 per cent of respondents who would give 'Don't know' responses when such a response is explicitly allowed, give a substantive response when it is *not* explicitly provided. Schuman and Presser invented the label 'floater' to refer to these respondents.

The 'non-attitude' problem could, of course, be ignored if it could be shown that respondents who give non-substantive responses when they are explicitly allowed but give substantive responses when they are not, are drawn equally from all of the substantive options. If this were the case, even if the absolute size of the percentages for each substantive option were to change, the relative differences between these percentages would not. It would also mean that any patterns of association in any cross-tabulations would not be disturbed. The last point defines what Schuman and Presser call the hypothesis of form-resistant correlations.

Unfortunately, a number of investigations have thrown up examples of questions for which the provision of an explicit, non-substantive response option has had the effect of radically changing the distribution of responses across all categories of the variables being investigated (e.g. Bishop *et al.*, 1980, 1983; Kalton *et al.*, 1980; Schuman and Presser, 1981). In some instances, the changes have been great enough to actually reverse patterns of association with other variables. Although most of the instances in which this has happened involve filters of the 'middle alternative kind' (e.g. 'Makes no difference', 'Undecided'), some involve stronger filters (e.g. 'Don't know' — Bishop *et al.* 1986:247). Table 8.1 (below) illustrates how the provision of a middle response alternative can affect responses.

In summary, we have learnt that typically up to 20 per cent of respondents will give a non-substantive response if they are allowed to but give a substantive response if a non-substantive option is not offered. We have learnt, too, that the

Table 8.1 *Responses for filtered and unfiltered versions of the question: 'do you think that drinking alcohol in moderation is good for your health or bad for your health?' (filter: 'or do you think that it makes no difference?') by gender*

	With filter 'Makes no difference' option explicitly provided		Without filter 'Makes no difference' option not explicitly provided but accepted if volunteered	
	Males	**Females**	**Males**	**Females**
Good	40.1%	22.6%	64.0%	57.6%
Bad	9.2	14.0	17.5	18.5
Makes no difference	50.7	63.4	18.5	23.9
	100%	100%	100%	100%
	(n 217)	(n 541)	(n 189)	(n 524)
	p<.01		N.S.	

Source: Kalton *et al.*, 1980:76, table 3. Title and captions by author.

provision of a filter can completely change the distribution of responses to a question. Both of these findings raise the problem of how non-substantive responses should be interpreted. On what basis do those respondents who give non-substantive responses when these are allowed give substantive answers when they are not?

Work done by Bishop *et al.* (1980:86) is relevant to the question that has just been asked. They presented respondents with a number of questions about fictitious issues (i.e. issues invented by researchers). The example set out in table 8.2 (below) illustrates the kinds of results produced.

Bishop *et al.*'s (1980, 1986) findings are noteworthy because they are very similar to those reported by Schuman and Presser, except their results were obtained using questions concerning *fictitious issues*. It is one thing for 10–20 per cent of respondents to give substantive responses to obscure issues. It is another matter altogether that a similar percentage would give substantive responses to questions concerning topics about which they can know nothing because the researcher has invented them!

Reviewing studies of responses to fictitious issues, Smith (1984:223) reasons

Table 8.2　*Responses to filtered and unfiltered versions of the question: 'Do you agree or disagree with the idea that the Public Affairs Act (a fictitious Act) should be repealed?' by trust in the government or public sector*

Trust in the government or public sector (measured using the SRC 3 item scale)

	Filter condition (table excludes those who said they are not interested in politics)		Unfiltered condition (table includes those who said they are not interested in politics)	
	High	**Low**	**High**	**Low**
Response to question about repeal of PAA				
Agree	25.0%	70.0%	35.0%	41.9%
Disagree	75.0	30.0	65.0	58.1
	100%	100%	100%	100%
	(n 16)	(n 20)	(n 20)	(n 43)
	p<.05		N.S.	

Source: Bishop *et al.* (1980:207, table 6. title and captions by author.

that respondents who give substantive responses to fictitious issues might
be:

(a) mistaken in their interpretation of the question;

(b) blindly choosing a response to avoid admitting ignorance; or

(c) imputing meaning to the question on the basis of contextual clues or their
own general dispositions (e.g., in essence, be saying to themselves, 'I'm
not certain what this question is getting at, but the others that I've just
answered were all to do with government responsibility for X, and I'm
for/against X . . . so I guess I would be for/against this issue).

Smith goes on to argue that the results of the relevant studies reported by
Hartley (1946), Schuman and Presser (1980) and Bishop *et al.* (1980) all indicate
that such responses can, in the main, be attributed to the third possibility:

> Respondents read meaning into the question and answer in terms of some general
> predisposition toward the economy, the government, or tolerance. In one sense,
> when people rely on such predispositions they are showing ideological or con-
> strained attitudes, since they are using general attitudes to supply responses to
> specific questions. On the Monetary Control Act example of Schuman and Presser,
> many of the tricked respondents were applying something like the following syllo-
> gism: Major premise: I support programs to curb inflation. Minor Premise: The
> Monetary Control Act is a program to curb inflation. Conclusion: I support the
> Monetary Control Act. The problem is that the minor premise that they imputed
> from the bill's name is wrong. (Smith, 1984a: 223–224)

The phenomenon of responding to fictitious issues is clearly similar to Converse's concept of 'non-attitudes'. But, as Smith asserts, they differ in that such
responses are not random since they correlate with the answers given to related,
more general questions.

Yet even if forced substantive responses are not random, it does not follow
that they should be equated to unforced substantive responses that are more
likely to be grounded in the respondents' experiences. It is relevant to note that
the best predictors of non-substantive responses have been found to be education and involvement. Francis and Busch's (1966) analysis of Michigan Survey
Research Center data disclosed negative correlations of around 0.4 between
non-substantive responses and both education and involvement. And Converse
(1976) reports that non-substantive responses in both the Gallup and the Harris
polls are negatively associated with respondents' levels of education. The relevant results reported by Converse are set out in table 8.3 (p. 106).

It is worth noting, too, that after re-evaluating the 1956, 1958 and 1960
Michigan Survey Research Center's panel data analysed by Converse (1964),
Smith comments that:

> looking at people who gave one 'Don't know' in 1956 or 1958 and those who gave
> 'Don't know' both times to the power and housing question, we found that they had

decidedly less political interest and lower education than respondents who were either consistent or who switched responses. While 52 percent of those who gave substantive responses engaged in no political activity, 67 percent of those with one 'Don't know' and 68 percent with two 'Don't knows' had less than a high school education. Similar patterns appeared on voting, political interest, and political knowledge. (Smith, 1984a:234–235)

Smith (1984a:236) goes on to summarise the respondent characteristics associated with 'Don't know' responses in the SRC's panel surveys — they were low education, low occupational prestige, low income, female, old, low political activity, low political efficacy, housewife, and member of the general public rather than opinion leader.

The finding that both less well-educated and less involved respondents are the most likely to endorse filter options (when they are provided) is in line with the hypothesis that the main reason for respondents endorsing non-substantive options is that they lack the information sought by the researcher. Of course, it would be dangerous to conclude that this is always the case. Although the available evidence suggests that most non-substantive responses reflect either ambivalence or the lack of a substantive answer, it is possible that some respondents may use explicitly offered non-substantive response options as vehicles for other answers (e.g., 'I don't want to answer that question', 'I don't understand what you are asking', etc.).

Experiments designed to differentiate those respondents who genuinely have no opinion from those who are ambivalent suggest that, typically, between one- and two-thirds of the respondents who endorse an 'Undecided' option are really ambivalent, while most of the remainder have no opinion. Dunnette *et al.* (1956) compared the response distributions for a set of questions that included the filters 'Undecided' and 'I don't know enough to answer', with the response distributions for the same set of questions without the 'I don't know enough to answer' filter. Whereas between 20 and 40 per cent of the respondents endorsed the 'Undecided' filter when it was the only one provided, the percentage fell to

Table 8.3   *The relationship between non-substantive responses and education*

| | % Giving 'No Opinion' & 'Don't Know' responses | |
	Gallup Polls	Harris Polls
Highest level of education		
College	7	8
High school	10	12
Primary school	15	22

Source: Converse, 1976:976.

less than 20 per cent when the 'I don't know enough to answer' filter was provided as well. Smith (1984a) re-analysed the non-substantive responses to fifteen of the attitude items used in the Michigan Survey Research Center's panel surveys in which respondents had been explicitly offered the non-substantive response options 'Not sure', 'It depends', 'No opinion' and 'Don't know', and makes the comment that on average about 34 per cent of the respondents who gave non-substantive responses could be categorised as being ambivalent (because they had either answered 'Not sure' or 'It depends'), and 60 per cent could be categorised as having 'No opinion'. The meaning of the remaining 6 per cent was less clear but Smith speculates that the 'Don't know' option appears to have been used by people who have an opinion but do not know what it is! Smith (1984a:229) concludes, 'it is clear that ambivalent responses are common and may, on average, account for a third to one half of all non-substantive responses'.

In sum, *it appears that many respondents give substantive answers, if they have to, that are not directly based on experience.* Thus, if filters are not used, the meaning of the substantive answers will inevitably be vague. This conclusion reinforces the view that filters should always be employed. It has to be acknowledged, however, that when filters are used, the meaning of their endorsement is itself often unclear. It is pertinent to add that the ambiguity of non-substantive responses usually arises either because respondents are forced to use particular response options to express quite different meanings (as when the researcher has failed to provide a complete array of non-substantive options) or because those non-substantive options that are provided are ill-defined. The sensible course of action is to include two filters: a 'No opinion' filter plus an 'I'm not sure' or 'It all depends' filter.

What kind of 'No opinion' filter should be used?

This is not a simple question because the meanings of the commonly used 'Don't know' or 'No opinion' filters are not as clear as they might, at first seem. Bishop and his colleagues (1980, 1983) have investigated the endorsement rates for different filters accompanying a list of fictitious items which might be expected to generate high rates of 'Don't know' and 'No opinion' responses. The following results are for the three filters endorsed most often when paired with a question about whether or not the respondent agreed that the fictitious Public Affairs Act should be repealed (i.e. a question that should generate very high 'Don't know' or 'No opinion' rates):

'Have you been interested enough to favour one side or the other?'
'Don't know' = 76.6 per cent.

'Do you have an opinion on this or not?'
'Don't know' = 82.5 per cent.

'Have you thought much about this issue — or haven't you thought much about it?'
'Don't know' = 85.8 per cent. (Source: Bishop *et al.* 1980: table 1)
Subsequently, Bishop *et al.* conclude that a filter:

> which asks respondents how interested they are in an issue, or how much they have thought or read about it, will generally screen out more people than one which asks simply whether they have an opinion. And the more abstract or remote the issue, the greater the wording effect will be. (Bishop *et al.*, 1983:543)

It should be added that Bishop *et al.* do not define what they mean by the 'strength' of a filter. It is possible that, for example, phrases such as: 'or not', 'to favour one side or the other', 'have thought about it' and 'haven't thought about it' make it easier or less embarrassing to not give a substantive answer. To further complicate the matter, Hippler and Schwarz (1989) have reported that the more strongly a filter is worded, the more strongly it suggests to respondents that the question is important and should be answered only if they can provide well-considered answers based on fact. This finding is a complication because it raises the possibility that strong filters are likely to screen out respondents who have weak views which, in spite of being weak, still influence their daily behaviour, but which they believe are not what the researcher is after, as well as those respondents who have interpreted the question as indicating that the researcher is subsequently likely to ask an even more difficult question.

The positioning of filters

Poorly defined non-substantive options are prone to generate format effects. This is demonstrated by a study carried out by Holdaway (1971). This study showed that the percentage of respondents using the 'Undecided' option in 5-point, 'Strongly agree' to 'Strongly disagree' rating scales was almost 22 per cent higher when it was placed in the middle than when it was placed at the end. Holdaway suggests that respondents were more likely to interpret the 'Undecided' category as 'neutral' when it was placed in the middle — that is, it appears that respondents used the position of the non-substantive option as a clue to its interpretation. A similar finding has been reported by Bishop (1987a). He and his fellow researchers investigated the effect of positioning the response option 'Continued at its present level' in the middle versus at the end of a number of questions. 'Do you think social security should be: increased, decreased, continued at its present level?' is an example of the questions they investigated. For four of six questions, the percentage of respondents who endorsed the middle alternative was greater — on average 3.3 per cent greater — when it was listed at the end of the question. Bishop suggests that:

> the harder it is to choose between two opposite alternatives on an issue . . . the more likely a person is to select the middle alternative when it is offered. This is particularly so when it is presented at the end of the question, because it appears more clearly to be a compromise between two equally attractive, or unattractive, alternatives . . . (Bishop, 1987a:227)

Thus the interpretability of responses is not increased a great deal by using ill-defined non-substantive options.

Having observed that respondents were somewhat more likely to endorse the middle alternative when it was placed at the end of the question, Bishop (1987a) does not offer any advice on its ideal positioning. Responses that are so weak that altering the ordering of the response alternatives affects their likelihood should not be confused with substantive responses. *The conservative decision would be to always place the middle option (e.g. '. . . or continued at its present level') at the end.* For example:

> Some people say that the United States needs to develop new power sources from nuclear energy in order to meet our needs for the future. Other people say that the danger to the environment and the possibility of accidents is too great. What do you think — are you in favour of building more nuclear power plants, would you prefer to see all nuclear power plants closed down, *or would you favour operating only those already built* or would you rather say that you 'Don't know' or 'Have never really thought about it'?

Should a middle category be offered at all?

It is tempting to avoid worrying about the positioning of middle categories by adopting the course of action suggested by Converse and Presser (1986:36) who argue that, because the 'intensity' of the views held is the major characteristic distinguishing respondents who are affected by the presence of a middle category from those who are not, the researcher should:

> not explicitly provide the middle category, and thereby avoid losing information about the direction in which some people lean, but follow the question with an intensity item, thus separating those who definitely occupy a position from those who only lean toward it. (Converse and Presser, 1986:37)

They recommend measuring 'intensity' by asking the main question and following it up with a question of the sort: 'How strongly do you feel about that?

— Extremely strongly, Very strongly, Somewhat strongly, or Not at all strongly'. One shortcoming of this approach, however, is that respondents who are truly neutral or ambivalent are equated with those who hold a substantive answer but indicate that they do not hold it very strongly. The use of both a 'Don't know' or 'No opinion' filter and an 'I'm not sure' or 'It all depends' filter in conjunction with some sort of 'intensity' measure would avoid this objection. Whether the researcher should use the 'intensity' filter suggested by Converse and Presser (1986) or choose some other filter, however, is not so clear. In 1944 Katz found that an accompanying 'sureness' scale (i.e. 'How sure are you that your opinion is right?': Not sure, Fairly sure, Very sure') produced higher correlations between responses to questions related to the focal substantive question and responses to the focal question itself than a 'How strongly do you feel on this issue?' scale. More recently, Schuman and Presser (1981:234–243) have reported the results of a comparison between an 'intensity' measure ('Compared to how you feel about other public issues, are your feelings on this issue: Extremely strong, Fairly strong, Not very strong?'); a measure of commitment to the issue in question ('Have you ever written a letter or given money in defence of the issue?'); and a centrality measure ('How important is this issue to you when you decide how to vote . . .?'). In conjunction with questions about gun control, they found that the 'intensity' measure was not as successful as either of the other two measures. They conclude that the 'intensity' measure failed because it was too easy for respondents to claim that they felt strongly about the issue being investigated. Thus, both the Katz and Schuman and Presser studies suggest that either a 'sureness' measure or an 'importance' measure is to be preferred over an 'intensity' measure.

Summary

It has been observed that it is a common occurrence for 10 to 20 per cent of respondents to answer a question in a substantive fashion when a non-substantive response option is *not* explicitly offered, but to shift to a non-substantive option when one is provided. Further, it appears that the researcher cannot rely upon respondents to indicate when some sort of filter is required. In other words, the fact that most respondents will answer a question, if forced, cannot be interpreted to mean that the question is equally relevant to each respondent. Further, since it has been found that the use of filters often changes the pattern of results, the researcher cannot simply ignore the problem of whether or not to allow non-substantive responses.

Both Kalton *et al.* (1980) and Schuman and Presser (1981:311–312) have argued that a 'Don't know' response option should not be included if a general indication of community values, ideological biases, or stereotypes is required.

Yet this suggestion is not well founded. There is no justification for the practice of collecting and pooling answers that are uninterpretable in the sense that, although empirically the same, they mean quite different things to different respondents. For this reason, Sudman and Bradburn's (1982:141) suggestion that 'Don't know' and 'No opinion' options should always be included, because they generate additional information, is a much more defensible position. Following Hippler and Schwarz (1989), the researcher might consider using *moderately* strong filters that are less likely than very strong ones to inhibit respondents from answering even when they could give legitimate answers. On the other side of the coin, Kahn and Cannell (1957) are probably correct in suggesting that filters should be chosen to minimise the psychological impact of not being able to answer. For example, saying to respondents: 'Many people have not had the opportunity to learn about X while others have picked up information about it — do you happen to know about X?' is probably better than requiring respondents to admit that they do not have an answer because they have never heard about X and have never thought about it.

Furthermore, it makes no sense to make a filter do several jobs at once. The task of a filter should be to establish the relevance of the question to each respondent. Middle alternatives (e.g. 'Neutral', 'Undecided', 'Ambivalent') should be treated as legitimate substantive options and explicitly offered to respondents along with the standard 'Don't know' option. For this reason, it makes sense to include an unambiguous 'Undecided' or 'It all depends' option. Again there is little justification in collecting uninterpretable answers, and even less in pooling them together.

In conclusion, it should not surprise anyone that Andrews (1984), after applying a sophisticated, multi-correlational, structural statistical modelling procedure to assess the validity of the data collected in six different surveys (totalling 7706 respondents), reaches the conclusion that:

> The second most important survey characteristic is whether the answer categories include an explicit 'Don't know' option. The effect of this design matter is clear and consistent: inclusion of an explicit 'Don't know' category was associated with better data, higher validity ... The idea that one should let respondents 'opt out' if they lack the requisite information receives strong endorsement ... (Andrews, 1984:431)

It should be added that Andrews looked only at the effect of the inclusion of the 'Don't know' filter. There can be little doubt that his conclusions would have been even more emphatic had he been able to analyse data collected with the use of questions which included filters and middle alternatives that generate clearly interpretable answers!

Chapter 9

*R*EDUCING QUESTION THREAT

Social researchers tend to take it for granted that respondents are, or can be, motivated to give them the information they require. In this chapter, however, we will look at the possibility that questions *per se* sometimes threaten respondents in a way that either influences their willingness to give answers at all or determines the nature of the answers that they do give.

> It is well documented that material that is likely to be sensitive or embarrassing tends to be underreported in surveys. Locander *et al.* (1976), for example, showed that bankruptcy and arrest for drunken driving were reported at very low rates, despite the fact that they were unlikely to be forgotten. Cannell *et al.* (1965, 1977) showed that hospitalizations associated with diagnoses that were likely to be threatening or embarrassing were reported at lower rates than others. (Fowler and Mangione, 1990:78)

While it is generally recognised that respondents sometimes give biased answers and sometimes refuse to answer at all, it is nevertheless generally assumed that these problems can be overcome by one means or another.

In fact, a number of discussions of how to overcome the effects of question threat have been published over the years (e.g. Barton, 1958; Williams, 1964; Blair *et al.*, 1977; Bradburn *et al.*, 1978; Sudman and Bradburn, 1974, 1982; DeLamater, 1982). In Barton's words (1958:67), 'the pollster's greatest ingenuity has been directed to asking embarrassing questions in non-embarrassing ways'. Early advice to researchers was mainly aimed at trying to reduce question threat through the use of one or more of a number of unrelated, alternative techniques (e.g. Barton, 1958; Skelton, 1963). It was stock advice to tell respondents that any answers they gave would be treated in confidence. And researchers were encouraged:

- to adopt a casual, everyday approach ('Do you happen to have . . .');
- to lessen any imputation of deviance (e.g. by the use of statements such as 'As you know, everyone does X sometimes . . . how often have you done X?', and by making sure that the range of response alternatives encompasses the respondent's likely position, so that the respondent is not put in the position of having to endorse the lowest or highest category);
- to let respondents answer anonymously (e.g. by employing a secret ballot procedure);
- to lessen the psychological immediacy of the question (e.g. by letting respondents report the behaviour of other people rather than their own behaviour and by allowing respondents to refer to response alternatives by number);
- to decrease the specificity of the information called for (e.g. by using broad response categories);
- to adopt a 'knowing' or direct approach so that respondents have to confirm rather than volunteer that the question is relevant to them (e.g. 'Have you stopped beating your wife?');
- to employ the 'Kinsey' technique of looking the respondent straight in the eyes and boldly asking the question so that respondents find it difficult to lie;
- to adopt an indirect approach so that the respondents give the required information without realising that they have (i.e. by using projective techniques); and,
- to place threatening questions at the ends of questionnaires and interviews so that respondents' answers to initial, less threatening questions will not be disturbed.

More recent advice has not so much challenged these ideas as added to the array of suggestions. Jones and Sigall (1971) and more recently Arken and Lake (1983) have proposed the use of the 'bogus pipeline' technique which has respondents believe that their answers are to be assessed by a lie-detector machine. The underlying hypothesis to this is that respondents would rather reveal socially undesirable information than risk being found out to be liars. Zdep and Rhodes (1976) and Fidler and Kleinknecht (1977) have proposed use of the randomised response technique which allows respondents to toss a dice to determine whether they will answer (in a yes or no fashion) a question about either a potentially threatening topic or a completely non-threatening topic. In the case of each interview, only the respondent knows for sure which question is being answered, although the response distributions for the survey sample can subsequently be statistically estimated by the researcher. In essence the randomised response technique allows respondents to answer anonymously. In addition, Blair *et al.* (1977) have reported that potentially embarrassing questions are less threatening if they are cast in a lengthy, open format, and phrased using the respondents' own words for the topic being investigated. And Bradburn *et al.* (1978) have suggested that questions should concern past rather than current behaviour. They also recommend that an additional set of questions should be asked with potentially threatening questions, allowing respondents to indicate the level of threat that is associated with them so that the researcher can later make adjustments to any estimates of the rates of occurrence of the behaviour(s) in question. Bradburn and his colleagues used the following question to measure the level of threat that topics generated in respondents:

> Questions sometimes have different kinds of effects on people. We'd like your opinions about some of the questions in this interview. As I mention groups of questions, please tell me whether you think those questions would make *most* people very uneasy, moderately uneasy, slightly uneasy, or not at all uneasy. How about the questions on . . .?

Most recently, Hippler and Hippler (1986) have developed their 'door in the face' technique. This technique involves using an open question to get respondents to give exact answers (e.g. their exact income) and then asking those respondents who have refused to answer the open question a less specific closed ended question — the underlying reasoning being that the societal norm of reciprocity dictates that respondents who have refused to answer the open question should make concessions to the researcher who has made concessions to them.

No doubt most of the suggestions listed above have at least some measure of validity. Still it is notable that many of the threat reduction strategies in the list appear to conflict either with one another or with other generally accepted question construction principles. For example, the advice to adopt a 'direct' or 'knowing' approach clearly conflicts with the advice to increase the psychological distance between the researcher and the respondents. And the advice to use lengthy, open ended questions clearly conflicts with the generally accepted principle that questions should be as simple and short as possible. To make matters worse, there are no guidelines to help the researcher choose one strategy over another.

The lack of guidelines is probably the result of two problems. First, there has been little consensus over what is meant by the concept of 'question threat'. Second, there has been little effort put into developing a theoretical framework within which choice decisions can be made.

The second problem is nicely illustrated by the idea, which is in danger of being widely accepted, that lengthy, open questions that are worded using the respondents' own concepts produce higher response rates than either short or closed questions (e.g. Blair *et al.*, 1977; Sudman and Bradburn, 1982; Van der Zouwen and Dijkstra, 1982b; Converse and Presser, 1986; and see table 9.1

(p. 125) for an example). It is not at all obvious what theoretical principles are embodied in this recommendation. Allowing that it might be true that explicitly listing threatening response options might emphasise their potential to threaten respondents, it is still not clear how the use of open questions avoids the introduction of related problems, such as the tendency to give non-valid, irrelevant or deliberately vague answers. In other words, there is no explanation for why respondents would be more willing to give honest and complete answers to open questions when they refuse to answer comparable closed questions. Moreover, any explanation would need to be both theoretically coherent and congruent with the available empirical evidence. In fact, as will be seen in chapter 10, the empirical evidence suggests that closed questions generally produce more usable data than do open questions. An example that was cited in chapter 1 underscores this point. Peterson (1984) found that when respondents were asked to report their ages by selecting age categories there was a 1.1 per cent non-response rate. In comparison, there was a 3.2 per cent non-response rate when respondents were asked the open question: 'What is your age?'; and a 9.7 per cent non-response rate when respondents were asked the open question: 'How old are you?' While the last version of the age question probably emphasises the negative aspect of age (i.e. being 'old') and for this reason may be more threatening for respondents, it is not at all obvious why the second version should produce a higher non-response rate than the first.

In trying to explain the effect of lengthening questions on respondent recall, Cannell *et al.* (1981:406) argue that long questions may aid recall because they:

(a)   essentially repeat the question;

(b)   give the respondents more time to think; and

(c)   encourage the respondents to take their time.

Whether these arguments can somehow be generalised to the strategy of handling question threat by employing lengthy, open-ended questions is moot. It is possible that a longer question may somehow desensitise the topic in respondents' minds, either by increasing their level of familiarity with it or by indicating that, if the interviewer is able to talk at length about the topic without being embarrassed, they, too, can talk about it without embarrassment. But such speculative explanations would need to be empirically tested before being accepted. There is a danger in accepting and generalising from *ad hoc*, non-theoretically based, empirical findings.

It is not hard, for example, to formulate less flattering alternative explanations to account for the apparent success of lengthy, open questions that have been worded in the respondents' own concepts. One can argue that the translation of short questions into long ones is likely to change them in fundamental ways (e.g. by adding justifications for particular responses). This possibility is clearly present in the example taken from Blair *et al.* (1977:318) that is set out below.

An example of short versus long versions of the same question from Blair *et al.* (1977)

Short version:
'In the past year, how often did you become intoxicated while drinking any kind of alcoholic beverage?'
Respondents were handed a card listing these response categories:
Never
Once a year
Every few months
Every few weeks
Once a week
Several times a week
Daily

Long version:
The respondents first provided their own word for 'intoxication' by answering the following question:
'Sometimes people drink a little too much beer, wine, or whisky so that they act differently from usual. What word do you think we should use to describe people when they get that way, so that you will know what we mean and feel comfortable talking about it?'
The intoxication question then read:
'Occasionally, people drink on an empty stomach or drink a little too much and become . . . (respondent's word) . . . In the past year, how often did you become . . . (respondent's word) . . . while drinking any kind of alcoholic beverage?'
(Source: Blair *et al.*, 1977:318)

Whereas 'intoxicated' might be seen to cover 'blind drunk' to 'tipsy', 'a little too much . . . on an empty stomach' probably limits the question to the 'mildly tipsy' end of the scale. Moreover, the reference to 'an empty stomach' would appear to provide a legitimisation or justification for the responses that fall at the mild end of the scale, making it easier for respondents to report this class of events. In other words, the higher response rates may simply have been due to the fact that a less threatening question had been asked.

Rather than employing a technique that is not understood, it would be safer to identify the possible reason(s) for the apparent success of longer questions and then devise and test alternative strategies which take these into account. If redundancy helps because it helps respondents understand complex questions, it would be better to find ways of efficiently increasing question comprehension without introducing additional problems — for example, by letting respondents read the question at the same time as it is read to them (see chapter 7). If long questions work because they imply the meta-level message that respondents can take their time, just as the interviewer is, then it would be better to directly inform the respondents that they should take their time, as Cannell *et al.* (1977, 1981) have done with considerable success. But beyond doubt the most serious problem with deliberately lengthening a question is the high probability that biasing factors will unwittingly be introduced. The fact that lengthening mildly threatening questions has been found to result in a lowering of response rates (Sudman and Bradburn, 1982:62) is congruent both with the general case for simplicity and brevity in questions and with the possibility that length lessens respondent comprehension. It is also relevant that Blair *et al.* (1977:316) note that response effects generated by threatening items have been shown to increase sharply with increasing average word length. Although it should be admitted that they do not say whether this is because difficult language itself is threatening (i.e. makes respondents feel incompetent or inferior), or whether lack of comprehension interacts with perceptions of threat associated with the topic.

All of the above comments merely reinforce the general view that there is a need for more theory to guide the selection of threat reduction strategies.

The definition of question threat

There can be little doubt that the fact that we lack a clear definition of the concept of 'question threat' is a major problem. Different writers have used different words. Barton (1958) refers to 'embarrassing' questions. Williams (1964) argues that the motivation on the part of the respondent to give 'false' responses arises from the anticipation of either being rewarded or being punished, and that questions threaten respondents when they ask for information that could be used to harm them. Weis (1968) talks about 'bias' — meaning the tendency of respondents to over-report socially desirable behaviour. Jones and Sigall (1971) refer to the likelihood of respondents reporting their 'true' or 'deeper' feelings. Locander and Burton (1976) refer to respondents' willingness to give 'personal' information. Fidler and Kleinknecht (1977, after Warner, 1965) refer to respondents' willingness to talk about 'private', 'sensitive' or, 'stigmatising' information. Bradburn *et al.* (1978) define threat in terms of the feelings of 'unease' generated by questions. And Sudman and Bradburn (1982) define question threat in terms of 'social desirability' and the likelihood that the questions will lead to either over-reporting or under-reporting of the behaviour being investigated. A quick look at the sorts of items Sudman and Bradburn (1982) have in mind will indicate the fuzziness of the general concept of question threat (see p. 118).

Sudman and Bradburn's list of threatening topics

Topics that are seen to be 'socially desirable' and are therefore over-reported:

Being a good citizen
    registering to vote and voting
    taking a role in community affairs
    knowing the issues
Being a well informed and cultured person
    reading newspapers and books, and using libraries
    going to concerts, plays and museum exhibits
    participating in educational activities
Having fulfilled moral and social responsibilities
    giving to charity
    helping friends and relatives
    being employed

Topics that are seen to be 'socially undesirable' and are therefore under-reported:

Illness and disabilities
    cancer
    venereal disease
    mental illness
Illegal and contra-normative behaviour
    committing a crime
    tax evasion
    consumption of alcohol
    sexual practices
Financial status
    income
    savings and other assets

(Source: Sudman and Bradburn, 1982:32–33. New format by the author.)

Few, if any, methodologists have taken exception to any of the items Sudman and Bradburn have included in their list. Indeed, other methodologists have advanced very similar lists. Lee and Renzetti (1990:512), for example, state that 'experience suggests that there are a number of areas in which research is more likely to be threatening than others'. These areas include questions that intrude into private spheres and personal experiences; concern deviance and social control; raise fears of identification; impinge on the vested interests of the powerful; raise the fear of coercion or domination; or concern sacred issues which respondents do not want to profane. Yet herein lies the problem. It is difficult to see a common dimension running through the different classes of items that are included in these lists.

It is not hard to think of a variety of motives for respondents giving incorrect or biased answers, besides the desire to be socially accepted. Some respondents may lie to avoid physical punishment or the loss of material benefits. Others may avoid answering a question altogether because thinking about it is psychologically distressing.

It is possible, too, that question threat might be generated by a number of different factors — some that are idiosyncratic to the particular respondent; some that arise out of characteristics of the questions *per se*, and some that arise out of the nature of the relationship between the researcher and the respondent. At the same time, it seems unreasonable to assume that the kinds of threats associated with each of these factors are necessarily the same. Further, it seems unreasonable to assume that different kinds of threats necessarily call for the same kinds of threat-reducing strategies.

All of this simply adds up to the fact that there is a need to go beyond past discussions of question threat. There is a need for a theoretical framework that allows the different particular techniques to be paired with the different particular types of threat.

Question threat generated by factors that are idiosyncratic to particular respondents

It can easily be appreciated that some of the items that were listed by Sudman and Bradburn (for example, 'cancer' and some forms of 'sexual behaviour') might generate purely personal fears or feelings of guilt. Some individuals, for example, may find it defiling to think about some kinds of sexual activities, while others may not be disturbed at all by thinking about them. Presumably there is no way to predict, ahead of time, whether or not an item will be psychologically disturbing to this or that respondent. At best, the effects of such threats, when they do occur, might be minimised by sensitive interviewing practices, for instance, by adopting the social worker's adage of working at the client's pace (i.e., by putting the demands of the interview to one side and trying to bolster the respondent's level of trust and self esteem whenever she or he shows signs of psychological distress).

Characteristics of the questions per se that threaten respondents

A number of question characteristics *per se* can make respondents uncomfortable. Sudman and Bradburn (1974) tentatively advance the conclusion that 'difficult' vocabulary threatens respondents (presumably because it makes them feel uneducated and socially inferior), which in turn increases the probability of 'Don't know' and socially desirable responses. And Payne (1951) presents results which suggest that 'vocabulary difficulty' relates to the tendency to endorse the last item heard. These findings, in turn, point to the conclusion that respondents will give non-substantive or incorrect answers rather than admit that they can't understand the question or are so poorly informed that they have never heard of the topic.

Certainly, it is plausible that respondents who are asked to respond to questions that they find difficult to interpret because of difficult vocabulary, excessive question length, grammatical complexity or difficult instructions, will feel that their sense of competence and self worth is being attacked. Presumably, threats that are associated with such question characteristics can be minimised by making sure that questions are simple enough to be understood by all respondents.

Other potentially threatening features of questions *per se* are key words that have negative stereotypic or cultural connotations. Survey methodologists have long recognised that respondents react to words with negative cultural nuances as if they are 'things'. For instance, any reference to 'communists' or 'homosexuals' in the United States during the 1950s would have stimulated excessive negative responses. It seems reasonable to assume, however, that question threat generated by the use of emotionally loaded or taboo words can be minimised, if not entirely avoided, by avoiding the use of terms that have negative, stereotypic connotations (e.g. by referring to 'men who prefer having sexual relationships with other men' rather than 'homosexuals').

Threat associated with the nature of the relationship which exists between the researcher and the respondent

A question can also threaten a respondent if the nature of the relationship that exists between the researcher and the respondent gives rise to fears of negative sanctions. But this statement is too simple in itself both because there are different kinds of sanctions and because the sanctions that operate in one relationship can be quite different from those that operate in other relationships. Respondents may fear being either socially rejected or thought less of by the researcher, or they may fear being materially sanctioned or physically punished in some way. Moreover, it is reasonable to assume that fear of social rejection is most likely to be an issue when the respondents see themselves as the interviewer's equals, while fear of either material or physical punishment is most likely to arise when respondents perceive that the interviewer is in a position to exercise political or economic power over them. It is worth looking at each of these possibilities in greater depth.

The fear of rejection when respondents perceive themselves to be the interviewer's social equal

Festinger's (1954) theory of social comparison processes predicts that social actors constantly seek to validate their attitudes and opinions by comparing them to those held by other social actors whom they define as being socially similar to themselves. Further, when social actors perceive discrepancies between their own attitudes and opinions and those held by socially similar others, they are motivated to try to reduce these discrepancies in one of three ways: by changing their own views; by trying to change the views held by the others with whom they compare themselves; or by rejecting the initial comparison with others in favour of new ones. It follows (especially from the implications of the last possibility) that social actors will learn to conform to group norms to avoid being socially rejected. Applied to the interview situation, this means that it can be predicted that respondents will be under psychological pressure to give answers that they think are normatively acceptable to the interviewer when they perceive the interviewer to be socially similar to themselves. It also seems reasonable to hypothesise that the questions themselves will have a tendency to make researchers and respondents define one another as social equals when they deal with general normative issues that can be seen to be of equal concern to all social groups in the researcher's and respondents' community (e.g. matters of hygiene or social morality). In such situations, the question threat that is generated will be reduced if the threat of being socially rejected is reduced.

A number of strategies have been invented which probably do this. Fear of being socially rejected can be reduced either by increasing the psychological distance between the interviewers and respondents or by ensuring the respondents' answers are anonymous. Both the 'secret ballot' technique (Benson, 1941: Turnbull, 1944) and the 'randomised response' technique (Zdep and Rhodes, 1976: Fidler and Kleinknecht, 1977) allow respondents to answer knowing that it is impossible for the interviewer to know how they have answered. The psychological distance between the interviewer and the respondents can also be increased by removing the physical presence of the interviewer from the research situation. This can be done by conducting interviews over the telephone, using mail questionnaires or letting respondents type answers to questions that are displayed on a computer monitor directly into the computer. Duffy and Waterton (1984), for example, explored the efficacy of the last technique and found that respondents' reports of alcohol consumption 'over the last seven days' was 33 per cent higher when the respondents typed their answers directly into a computer than when respondents had to personally respond to an interviewer. The psychological distance between the interviewer and respondents can also be increased by making sure that the response categories used are no more precise than is needed, given the objectives of the research. It can also be increased by ensuring that the questions do not contain clues about what the researcher thinks is 'normal'. Hippler and Schwarz (1987) suggest that this can be done by using open questions to obtain data on behavioural frequencies (e.g. average number of beers drunk at a sitting). Alternatively, it can be done by making sure that the response categories generously encompass even the most extreme behaviour, so that no clues are given as to what the researcher thinks is deviant.

The fear of political or economic sanctions

Both Katz (1942) and Williams (1964) have suggested that interviewers who have higher social status than their respondents can pose either a political or an economic threat for the respondents. Williams comments that questions can range from requests for information that could have few consequences for their respondents, to requests for information that could be used to either help or harm them. Such would be the case if a social worker were to ask a client for information that might put in jeopardy a benefit that the respondent was receiving. While it is undoubtedly possible for higher status researchers to threaten lower status respondents in this way, it should also be recognised that researchers can, for much the same reason, threaten respondents who have higher status than themselves. For example, a newspaper reporter's questions might threaten a rich industrialist because the industrialist fears the social consequences that might flow from the publication of the information being sought by the reporter.

In situations in which respondents fear either political or economic sanctions, the use of techniques that increase the psychological distance between the respondents and the researcher are not likely to be appropriate because they do not reduce the kind of threat that has been invoked. Instead, situations that pose economic or political threats to respondents require procedures that maximise trust on the part of the respondents (e.g. guarantees of confidentiality and assurances that their answers will not lead to either political or economic sanctions). In addition, anything that researchers can do to indicate a lack of naivety on their part may help to override the effects of the respondents' fears. The use of leading questions in the context of a demonstrated broad background knowledge of the topic on the part of the researcher, for example, is likely to lessen the temptation to give misleading answers (Richardson, 1960; Hunt *et al.*, 1964; Zuckerman, 1972). And stressing the fact that the respondents' views are too important to be incorrectly recorded may help to counteract the temptation on the part of the respondent to refuse to answer at all (see Manning, 1966–67).

A complicating fourth factor: the respondents' definition of the situation

In discussing the consequences of the fact that different topics are likely to generate different kinds of threats for respondents, we have ignored the possibility that any topic might generate two or even all three types of threat. A question about 'age' for instance, might be psychologically disturbing if it raises fears of mortality; generate fears of social rejection if the respondent is personally 'attracted' to the interviewer; or generate fears of economic sanctions if the respondent is applying for a job for which she or he might be considered to be either too old or too young. Clearly, many — if not all — topics are capable of triggering off more than one type of threat at the same time. Questions about sexual behaviours, for example, simultaneously relate to social mores as well as to prevailing laws. Questions about income can be reminders that one has 'failed one's family'; can generate invidious social comparisons between self and interviewer; or can threaten a material benefit (e.g. a pension). A question about how many people live with the respondent can trigger off feelings of loneliness or vulnerability to attack; stimulate invidious social comparisons; or raise fears of economic or political sanctions (e.g. jeopardise receipt of a welfare benefit). A question about which political party the respondent voted for can challenge the respondent's loyalty to the social class that she or he and the interviewer belong to or emphasise the conflict in political interests that exists between the respondent and the interviewer if they belong to different social classes.

Given the comments that have just been made, the question that arises is: What should be done to minimise question threat when it is suspected that the question may generate more than one type of threat? There are really a number of parts to this problem. First, the kinds of threats that are likely to operate have to be guessed at on the basis of an appraisal of the way in which the respondents are likely to define the question–answer situation. Second, the researcher has to decide on the best way to tackle the threats that have been identified. Then the researcher can decide whether to concentrate on the problem of minimising the threat that is most likely to be dominant in the situation or employ a number of threat-reducing strategies at the same time.

All of this is not to suggest that the problem of question threat is easily solved. Indeed, survey researchers have been all too susceptible to taking it for granted that respondents are, or can be, motivated to give the researcher the required information. As has already been said a number of times, respondents must be able to *trust* the researcher not to use the information against them and define the request for information as being *legitimate*. Neither of these requirements can be taken for granted, even if they hold true at the start of the question–answer process. There is a great deal of sense in the view expressed by Douglas (1985:25):

> Creative interviewing ... involves the use of many strategies and tactics of inter-action, largely based on an understanding of friendly feelings and intimacy, to optimise *cooperative, mutual disclosure and a creative search for mutual understanding*. It certainly does not always start out with a high degree of cooperation; and like any relationship, including the most friendly, it always involves some potential, or actual, conflicts that must be assiduously and creatively managed. However, it always in-volves *some trust and cooperation* ... (and) ... cooperation, like everything else, is created and recreated as we go along. (Douglas, 1985:25–26) [my emphasis]

Along with the complication that the respondent's level of *trust* is a con-stantly varying quantity, the issue of whether respondents will define a researcher's request for information as a legitimate one needs to be addressed. A number of factors bear on respondents' willingness to define requests for information as legitimate. Presumably, requests that are defined as illegitimate will threaten respondents because they raise the possibility of either having to offend the interviewer by refusing to answer or of having to feel guilty for being disloyal to fellow social actors. They may also raise fears of being punished by one's fellows for divulging the information to the researcher.

A number of writers have discussed the phenomenon of group loyalty and status barrier rules that dictate what a member of one group can say to another (Benney *et al.*, 1956; Goody, 1978; Wax, 1979). An example from Wiedner (1983) is illustrative. Wiedner found that the residents in a hostel for newly released prisoners would not talk to him (especially when the other residents could see them talking) lest they be defined as breaking the residents' 'code' of not talking to the management. Cicourel (1982) adds that 'norms of politeness' can determine both what, and to whom, information is given. These status barrier rules are likely to be just as difficult to eliminate as the political or economic threats that arise when questions concern these issues and when the researcher and respondents are unlikely to see one another as social equals.

Summary

Sudman and Bradburn (1982) advance the idea that question threat equates to the level of unease generated in respondents. They fail to explain, however, why some questions make respondents feel uneasy, except to suggest implicitly that such questions are perceived by respondents to have 'socially correct' or 'socially desirable' answers. It has been argued here that several factors deter-mine the level of threat. The list includes: the nature of the topic itself; idiosyncratic associations the topic might have for particular respondents, characteristics of the question *per se* (e.g. length, difficulty of vocabulary, grammatical complexity), and the nature of the relationship between the researcher and the respondents, as well as status barrier rules. It has also been suggested that the different types of threat are likely to be best managed by the use of different threat reduction strategies. The suggestions that were made concerning the selection of appropriate strategies are summarised in table 9.1 (below).

Table 9.1   *Pairing different threat-reducing strategies with different types of question threat*

Types of questions	Types of threat generated	Appropriate threat-reducing strategies
Questions that concern normative issues, e.g.: matters of hygiene, social morality, social responsibility, aesthetic judgement, group loyalty	Fear of being socially rejected by the interviewer	• Allow respondents to answer anonymously • Decrease the likelihood that respondents will see the interviewer as a social peer • Use interviewing procedures that increase either the physical or psychological distance between the respondents and the interviewer
Questions that concern either political or economic interests	Fear that the interviewer will impose either economic or political sanctions on the respondent	• Increase respondent's level of trust • Stress confidentiality • Establish lack of interviewer gullibility • Emphasise social significance of respondent's answers

Chapter 10

*T*HE OPEN VS. CLOSED QUESTIONS DEBATE

Coding responses to open questions and formulating sets of response options for closed questions

Since the initial development of modern social survey techniques at the start of the twentieth century, social scientists have fallen into two camps: those who have been attracted to the use of open questions, and those favouring the use of closed questions. These two camps have become more entrenched with the passing of the decades.

On the one hand, advocates of open questions have been fortified by the thoughts of a number of the early sociologists (such as Max Weber and William Thomas), ethnographical anthropologists (such as Clifford Geertz) and more recently by ethnomethodologists (such as Harold Garfinkel, Aaron Cicourel, Jack Douglas and Charles Briggs). All of these social scientists have stressed the cultural relativity of meaning — that is, that respondents' acts must be understood in terms of the meanings that the respondents themselves assign to them — coupled with the idea that the meanings that are ascribed to an act in one situation can be very different to the meanings ascribed to it in another situation.

On the other hand, although advocates of closed questions were initially led by those involved in the development of large scale, national survey techniques and by market researchers who needed to conduct surveys quickly (e.g. Paul Lazarsfeld and George Gallup), during the last few decades the emergence of computer technology has, if anything, increased the attractiveness of closed questions for them.

It is also probably fair to say that the arguments put forward by the two opposing camps have often looked more like 'articles of faith' than conclusions based on reason and evidence. Yet the methodological issues raised by the use of open and closed questions are fundamental and deserve careful consideration.

So that we will not lose our way or become bogged down in the 'fire' between the camps, the rest of this chapter has been structured according to the following plan:

1 The principal advantages and disadvantages associated with the two formats.
2 An evaluation of the assumptions underlying the use of open questions.
3 Problems associated with 'probing' inadequate answers to open questions.
4 Problems associated with coding responses to open questions.
5 An evaluation of the assumptions underlying the use of closed questions.
6 Problems associated with developing sets of response options for closed questions.
7 Problems associated with recording responses to closed questions.
8 Problems associated with interpreting responses to closed questions.
9 An evaluation of three additional uses claimed for open questions.

The principal advantages and disadvantages associated with the two formats

Proponents of the use of open questions argue that they allow respondents to say what is really on their minds without being influenced by suggestions from the researcher, whereas closed questions lock respondents into arbitrarily limited alternatives. They see closed questions as being typically decontextualised and as typically providing incomplete and arbitrarily closed sets of response options which are almost bound to distort respondents' answers. Survey researchers, on the other hand, think that open questions tend to produce material that is extremely variable, of low reliability and difficult to code.

Of course, not all social researchers have taken such clearcut positions. There have been those who have tried to adopt a compromise position. Lazarsfeld (1944), for instance, suggested that open questions should be used at the initial stage of a project, so that the appropriate response categories could be identified for use with closed questions, and also, at later stages in the research, to throw light on apparently deviant answers to the closed questions. In fact, most researchers would at least pay lip service to the first of these suggestions. The current normative position is implied in the following excerpt from Schuman and Presser (1979a:710):

[D]ifferences (in response distributions for open and closed versions of the same questions) will be minimised if investigators begin with open questions on large samples of the target population and use these responses to construct closed alternatives that reflect the substance and wording of what people say spontaneously. This point is so obvious as to be embarrassing to state yet it is probably violated in survey research more often than it is practised.

The most important of the claims that have been made regarding the two formats are summarised in table 10.1 (below). Although the relative merits of open and closed questions have been debated for much of this century, few attempts have actually been made to compare the kinds of answers actually produced by the two formats. Moreover, those that have been made (see Link, 1943; Crutchfield and Gordon, 1947; Dohrenwend, 1965; Schuman and Presser, 1979a) have reached conclusions which seem to be grounded more firmly on 'common sense' than on empirical findings.

Table 10.1   *The most important claims that have been made regarding open and closed questions*

Open questions	Closed questions
(a) Allow respondents to express themselves in their own words.	(a) Allow respondents to answer the *same* question so that answers can be meaningfully compared.
(b) Do not suggest answers — indicate respondent's level of information — indicate what is salient in the respondent's mind — indicate strength of respondent's feelings.	(b) Produce less variable answers. (c) Present a recognition, as opposed to a recall, task to respondents and for this reason respondents find them much easier to answer.
(c) Avoid format effects.	(d) Produce answers that are much easier to computerise and analyse.
(d) Allow complex motivational influences and frames of reference to be identified.	
(e) Are a necessary prerequisite for the proper development of sets of response options for closed questions.	
(f) Aid in the interpretation of deviant responses to closed questions.	

An evaluation of the assumptions underlying the use of open questions

Open questions do not suggest answers to respondents

Perhaps the most persistent criticism of closed questions is that pre-set response options are likely to cause respondents to give answers they would not give if they had to provide them for themselves. The difference between the workings of open and closed questions in this respect is indicated by the results of a study that was referred to in chapter 1. Schuman and Presser (1979a) report that, whereas 22 per cent of the respondents who answered an open question about 'the most important problems facing the country,' mentioned food and energy shortages, only one out of 592 respondents used the 'other' category to give this answer to a corresponding closed question that did not include it as an option. What is especially interesting about these results is that they were obtained just after a severe winter that had caused food and energy shortages which had received a lot of media attention. Schuman and Presser are driven to remark:

> [These] ... results bring home an obvious and yet profound point about survey questions: almost all respondents work within the substantive framework of priorities provided by the investigators, whether or not it fits their own priorities ... (Schuman and Presser, 1979a:707)

Even so, the implied suggestion that open questions do not suggest answers to respondents is not necessarily valid. Indeed, the common practice of using 'probes' to clarify the meaning of responses to open questions comes close to turning them into closed ones. (Note that this problem is taken up again below, pp. 134–8.) Further, the implied view that answers to open questions are sometimes more valid than answers to closed questions can be correct only if the answers to open questions can be interpreted and coded properly. Both of these requirements assume a lot, as will be made clear later (see pp. 138–9).

Answers to open questions indicate respondents' levels of knowledge about the topic

This assumption is suspect on a number of grounds. Most generally, open questions rest on the assumptions that they are relevant to respondents and that respondents can give correct answers within the question–answer situation. But it is easy to imagine that respondents can forget appropriate answers in the heat of the moment and there is little evidence that respondents necessarily mention the things that are most important to them first. Post-Freud, it is widely taken for granted that people often repress, or refuse to disclose, psychologically or socially sensitive concerns. The overall situation is much more complex than is implied by the assumption that answers to open questions indicate respondents' levels of information. In fact this assumption rests on three more basic assumptions:

(a) respondents will answer an open question if they 'know the answer';

(b) respondents will not try to answer an open question if they do not know the answer; and,

(c) respondents will answer closed questions even when they do not know the answer.

It should be obvious that not one of these assumptions is likely to be invariably true. Consequently, the assumption that open questions indicate respondents' levels of knowledge about the topic will seldom be true.

Answers to open questions indicate the salience of the topic in the respondents' minds

Most methodologists have unquestioningly accepted the claim that answers to open questions indicate what issues are salient in the respondents' minds (e.g. Lazarsfeld, 1944; Dohrenwend, 1965; Schuman and Presser, 1979a; Converse and Presser, 1986; Schwarz and Hippler, 1987; Fowler and Mangione, 1990). Few, if any, methodologists, however, have bothered to define the concept of 'salience'. This would be unproblematic if the meaning of the concept were clear, but it is not. Should it be taken to mean: 'importance to the respondent', 'most easily remembered', or 'central to the respondent's thoughts at the moment'? Fowler and Mangione (1990:90) beg the issue by recommending that the variability in the number of points made by respondents in response to an open question should be controlled by asking for the 'main' reason rather than 'all' reasons.

Assuming that salience is taken to mean 'importance to the respondent', there is little reason to believe that the first items mentioned by respondents in response to an open question are among the most important to them. In fact, some issues may not only be important but be so threatening that respondents either repress them or avoid talking about them altogether, while other issues may be so salient that respondents do not bother to mention them simply because they think that they are too obvious to mention.

The last possibility probably explains why responses to the 'twenty statements test' used in symbolic interactionist studies of the 'self', typically lack references to social roles that one would think should be central to respondents' self concepts (see Zurcher, 1977). The twenty statements test requires respondents to make up to twenty statements in answer to the open question, 'Who am

I?' Respondents are told to list their answers in the order that they occur to them, not to worry about importance, and to go along 'fairly fast'. Although, a respondent might be expected to list such things as: (I am) male, a student, 20 years of age, . . . and so on, typical response patterns have been found to include a surprisingly low proportion of references to gender and to work roles, even though there is no evidence to think that these have lessened in importance in Western societies during the last few decades. Hence, it is difficult to look at answers to the twenty statements test and not suspect that respondents have neglected to list such things as gender and work roles because they have assumed that these are too obvious to mention within the test situation (i.e. because it can be assumed that the researcher already knows these things).

Following on from this observation, respondents may also either mention or not mention items because the test situation either accentuates or does not accentuate them. McQuire and McQuire (1982), for instance, report that the likelihood that a respondent will mention a particular status factor in answers to the twenty statements test increases if the respondent is different in terms of that status factor from the others taking the test (e.g. is the only female, is the only black person, is the youngest or oldest person, etc.).

The commonly observed phenomenon of job applicants walking out of interviews 'kicking themselves' for forgetting to make 'this' point or 'that' point also indicates how situational pressures and distractions can change the salience of different issues.

Respondents' answers to an open question indicate the strength of their feelings about the topic

Although this assumption is as widely held as the 'salience' assumption is, it too has little, if any, published evidence to substantiate it.

Open questions avoid the format effects that have been associated with closed questions

The format effects that have been of concern include: the tendency to tick in the middle of rating scales, the tendency to endorse the most socially desirable or acceptable answer, the tendency to endorse the first response option seen, the tendency to endorse the last option heard, and the tendency for judgements to be affected by end items or anchor points.

Some of these effects (e.g. the tendency to endorse the first response option seen or the last one heard) are easily controlled by varying the order in which response options for closed questions are presented to respondents. And anchor effects (i.e. contextual effects) can be minimised by making sure that the range of responses that is offered to respondents is appropriate. Schwarz and Hippler (1987:174) may be right when they suggest that the range covered by response options can be a source of information for respondents about the sorts of answers that the researcher sees as 'normal'. But in these cases the researcher has only to make sure that the range of responses offered sensibly encompasses the likely range of respondents' positions in regard to the topic so that they are not made to feel deviant to minimise the problem. (Note this was discussed in chapter 5 and is discussed again in chapter 11.)

As for any tendency for respondents to avoid strong evaluations and to endorse socially desirable response options, it has never been shown — nor is it clear how it could be shown — that closed questions are likely to suffer more than open questions from such problems. Indeed, if the researcher does not specify the array of possible answers, it would seem to be impossible to assess the strength of such tendencies.

Thus the criticism that closed questions are more susceptible to format effects than open questions has little basis.

Answers to open questions allow complex motivational influences and frames of reference to be identified

Lazarsfeld (1944) was one of the first to specifically suggest that open questions are useful for:

(a)   clarifying the meaning of respondents' answers;
(b)   discerning influences on opinions (for example, the dimensions of the topic and personal motivations that have influenced respondents); and
(c)   clarifying the nature of the relationship between variables.

These presumed benefits of questions are clearly not independent. More to the point, they imply that the answers to an open question indicate:

(a)   how a respondent has interpreted it;
(b)   the underlying motivation(s) influencing the respondent's orientation to the topic; and
(c)   the frame of reference that the respondent has employed.

Each of these implications awaits critical evaluation.

An answer to an open question indicates the way in which a respondent has interpreted it

In chapters 3, 4, 5 and 6 we looked at the conditions that must be met if questions are to elicit interpretable answers. It was argued that each respondent must both define the topic in the same way as the researcher and also give the kind of answer the researcher requires. In regard to the latter requirement, it was argued that there are a number of degrees of freedom that respondents can exercise when formulating answers to either open or closed questions and that the only way to avoid having different respondents give different kinds of answers is to specify the kinds of answers required. It was argued that this has to be done because the ways in which respondents have defined a topic and the perspectives they have adopted are not necessarily apparent in their answers. If anything, however, this argument is even more pertinent to open questions than closed questions because open questions afford fewer clues as to what kind of answer the researcher expects. In other words, there are good reasons for rejecting the hypothesis that answers to an open question indicate the ways in which respondents have interpreted it.

An answer to an open question indicates the motivation(s) that have influenced the respondent's orientation to the topic

Many researchers have been unwilling to accept the assumption that open questions are useful for exploring complex motivational states:

> [The] normal human being in Western civilisation is usually quite unable to realise
> — even to himself — what are the motivations for many of his actions . . . many of
> these motives are in fact relatively simple and may be ascertained if the problem is
> tackled scientifically . . . (e.g. with projective tests) . . . but to attempt to ascertain
> them by asking point blank: Why do you do this? is not only a waste of time and
> money but also a course of proceeding which any reputable practitioner or market
> researcher should regard as unethical. (Henry, 1971:294)

As was noted in chapter 7, Henry reports the results of several market research experiments that suggest respondents had been influenced by factors of which they had not been aware. It should be added that, even if respondents had been aware of their motivations, there is no reason to expect them to disclose them unless they had been explicitly asked to do so.

The answer to an open question indicates the frame of reference used by the respondent

The fact that respondents can formulate responses from a large (if not infinite) array of perspectives (see chapters 4 and 5), makes it theoretically nonsensical to pick on any one and treat it as the only 'real' explanation. Requests for explanations are generally likely to simply pressure respondents into giving answers that they think will satisfy the researcher. Not necessarily at odds with this argument is the tendency, identified by attribution theorists in social psychology (see, e.g., Monson and Snyder, 1977) for respondents to give answers from their own standpoint. Menzel (1978) gives an example that illustrates how this works. He notes that soldiers questioned about the reasons for the My Lai massacre might have talked about how it was impossible to distinguish the Viet Cong from the South Vietnamese and how they had merely carried out their orders. An equally good explanation (though less likely to be actually given according to attribution theory) could have been cast in terms of the political processes current in the United States at that time — for example, the pressure to produce evidence to demonstrate that the war was being won (e.g. such as documenting rising daily body counts). In the final analysis, causes that are taken into account reflect both implicit and explicit interpretative decisions made by both the researcher and the respondents. This implies that the response framework that should be used needs to be specified by the researcher or that the researcher must attempt to delineate the types of explanations which different kinds of respondents typically give in different kinds of situations, if answers are to be both interpretable and comparable. The need to identify the nature of the perspectives used by the respondents stands as a problem that cannot be avoided.

Problems associated with probing inadequate answers to open questions

Perhaps because open questions require respondents to first decide 'how' to answer before answering, answers to open questions are much more variable than answers to closed questions (e.g. Cantril and Fried, 1944:11; Schuman and Presser 1979a:704; Potter and Mulkay, 1985). This puts pressure on interviewers to continually ask themselves whether or not particular answers are of the sort they require: can they understand the answers respondents have given; have the respondents provided the information they want?

The solution usually suggested, both for the tendency of respondents to stray from the topic when answering open questions and for the high frequency of incomplete answers, is to make sure that interviewers clearly understand the researchers' goals so that they can 'probe' respondents' minds to clarify obscure answers. Campbell (1945:347), comments that the open question:

is by no means an infallible instrument: the freedom of response which it permits can lead to ambiguity rather than clarity. The successful use of this technique requires precise and thoughtful formulation of questions and careful, intelligent interviewing . . .

Converse and Presser (1986:67) echo Campbell's view when they assert that rough codes for the possible responses to open questions should be designed in advance and explained to the interviewers so that they can recognise when a question has been adequately answered. And Zeisel (1985:205) writes:

The major interviewing problem derives from the difference between what the respondent thinks is a satisfactory answer and what the interviewer regards as satisfactory. The interviewer must be familiar with the accounting scheme because she must try to obtain answers for each dimension.

To this purpose, the interviewer must help her respondent along by encouraging more specific or more complete answers or by asking for the resolution of contradictions . . .

The irony of this line of advice is that it begs the question of whether open questions are better or worse than closed questions because, in essence, it turns them into closed questions.

Just as important as the principle that interviewers should know the required sorts of answers is the principle that interviewers should attempt to get adequate answers. Fowler and Mangione (both of the Massachusetts Center for Survey Research, 1990:41) draw attention to the fact that existing manuals vary greatly in the advice they give about how inadequate answers should be dealt with: 'Some organisations seem to accept, or even encourage, interviewers to find a variety of conversational ways to get respondents to clarify or elaborate their answers'. They go on to say that:

Our preference is to have interviewers stick with a very small list of probes.
In fact, we train interviewers that in addition to repeating the question, they only need to use three probes:
1. How do you mean that?
2. Tell me more about that.
3. Anything else?

These three probes are easy to remember. They are non directive. they do not give interviewers any opportunity to innovate in ways *that would make their interviews different across respondents or interviewers.*

The interviewer's task is to decide which of these probes is appropriate, and that involves analyzing the respondent's answer. The four probes, including repeating the question, correspond to the four ways in which a respondent's answer can be inadequate:

1. The response can fail to answer the question; it answers some other question. The interviewer should repeat the question.

2. The answer contains unclear concepts or terms that make its meaning ambiguous. The interviewer should probe, saying, 'How do you mean (that)?'

3. The answer is not detailed enough or specific enough. The interviewer should probe saying, 'Could you tell me more about (that)?'

4. A perfectly appropriate answer has been given, but there is a possibility that there are additional points that the respondent could make in answer to the question. The interviewer should ask, 'Is there anything else?' (Fowler and Mangione, 1990:41–42) [my emphasis]

The idea that probes should be non-directive is obviously crucial. Yet how well do the limited, standardised probes suggested by Fowler and Mangione meet this requirement? An analysis of an illustrative example that Fowler and Mangione (1990:42–43) discuss at length is instructive. A precis of this example follows:

Q. From your point of view, what are the best things about living in this neighbourhood?

A1 In the last neighbourhood in which we lived, it was very transient. People didn't care about keeping up the neighbourhood.
   [Decision — answer does not answer question — use probe: repeat question]

A2 The people.
   [Decision — answer is unintelligible — use probe: Tell me more about that.]

A3 The people are good neighbours.
   [Decision — answer needs further clarification — use probe: How do you mean 'good neighbours'?]

A4 They keep to themselves. They leave you alone. You don't have to worry about being sociable and you don't have to worry about what they think.

Notice that in this example the respondent's focus of attention in A1 is quite different from that in A4. In A1 the focus is on the way the neighbours keep up the neighbourhood; in A4, it is on the way the neighbours keep to themselves. Fowler and Mangione claim that A1 is not relevant. But it is not clear why it is not relevant. It is true that the focus is upon the last neighbourhood the respondent lived in rather than upon the new one. Nevertheless, the respondent may very well be saying something about the new neighbourhood by comparing it to the last one. Likewise, although A4 is overtly about the new neighbourhood, it may nevertheless contain elements of comparison with the last neighbourhood. In other words, it is not necessarily the case that A4 is any more relevant to the question than A1. What must be said, however, is that the dimension focused upon in A1 is quite different from that being focused upon in A4. Just why this shift of focus occurs is not clear. But the most likely explanation would seem to be that the interviewer's probing caused it to happen. It is as if the probes signalled to the respondent that the answer given first is somehow inadequate so that the respondent has 'tried again' to find an answer that will satisfy the interviewer. The most obvious explanation for this is that the respondent was not told, when the question was first presented, what sort of answer was required.

If the task of ensuring that answers to open questions are relevant poses methodological difficulties, the task of ensuring that they are complete raises similar problems. Link captures the problem succinctly:

> [The] depth interviewer is supposed to use his own ingenuity in asking impromptu questions, and to keep up this process until the particular subject seems to have been wrung dry . . .
>
> Obviously, from this description, the responses obtained by a depth interviewer reflect the mind of the interviewer as well as the mind of the person interviewed. When we come to evaluate such interviews, we are at once confronted by this problem, namely: which of the ideas expressed represent the real thoughts of the respondent, and which represent the thoughts which the interviewer, by suggestion, has construed to elicit? (Link, 1943:269)

Similarly, Smith and Hyman (1950) report the results of a study which indicate a tendency on the part of interviewers to record the results that they expect to hear rather than those they are actually given.

In addition, a related difficulty arises because different respondents give different amounts of information. Some respondents are capable of giving lengthy, multi-stranded answers while others respond with the briefest of answers to the same questions. Adverbial questions — that is, 'how', 'where', and 'why' — questions are particularly prone to eliciting answers of varying length. Fowler and Mangione (1990:90–91) suggest that the researcher can avoid this problem by narrowing the discretion of both interviewers and respondents about the kinds of answers that count. They recommend translating general, adverbial questions into more specific questions. For example, 'How do you get to work?' might become:

'What kind of transport do you use to get to work?'; or

'By what route do you proceed to work?'

And, as has already been noted, they suggest limiting the number of responses to 'why' questions by asking for the main reason rather than for all reasons, so that each respondent only gives one answer.

Again, no matter how sensible the advice that has been given about how interviewers should 'probe' to improve the adequacy of respondents' answers, such advice avoids the question of whether or not open questions are more useful than closed questions as indicators of what issues are important to respondents and of how their answers should be interpreted. The problem is that the use of 'probes' inevitably comes close to turning open questions into loosely formulated closed questions.

Problems associated with coding responses to open questions

Advocates of open questions usually hold that a satisfactory coding schema can be formulated by going through a sample of responses several times to get a sense of the sort of categories into which the responses naturally fall (e.g. Silvey, 1975:38; Montgomery and Crittendon, 1977; Mostyn, 1985). Once a set of consistent categories has emerged, the remaining responses are coded. If one adopts this view, one implicitly assumes that respondents' answers speak for themselves. But this simple approach ignores all of the issues that have been raised in chapters 4 and 5, and in earlier sections of this chapter.

Consider, for instance, the deceptively simple question: 'What is your father's occupation?' The author had a sample of students answer this question. The answers given are set out in table 10.2 (p. 139). How should such answers be coded? The coding system chosen should reflect the reason that the research was carried out in the first place. If the intention had been to use the answers as indications of social class, they could be coded according to the ranking of each occupation mentioned on an established occupational prestige scale. If the intention had been to look at the impact of the fathers' occupations on the respondents' lives, the information might be classified according to the hours worked. If the intention was to classify fathers in terms of their probable relationship to different economic interests, the answers would need to be classified in yet another way. And so on.

Looking at table 10.2 it can be seen that most answers contain insufficient information to allow them to be classified properly in terms of any one of the possible ways suggested above. Even for the relatively simple goal of classifying paternal occupational prestige, many of the answers do not contain all the information that would allow this to be done. The obvious conclusion that has to be drawn here is that a question should be put to respondents in such a way that it elicits complete answers of the kind required. More generally, in the absence of clear guidelines about what sorts of answers are required, respondents can, and will, focus upon such a variety of aspects of the topic that their answers are neither comparable nor codable.

Table 10.2 *A sample of answers to an open question regarding father's occupation*

The question:*
Your father's occupation is (or was)? *Give details:*
Nature of business:_____
Size of business:_____
Owner____ Employee____

A sample of the answers given:

1	Real estate agent	—	Employee
2	Tailor	—	Employee
3	Taxi	Medium	Unknown
4	Motor mechanic	—	—
5	Timber merchant	Small	Owner
6	Commercial manager telecommunications	Philips	Employee
7	Farming	3000 acres	Owner
8	Research organisation	Small	Gov't of Aust.
9	Bus driver	—	—
10	Exploration company	Large	Employee
11	Stipendiary magistrate	—	—
12	Builder	Small-medium	Owner
13	Plumber	2 people	Owner
14	Car manufacturer	Very Large	—
15	Foreman	Large	Employee
16	Small bus. plastic components manufacturer	Small	Owner
17	Doctor/ GP	—	—
18	Tool setter	Big	Employee
19	Builder	Medium	Self-employed
20	Garage proprietor	1 employee	Owner
21	Shop assistant	—	—
22	Imports and exports	Medium	Owner
23	Manufacturing firm	200 people	Owner
24	Teacher/ library asst	—	—
25	Photography	—	—
26	Wheat production	Family	Self-employed
27	Clerical	Multi-national	Employee
28	Teacher/catering	—	—

***Note:** Responses to this question are set out here to demonstrate the general point that has been made. Although more complex question sequences have been developed to establish respondents' occupational status — see chapter 3, pp. 27–8 — it could be argued that they, too, suffer from the same problems as the question used here.

An evaluation of the assumptions underlying the use of closed questions

Assumption 1: Because all respondents answer the question in the same way, the answers can be meaningfully compared

A great deal of evidence on the falsity of this assumption has been presented in earlier chapters. In chapters 3 and 4 it was noted that if different respondents are to interpret a question in the same way they must give the same meaning to key words. Yet even when they have done this, respondents seldom interpret questions literally. They adopt a perspective that includes, among other things, assumptions about the sort of information the researcher 'really' wants. If different respondents give different meanings to key concepts and adopt different perspectives, they will, in fact, be answering different questions. In other words, the fact that every respondent has been exposed to the same words is no guarantee that they will have understood the question in the same way. Thus it is clear that the researcher should try to ensure that respondents will both define key words in the same way and adopt the same perspective. While this may require some effort on the part of the researcher, it is not an impossible task (see chapters 3 to 6).

It is undoubtedly the case that closed questions go a long way towards limiting the kinds of answers respondents give because they require respondents to select responses from sets of response options. The provision of response options necessarily means that respondents are provided with clues as to the intended focus of the question, the required level of social generality of the answer, and so on. Nevertheless, it must be recognised that providing arrays of response options will not guarantee that key terms are defined in the same way or that the overall perspectives adopted by respondents are the same.

Assumption 2: Respondents find closed questions easier to answer

This assumption is easily supported. Besides helping respondents decide what sort of responses are appropriate, pre-set response options inevitably act as prompts which help respondents recall information that they might otherwise forget. For this reason, it is not surprising that Dohrenwend (1965:180) reports that the proportion of usable responses declined during the course of experimental interviews for open questions while remaining constant for closed questions. Likewise it is not surprising that Loftus (1982) has reported that when respondents are allowed to testify freely in legal cases they produce accounts that are far less complete.

Assumption 3: Answers to closed questions are more easily analysed

The claim that closed questions produce data that are more easily analysed than open questions is at one level almost true by definition. Respondents' answers are, after all, constrained by the categories that are provided and are therefore less variable. True, that is, if one is willing to assume that every respondent who selects a particular category has interpreted it in the same way. We have seen, however, that there are no guarantees that this is always the case. Indeed, it was because of this that Lazarsfeld (1944:48) argued that open questions are useful aids for making sense of apparently deviant responses elicited by closed questions. Discussing the way in which political scientists had used open questions, he noted:

> The general pattern of these studies proceeds from an empirical correlation which is not very high. We take cases which do not follow the majority pattern and try to gain an impression or to account for their irregularity. The political scientist is used to such a procedure. He knows, for instance, that the more poor people and Catholics live in a given precinct of a big city, the more Democratic votes he can expect. But here is a precinct which qualifies on both scores, and still it went Republican. What accounts for this deviation? Is the Democratic machine inefficient? Has a special local grievance developed? Was there a recent influx of people with different political traditions? This is quite analogous to what we are trying to do when we are faced with individual cases which went statistically out of line. With the help of open interviews we try to discover new factors which, if properly introduced, would improve our multiple correlation. (Lazarsfeld, 1944:48)

The point is, if closed questions can not be interpreted without the researcher having to fall back on to open questions, the superiority of closed questions may be more apparent than real.

Problems associated with developing response categories for closed questions

In the past, most methodologists have accepted the idea that the use of open questions is unavoidable during the initial stages of question design. Lazarsfeld (1944) argued that the respondents' motivations could be adequately explored with closed questions provided that they were well grounded in the results of pilot work based on open questions. Schuman and Presser (1979a), too, contend that closed questions do not suggest invalid answers to questions as long as the alternatives that are presented to respondents have been properly developed through pilot work with open questions followed by pre-testing to ensure that the set of response options is appropriate in the sense that all of the required categories, and no inappropriate categories, have been included. Fowler and Mangione (1990:18–19), too, assert that:

> Exploratory research usually is not done best using standardized interviews. By design, in a standardized interview one only learns the answers to the questions that are asked. At the exploratory stages of research, finding out which questions to ask is a major goal . . . Restricting or structuring answers . . . should not be done until the researcher is sure the answer options are comprehensive and appropriate.

It is worth observing again that few methodologists have raised any objections to Lazarsfeld's (1944) recommendation that researchers should begin with open questions in pilot work and use the resulting responses as a basis for developing meaningful and exhaustive sets of response alternatives for closed questions.

Clearly, the completeness of the response set that accompanies a closed question is a critically important issue. Moreover, it is an issue that is made even more important by the finding that the widespread practice of including an 'Other' category does not seem to suffice (see Belson and Duncan, 1962; Schuman and Presser, 1979a:707).

Cantril and Fried (1944:11) present a convincing example of what happens when response options are not appropriate. They cite the results of a national survey conducted by the United States Office of Public Opinion Research in which the question was asked, 'If Russia should defeat Germany, which of these things do you think Russia would then try to do — try to spread Communism all through Europe, or work with Britain and the U.S. in making it possible for the countries of Europe to choose their own form of government?' Forty-one per cent thought Russia would try to spread Communism, 36 per cent thought she would try to work with Britain and the United States and 23 per cent had no opinion. Cantril and Fried then note that the Office of Public Opinion Research subsequently had a sample of forty respondents answer an open version of the closed survey question — that is, the forty respondents were asked, 'If Russia should defeat Germany, what do you think Russia would try to do next?' Only three of the 40 gave answers that could be said to fall into either of the survey alternatives. Seven (17.5%) couldn't answer. The remaining thirty respondents' answers were spread quite evenly over another sixteen categories. As Cantril and Fried remark: 'With respect to issues that are not clear-cut . . . armchair attempts to design alternatives may prove extremely misleading'.

The danger is that it is very easy to invent a set of categories on an a priori basis which appear to be self-evidently adequate. Another example will serve to reinforce this lesson. A researcher might feel that the categories 'Very good', 'Good', 'Fair', or 'Poor', might be appropriate response options for the question, 'How would you rate the school your child attends?' What should one conclude, however, if a respondent answers as follows?

> That is complicated for me. My child is in the second grade, I do not think they are doing a very good job in areas such as numbers and reading skills. However, at this age, I do not think that the content of what they learn is all that important. Kids can catch up in that respect. On the other hand, I think they do an excellent job in recreational areas such as gym and recess, where there is good equipment and a lot of opportunities for the kids to do things together. I think that is very important at this age. (Fowler and Mangione, 1990:15)

And the following example illustrates the same problem. While most respondents in Western societies can be made to place themselves in one of the following age categories: 10-19, 20-29, 30-39, etc., Carter (1971:24 — cited by Pawson, 1989:43) has suggested that the categories: 'Infancy', 'Adolescence', 'Young adulthood', and 'Old age' might better reflect the age-related distinctions that are actually made; and the categories: 'Child', 'Warrior', and 'Elder', might be preferable in certain pre-industrial societies.

It must be emphasised that it is all too easy to formulate inappropriate categories for use with closed questions. It is also very easy to fail to properly list a complete set of appropriate response options. One class of questions for which this basic requirement is commonly overlooked is discussed by Payne (1951: chapter 4). Payne refers to this class as 'two-way', 'dichotomous' or 'bifurcated' questions. Questions of this type suggest only two possible alternatives (e.g. yes or no, approve or disapprove, favour or oppose, etc.). Payne observes that:

> This type of question is by far the most commonly used of all. It appears to fit the largest number of situations. It reduces issues to their simplest terms and its advocates say that it comes closest to duplicating the types of decisions that people are accustomed to making. And whether we realise it or not, it is probably correct that even our complicated decisions are broken down into many separate two-way issues. (Payne, 1951:55)

The inherent fault with dichotomous questions is that they imply rather than explicitly state one of the alternatives and thus underemphasise it. For example, the question, 'Are you going to the game — yes or no?' does not give equal weight to the possibility that the respondent is not going to the game (i.e., 'Are you going to the game *or not?*'). Payne reports the results of an investigation into the effect of adding 'or not' to such questions. Whereas 77 per cent of one sample of respondents agreed with the statement, 'Do you think anything could be done to make it easier for people to pay doctor's or hospital bills?', 74 per cent of another similar sample of respondents, for whom the phrase 'or not' was added, responded in the same way. No doubt the proportion of respondents agreeing would have been even larger if the second option had been given its full weight (e.g., '. . . or do you think there is nothing that could be done to make it easier for people to pay doctor or hospital bills?'). Given this, one might predict that simple yes–no questions would be biased towards 'Yes' answers because the negative option is not given full weight. In fact, this is the conclusion that Molenaar (1982:58–59) reaches on the basis of a review of the literature. Molenaar expresses the view that there is a greater tendency for respondents to endorse a response option when it is presented by itself in a yes–no format than when it is presented with fully explicated contrasting alternatives.

But to return to the basic issue that is being addressed in this section: is it true that a set of response options for a closed question will be both more appropriate and more complete if it is based on responses to an open question? Few studies have been conducted to address this claim. Of those that have been carried out, one in particular is especially revealing. It is Schuman and Presser's (1979a) attempt to use the responses to an open question to improve the response set for a corresponding closed question. Schuman and Presser begin by comparing the responses elicited by a closed question (first used by Lenski in 1963 to gauge what people value in their jobs) with the responses elicited by an open version of the same question. The two questions and associated response distributions are set out in table 10.3 (p. 145). The first thing to notice is that the responses to the open question are far more diverse than are the responses to the closed question. Indeed, the five closed question response categories account for less than half of the responses given to the open question. Second, it should be noticed that the differences between two response distributions vary greatly over the first five categories. In fact, they are so different that they correlate quite differently with both gender and education.

Schuman and Presser admit that it is not clear which question should be seen to have produced the most valid results. Nevertheless, they entertain the possibility that the discrepancies between the two response distributions might have occurred because the response options accompanying the closed question had not been appropriate. To test this possibility, they revised the response categories for the closed question to make them more like the codes that had been developed to classify the answers to the open question. In doing this, they dropped the third and fourth options because they had been endorsed by tiny percentages of respondents answering the open question, and they added the fifth and sixth codes for the open question responses. The eighth code for the open question was not added to the revised closed question response options even though it accounted for 17 per cent of the open question responses because it was a vaguely defined, general category. Finally, they relabelled the

Table 10.3   *First comparison of response distributions for open and closed versions of the work values question*

Closed question:
This next question is on the subject of work.
Please look at this card and tell me which thing on this list you would prefer in a job?

Open question:
This next question is on the subject of work.
People look for different things in a job. What would you most prefer in a job? —

Answers coded:

Closed		Open	
(1) High income	12.4%	(1) Pay	11.5%
(2) No danger of being fired	7.2	(2) Security — steady employment	6.7
(3) Working hours are short: lots of free time	3.0	(3) Short hours — time for other things	0.9
(4) Chances for advancement	17.2	(4) Opportunity for promotion	1.8
(5) The work is important and gives a feeling of accomplishment	59.1	(5) Stimulating work — Work that is challenging and gives a sense of accomplishment	21.3
		(6) Pleasant — enjoyable work	15.4
		(7) Conditions include control over work & physical conditions	14.9
		(8) Liking the job — non-specific — not codable as 5 or 6	17.0
		(9) Responses specific to particular job	3.0
		(10) More than 1 codable response	1.4
		(11) Other	2.1
(6) Don't know/no opin.	1.1	(12) Don't know/no opin.	4.1
	100%		100%
	(n=460)		(n=436)

Source: Schuman and Presser, 1979a:696. Original table abbreviated and retitled by author.

categories to more closely reflect the nature of the cases that had been sub-sumed under each of the codes for the open question. Two new surveys were then conducted to test the revised set of response options and codes. The response distributions for the revised procedures are set out in table 10.4 (p. 147).

A number of things are worth noting about the new results. In the first place, although the revised response options for the closed question account for a higher percentage of the responses to the open version, a large proportion (42%) of the respondents answering the open version still gave responses that were not anticipated by the response options for the closed question. Next, relabelling the response options for the closed question appears to have changed the percentage of respondents endorsing 'security' (from 7.2% up to 20.3%) and 'accomplishment' (from 59.1% down to 31.0%). In the third place, whereas 14.9 per cent gave answers that were coded under 'work conditions' in the first survey, a total of only 7.7 per cent fall into the two derivative categories 'control over work' and 'working conditions' in the second survey. And fourth, the fact that the increase in percentage of respondents endorsing the closed question option 'security' goes up would seem to be incongruent with the hypothesis that the closed question format *per se* generates social desirability responses (discussed earlier in this chapter).

In trying to make sense of the differences between the two response distributions, Schuman and Presser suggest that the 'pay' responses to the open question equate to the 'pay' plus 'security' responses to the closed question. As evidence for this suggestion, they note that the 'pay' responses to the closed question do not correlate with levels of education, while the 'security' responses correlate negatively. It is relevant to point out, though, that the 'pay' responses accounted for 24.3 per cent of the responses to the open question while the 'pay' and 'security' responses accounted for a total of 33.5 per cent of the closed question responses (i.e. 9.2 per cent more).

Similarly, Schuman and Presser suggest that the 'satisfaction' responses to the open question equate to the closed question 'accomplishment' plus 'pleasant' responses. In support of this suggestion, they cite the results of a small scale follow-up study in which eighteen of twenty-six respondents, whose responses to the original open question had been coded 'satisfaction', endorsed 'accomplishment' when responding to the closed question. Again, it is relevant to note that whereas a total of 44.6 per cent of the open question respondents' answers were coded 'accomplishment', 'pleasant' or 'satisfaction', a total of 50.8 per cent of the responses to the closed question were accounted for by the 'accomplishment' and 'pleasant' response alternatives (i.e. 6.2 per cent more).

Finally, Schuman and Presser interpret the fact that the response options for the revised closed question picked up 15.7 per cent more respondents than the response options for the original closed question as support for the hypothesis

Table 10.4   *Comparison of response distributions for the revised response options for the closed question and the revised codes for the open question*

Closed question:
This next question is on the subject of work.
People look for different things in a job, which of the following things would you most prefer in a job?

Open question:
This next question is on the subject of work.
People look for different things in a job. What would you most prefer in a job? (Codes 1–5 given high priority.) —

Answers coded:

(1) Work that pays well	13.2%	(1) Pay	16.7%
(2) Work that gives a feeling of accomplishment	31.0	(2) Feeling of accomplishment	14.5
(3) Work where there is not too much supervision & you make most decisions	11.7	(3) Control of work	4.6
		(4) Pleasant work (sociability & enjoyment responses)	14.5
(4) Work that is pleasant; other people are nice to work with	19.8	(5) Security	7.6
		(6) Opportunity for promotion	1.0
(5) Work that is steady with little chance of being laid off	20.3	(7) Short hours/free time	1.6
		(8) Physical working conditions	3.1
		(9) Benefits	2.3
		(10) Satisfaction/ liking the job (non-specific, not coded in 2, 4)	15.6
		(11) Responses specific to particular job	3.7
		(12) 2+ codable responses	4.0
Other	0.4		3.6
Don't know/no opin.	3.6		7.0
	100%		100%
	(n=1194)		(n=1153)

Source: Schuman and Presser, 1979a:700, table 4. Original table abbreviated and retitled by author.

that the categories for the original version had not been properly grounded in responses to the initial open question. But this conclusion must be kept in perspective. It is significant that the revised response options still failed to encompass over 40 per cent of the responses to the corresponding open question. In addition, the fact the answers to the corresponding open question were still much more variable than the answers to the closed question should not be forgotten. Further, although Schuman and Presser are clearly of the view that open questions are essential for obtaining the frames of reference used by respondents for formulating appropriate response sets (Schuman and Presser, 1979a:704 and 710), much of their discussion of the differences between the response distributions for the revised questions focuses on interpreting the responses to the open question — especially the 'pay', 'security' and 'satisfaction' responses. In other words, *one could just as well argue that the closed question responses were necessary to interpret responses to the open question as argue that the closed question was improved by grounding its response alternatives in the responses to an open question.*

Problems associated with recording responses to closed questions

> When a question calls for a respondent to choose answers from a list and then the respondent has not done so, the interviewer's job is to explain to the respondent that choosing one answer from the list is the way to answer the question (called training the respondent) and to read the list of responses again. (Fowler and Mangione, 1990:39)

Fowler and Mangione continue by suggesting that there are two kinds of mistakes that interviewers can make. The interviewer can:

(a) wrongly record answers; or

(b) neglect to read all of the response options.

> For example, if a question reads 'How would you rate your schools — Very good, Good, Fair, Poor', and a respondent answers, 'Not very good', the interviewer should read the whole question again rather than just saying, 'Well would you say, Fair or Poor?'

Fowler and Mangione insist that closed questions should be asked *exactly as they are written.* They reason that if interviewers do this and respondents have trouble answering the question the researcher at least, knows that any differences in respondents' answers have arisen out of the respondents' interpretations of the original question rather than out of the interviewers' behaviour, and that the measurement process has been consistent across respondents. For these reasons, Fowler and Mangione recommend that interviewers should be programmed with standardised explanations *to teach* respondents to use the response options that are offered. They say that this can be achieved by:

(a) starting an interview with a general instruction:

> Since many people have never been in an interview exactly like this, let me read you a paragraph that tells you a little about how it works. I am going to read you a set of questions exactly as they are worded so that every respondent in the survey is answering the same questions. You'll be asked to answer two kinds of questions. In some cases, you'll be asked to answer in your own words. For those questions, I will have to write down your answers word for word. In other cases, you will be given a list of answers and asked to choose the one that fits best. If at any time during the interview you are not clear about what is wanted, be sure to ask me. (Fowler and Mangione, 1990:51)

(b) Programming the interviewer to explain why it is necessary ask a question, even if the respondent has partly answered it already:

> The next question is one you have dealt with to some extent. However, the way the interview works I need to have you answer each question specifically, so that we can compare the answers you give with the answers everyone else gives. Also, sometimes we find the answer is different to a specific question, even though it seems that the question has been answered before. So let me read the question as it is worded here, and I would like you to make sure we have it right. (Fowler and Mangione, 1990:51)

And programming the interviewer to merely repeat a question if the respondent appears to have difficulty with it:

> I see what your problem is with the question. Even though these questions are carefully tested, sometimes we have one that is not quite clear to some people, or doesn't quite fit everybody's situation. Again though, the way the survey works, we need people's best answers to the questions as they are written. That way we can compare your answers with other people's. If we change the question for each respondent, we wouldn't be able to analyze the answers. Let me read the question again, and you give me the best, most accurate answer you can, given the way it is written. (Fowler and Mangione, 1990:51–52)

or:

> With this kind of question, answers are analyzed according to which of these alternatives people choose. I need to have you choose one of the specific answers so that we can compare your response with those others give. We know that in some cases none of the answers will fit the way you feel exactly; but other people will have that problem, too. The important thing is that we keep the question-and-answer process consistent across everybody, so we can see similarities and differences in the answers people give. (Fowler and Mangione, 1990:52)

The problem with instructions like these is that they clearly pressure respondents into answering in terms of the alternatives, whether or not these are appropriate for them.

Problems associated with interpreting responses to closed questions

It has been repeatedly stressed in previous chapters that a key assumption underlying the use of questions in social research is that the answers respondents give can be meaningfully compared with one another. This assumption is forcefully expressed by Crutchfield and Gordon:

> In order that opinion poll answers be valid, respondents must interpret the question in the same way. Respondents who read different meanings into a question are, in effect, replying to different questions. When this happens the investigator cannot make a valid analysis of his results, for he has no assurance that the tabulations would be similar if all respondents had construed the questions in the same way. (Crutchfield and Gordon, 1947:1)

It was argued in chapters 3 to 6 that unless respondents have a clear understanding of what the question is about and are told what perspective to adopt when framing an answer, different respondents will answer the same question in quite different ways. This is as true for open questions as it is for closed questions. Even though it might be added that the response options which make up a closed question put some restrictions on the kinds of answers respondents can give, it must be appreciated that the implied framework will be, at best, partial in nature. Implied response frameworks typically fail to provide respondents with information about why the researcher wants the information, what the researcher already knows or assumes, the perspectives that should be adopted, the required social generality of answers, and the standards of comparison which should be used if evaluations are called for. In other words, closed questions can be almost as deficient as open questions when it comes to the issues of the comparability and the interpretability of respondents' answers. The real problem is not in the different formats (i.e. 'open' vs. 'closed' formats) *per se* but in the failure to properly specify a response framework for respondents.

The inescapable, overall conclusion that one is forced to reach is that it is dangerous to argue that open questions necessarily produce more valid results than closed questions. On the other side of the coin, it is equally dangerous to argue that closed questions are more efficient — especially if the time taken to develop appropriate sets of response options is taken into account.

An evaluation of three additional uses claimed for open questions

Three more virtues have been claimed for open questions, each of which merits brief discussion.

First, Kidder and Judd (1986:248), for example, argue that open questions allow respondents to convey the fine shades of their attitudes to their own satisfaction instead of forcing them to choose one of several statements that may all seem more or less unsatisfactory. For this reason, they suggest that open questions may be more motivating for respondents. This suggestion aside, it is just as likely that respondents are more likely to feel frustrated rather than liberated if the meaning of an open question is obscure — that is, if the respondents are not told what sorts of answers they should give.

Second, Schuman and Presser (1979a:711) suggest that open questions are useful when a set of meaningful alternatives is too large and complex to present to respondents (presumably by reading them out to the respondents because length would seem to be less of a problem if the options are presented on a card). Unfortunately, this suggestion runs contrary to everything we know about human memory. If respondents are asked to search their memories for the most appropriate answer out of a large range of possible answers, there is no guarantee that their memories will not fail or that they will not give the first answer that occurs to them that seems to answer the question.

Third, Schuman and Presser (1979a:711) suggest that it may be necessary to use open questions when the researcher has reason to suspect that rapidly shifting external events will affect answers (i.e., when the relevance or adequacy of preset sets of response options are likely to be affected). If one takes the line that researchers have to make the most of all the opportunities that are open to them, rather than the line that open questions are problem free, this is plainly a defensible suggestion.

Summary

Open and closed versions of the same questions have been found to typically generate quite different response distributions (e.g. Schuman and Presser 1979a) and it is not obvious which format produces the most valid data. The meaning of responses to open questions can be just as obscure as the meaning of responses to closed questions. This is especially true when respondents are allowed to wander from the topic, which seems to be almost an endemic problem with open questions (Campbell, 1945; Dohrenwend, 1965). It is also true when respondents are not told what kinds of answers the researcher requires. In addition, answers to open questions are often less complete than answers to corresponding closed questions.

Methodologists who have considered the issues have tended to settle on the compromise position that a judicious mix of open and closed questions is best (e.g. Kahn and Cannell, 1957:158; Gallup, 1947). It has been widely taken for granted that qualitative, in-depth interviews should precede the formulation of fixed-choice questions so that response categories will reflect the respondents' worlds rather than the researchers' (e.g. Cicourel, 1982; Converse, 1984; Converse and Presser 1986). One might almost say that since the publication of Lazarsfeld's paper in 1944 every survey researcher has accepted the idea that open questions can play a useful part in interpreting responses to closed questions.

But the issues are not so easily settled. The observation that the distributions of answers to open questions often differ markedly from the distributions of answers to corresponding closed versions of the same questions is often taken as evidence that the response options for the closed questions must be inappropriate; but such an outcome can just as easily be the result of respondents having to guess what kinds of answers the researcher wants in response to open questions. The central issue is not which format produces the most valid responses but whether or not respondents know what kinds of answers they should give. And this is an issue that applies equally to both open and closed questions.

Chapter 11

*M*EASURING ATTITUDES

Researchers are often tempted to design and use questions that will allow them to measure the strength of respondent attributes instead of just noting their presence or absence. Working with non-dichotomous variables is a step toward greater precision which in turn allows the formulation and testing of more complex hypotheses using sophisticated statistical procedures (such as correlational and analysis of variance procedures).

One class of attributes in particular — that of 'attitudes' — has received a great deal of attention from methodologists. And a great many question devices have been invented to measure respondents' attitudes; see Sudman and Bradburn (1982:158–173) for a concise discussion of the most commonly used techniques. The list includes:

(a) Simple open ended questions (e.g. 'What are your feelings about X?')

(b) Simple rating scales which are presented as representing the attitude continuum underlying topics with instructions for the respondent to place ticks at the points on the scales which best indicate their attitudes toward the topics.

(c) The Michigan Survey Center's adaptation of Katz's (1944) 'ladder' and 'thermometer' rating devices, which require respondents to indicate where they would place themselves on pictorial representations of the attitude continuum. The ladder and thermometer presentations are attempts to make the rating task less abstract for respondents (figure 11.2 — 5 and 6, p. 157).

(d)   The National Opinion Research Center's ranking procedure for getting respondents to indicate the first, then second, then third . . . most important items in a list.

(e)   Rokeach's procedure of having respondents sort labels with values printed upon them until the labels have been ordered in ways that reflect the respondents' own orderings.

(f)   The 'Q sort' technique which involves respondents being given a deck of 100–200 cards, with a statement about the attitude object printed on each card, and instructions to sort the cards into a given number of piles that are subjectively equal distances apart.

(g)   The paired comparison technique that requires respondents to look at each of the possible pairs that can be generated by a set of items and to state which item in each pair is 'highest', 'best', 'preferred', etc.

(h)   Thurstone equal interval scales (sometimes referred to as 'differential' scales) which are formed by: (i) having a panel of judges sort several hundred statements about a topic into eleven piles ranging from the most negative to the most positive, and (ii) identifying a smaller number of statements (usually about 10–20) that are characterised by a high level of agreement among the judges and are spread evenly across the eleven piles. The selected items are then assigned values according to the piles in which the judges have agreed they should be put before being presented in a random order to survey respondents. Finally, the respondents are instructed to check the two or three statements that are closest to their own positions. In this way, the respondents are ordered according to the average value of the items they have endorsed. (See either Selltiz *et al.* 1965:359–365, or Kidder and Judd, 1986:205–207, for a more extended discussion).

(i)   Sets of statements about the attitude object (usually 10–20 in number) accompanied by rating scales which are either numeric (e.g. 1, 2, 3, 4, 5, or −2, −1, 0, +1, +2), verbal (e.g. 'Strongly agree', 'Agree', 'Neutral', 'Disagree', 'Strongly disagree'), face (e.g. lines of faces with expressions ranging from sad through neutral to happy) or line (e.g. lines with labels at each end) rating scales. Respondents are instructed to tick the response options that best reflect their positions on each item. Individual respondents are then given total scores on the basis of the sums of their ratings. These total scores are taken to indicate the respondents' positions in respect to the attitude object. Such sets of rating scales are usually called either 'Likert' scales or 'summated scales'. (See either Selltiz *et al.*, 1965:366–370, or Kidder and Judd, 1986:207–210, for a description of the procedure used to select items.)

(j)   Guttman unidimensional scales (sometimes referred to as cumulative scales). The Guttman scaling procedure can be thought of as a technique for checking to see that the items employed in either a Thurstone scale or a Likert scale all relate to the underlying attitude dimension that these scales are designed to measure. (See Selltiz *et al.*, 1965:370–377, or Kidder and Judd, 1986:207–210, for a fuller description.)

Most research technique manuals present a list like the one above. Almost all manuals do little more than list the various techniques as if they constitute a range of equally valid procedures that researchers can choose between as they fancy. The truth is that there has been little work directed toward comparing the relative strengths and weaknesses of the different procedures.

A number of factors are probably responsible for this situation, the most obvious of these being the fact that the techniques do not produce information that is logically equivalent because some are based on the ranking of items while others involve the rating of items.

Ranking devices clearly give information about the order in which each respondent would place items. They do not, however, provide information about the subjective importance or weight each respondent would assign to each item. Because of this, the researcher cannot sensibly compare different respondents' rankings. This problem is presented schematically in figure 11.1 (p. 156).

Rating procedures, on the other hand, presumably give rough information about the perceived significance of each item — rough because the items are classified into a small number of categories (usually 3–7). But, for at least two reasons, they fail to provide clear information about the relative importance of the items to the respondents. In the first place, items that are placed in the same rating category are by definition unordered. In the second place, the validity of inferences about the relative importance either of different items to the same respondent, or of the same item to different respondents, depends upon the extent to which the rating categories are given standardised meanings. For example, it has to be assumed that a 'Strongly agree' response to item X has the same meaning as a 'Strongly agree' response to item Y, and that a 'Strongly agree' response from one respondent has the same meaning as a 'Strongly agree' response from another. As will be argued later in the chapter, neither of these assumptions is invariably true.

Another factor that may explain the lack of studies seeking to compare the different measurement procedures is the sheer popularity of rating procedures. Rating scales — especially batteries of rating scales — have been used much more often than any of the other procedures (Bardo *et al.*, 1976). One can only guess as to why summated rating scales have been so popular. A possible explanation lies in the facts that they appear to be easy to prepare and that respondents seem to find them easy to use. Whatever the reasons for the overwhelming popularity of rating scales, however, their popularity is the reason that most of this chapter will be spent discussing issues relating to them.

Figure 11.1   *A pictorial comparison of the rankings of four items (i, ii, iii, and iv) made by four respondents (A, B, C, and D)*

Absolute values of the items (assuming that they can be measured)		Respondents			
		A	B	C	D
Highest possible	1	i		i	
				ii	
				iii	
	2	ii	i	iv	
		iii	ii		
			iii		
	3		iv		i
					ii
					iii
Lowest possible	4	iv			iv

In the case of ranking tasks, unless respondents are asked to indicate what weight they would give to each item, the researcher is neither given information about the importance of the differences between ranks for each respondent nor given information about the level of 'subjective' similarity between items which are nominally assigned the same rank by different respondents. Hence, for example, item i is ranked 'high' by each respondent but this rank does not mean the same thing to each respondent. Whereas respondents A and C would give item i the highest absolute weighting, respondent B would give it the second highest absolute weighting, and respondent D would give it the second lowest absolute weighting.

To simplify the discussion, we will begin by looking at issues related to single rating scales before moving on to issues that are peculiar to batteries of rating scales.

Single rating scales

Although rating scales come in several formats, all are designed to do the same job: to allow respondents to indicate the strength of their attitude toward a specified topic. Some of the more common alternative rating formats are set out in figure 11.2 (p. 157).

Because rating devices are questions, all of the issues that were raised in chapters 2 to 6 apply to them. In those chapters, it was argued that questions should satisfy three basic considerations:

(a) the topic of focus should be clearly defined;

(b) the relevance of the topic to the respondents should be established; and

(c) respondents should all give the same kinds of answers.

Figure 11.2 *A number of common rating scale formats*

(1) Tick the position that indicates your feeling about X:	Strongly agree _ _ _ _ _ _ _ _ _ _ _	Strongly disagree
(2) Place a tick at the point on the line that reflects your feeling about X:	Strongly agree _____	Strongly disagree
(3) Circle the number that indicates your feeling about X:	Strongly agree 1 2 3 4 5	Strongly disagree

(4) Circle the face that indicates the way you feel about X:

(5) Where do your feelings towards X place you on the 'feeling' thermometer?

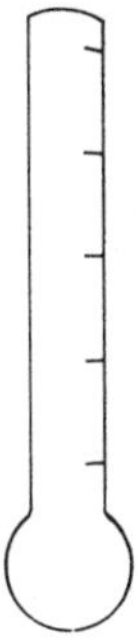

Very warm

Neither warm nor cold

Very cold

(6) Here is a picture of a ladder. Suppose we say the top of the ladder (pointing) represents the best possible life and the bottom (pointing) represents the worst possible life. Where on this ladder (moving finger rapidly up and down) do you feel you personally stand at the present time?

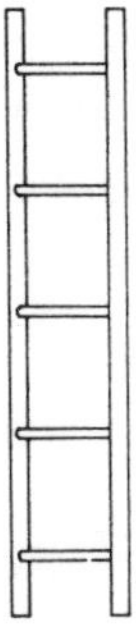

Best possible position

Worst possible position

It must be said, however, that the rating scales that have been employed in the past to measure respondents' attitudes have generally been inadequate in terms of all three of these requirements.

The topic should be clearly defined

Researchers have never managed to reach a consensus on how attitudes should be defined. This has caused Dawes and Smith to observe that:

> It is not uncommon for psychologists and other social scientists to investigate a phenomenon at great length without knowing what they are talking about. So it is with *attitude*. While 20,209 articles and books are listed under the rubric 'attitude' in the *Psychological Abstracts* from 1970 to 1979, there is little agreement about the definition of *attitude* and hence what aspects of attitudes are worth measuring. In fact, the typical article on attitude contains a discussion of various classical definitions of attitude, which then conclude with a statement of what the author himself or herself will mean by the term. How cumulative science can survive this Humpty Dumpty operationalism is not entirely clear. (Dawes and Smith, 1985:509)

To make matters worse, if one looks at how researchers have defined 'attitude' over the last fifty years, one cannot help but be struck by the growing complexity of these definitions.

In 1935, Allport reviewed over one hundred definitions of 'attitude' that had been advanced by various researchers and concluded that most investigators basically agreed that *an attitude is a learned predisposition to respond to an object or class of objects in a consistently favourable or unfavourable way*. This definition focuses upon the dimension of 'affect' which is assumed to be bipolar (i.e. negative–positive) and ignores other possible dimensions — for example, the beliefs held about the object as well as the 'intensity', 'extremity', and 'centrality' of these beliefs and feelings (see Petersen and Dutton, 1975).

Even though Allport's definition has commonly been paid lip-service by theorists and researchers, it has never really guided research. The principal reason for this is that attitude researchers have mainly been interested in the prediction of respondents' behaviour on the basis of their attitudes, and the link between attitudes and behaviour has never been demonstrated to be very strong. In their efforts to increase the size of their correlations, researchers have made many changes to both the definition of the concept of attitude and the devices they have used to try to measure this concept. Changes have usually involved adding dimensions rather than sharpening their focus upon a particular dimension.

Doob (1947), for example, agreed that an attitude is a learned predisposition to respond — but goes on to suggest that, once an attitude is learned, the individual also learns ways of expressing it. Warner and DeFleur (1969) add the idea that individuals take into account the contingent social pressures and not just their attitude when deciding how to behave toward an object. Thus they predict that the attitude–behaviour link will be strongest when the behaviour can occur in private rather than in public, since respondents will not fear negative social sanctions when expressing socially unacceptable views. Similarly, Fishbein (1967) proposed a model in which behavioural intentions are seen to be a joint function of the attitude toward performing a particular behaviour in a given situation and perceptions about the positive and negative social reinforcements associated with the social norms related to that behaviour.

The drift toward more complex definitions of attitude has probably been exacerbated by the relative lack of success of the logically more elegant measuring devices (e.g. Thurstone and Guttman scales which assume unidimensionality — see Tittle and Hill, 1967). It is ironic that scores on summated, multi-item rating scales (i.e. Likert scales) which imply the least precise definitions — in that they are like shotguns which fire many pellets at once at a target — have been found to generate scores which correlate most strongly (most, but not very strongly) with behavioural outcomes (see Tittle and Hill, 1967).

It should also be noted that theorists have paid some attention to the fact that, when respondents are asked to indicate how strongly they approve or disapprove of a particular item, the approve–disapprove dimension is confounded with other possible dimensions (e.g. 'importance', 'centrality' and 'sureness').

More than forty years ago, Katz (1944) drew attention to the need to measure the intensity of responses and suggested that measuring it would indicate the likely permanence of opinion (by which he meant the extent to which respondents' views were clearly formulated) and the degree to which respondents might be susceptible to suggestions. He went on to test a number of devices used by the American Institute of Public Opinion, including his own thermometer device (marked: 'Very strongly', 'Fairly strongly', and 'Don't care'). These were used in conjunction with the question: 'How strongly do you feel on this issue?' together with a 'sureness' scale: 'How sure are you that your opinion is right?' ('Not sure, Fairly sure, Very sure'). The results of his experiments indicated that responses on the 'sureness' scale were the best predictors of responses to related questions — especially questions regarding future events. More recently, Schuman and Presser (1981:234–243) have reported the results of experiments designed to compare 'intensity' (i.e. the subjective strength of feeling reported by the respondent), 'centrality' (i.e. the subjective importance of the issue to the respondent), and 'committed action' (i.e. whether or not the respondent had ever acted in defence of the item). For questions to do with gun control, 'intensity' was measured by the question:

'Compared with how you feel on other public issues, are your feelings on this issue: Extremely strong, Fairly strong, or Not very strong'. The intensity measure, however, was found to be not as useful as the 'centrality' and 'committed action' measures. The 'committed action' measure asked respondents if they had ever written a letter or given money in defence of the issue and the 'centrality' measure asked respondents: 'How important is a candidate's position on gun control when you decide how to vote in a Congressional election? : One of the most important, Very important, Somewhat important, Not at all important'. Schuman and Presser suggest that the 'intensity measure failed because it was too easy for people to claim inaccurately that they felt strongly about the issue being investigated — in this case, gun control.

The point that needs to be repeated is that the failure to identify and properly deal with significant component dimensions of attitudes has been a major obstacle to progress in attitude research. In particular, there has been a persistent tendency to confuse 'extremity' of judgements with the 'importance' of topics for respondents and with the 'certainty' or 'sureness' of their responses.

Besides a lack of consensus over the way attitudes should be defined, there is another sense in which the focus of rating scales is not clear. It is generally assumed that respondents interpret a rating task as a request to indicate how they stand in relation to the accompanying statement (i.e. to use the statement to measure themselves or make 'respondent centred' responses). Yet it is clearly possible for respondents to interpret the task as a request to rate the accompanying statement (i.e. to measure the accompanying statement or make a 'stimulus centred' response). The only obvious way that this basic ambiguity can be avoided is for the researcher to explicitly instruct respondents as to what kind of responses they should make — that is, either to ask respondents to indicate, for example, how strongly they either agree or disagree with each statement or to ask them to indicate how much 'Approval-or-Disapproval' each statement implies.

The applicability of the topic to respondents has to be established

Establishing the applicability of the topic to respondents is usually done by providing the filter response options of 'Don't know', 'Neutral' or 'Undecided'. As was pointed out in chapter 8, however, the meanings of these filters are generally far from clear. Holdaway (1971) reports, for instance, that respondents are more willing to use the category 'Neutral' than 'Undecided' and further that the number of respondents who are prepared to use the category 'Undecided' drops dramatically if it is put at the end of the rating scale rather than in the middle. Thus there is a need to offer response categories that generate less ambiguous responses than the categories that have been used in the past. In other words, there is a need to use response categories that clearly establish the basis, or lack of a basis, for respondents' opinions. This conclusion is in line with the general view that pervades this book — namely that the meaning of questions and response options must be made clear to respondents if their answers are to be properly interpreted by the researcher.

Respondents need to know what sort of an answer they should give

A number of issues were raised in chapters 4, 5, and 6 that are relevant to the way respondents interpret and respond to the categories making up rating scales. In particular, attention must be paid to the required level of generality of responses, and the specification of the standards of comparison that respondents are to use.

The level of generality of responses

Most rating devices implicitly require personal rather than cultural or stereotypical responses. If this is the case, an initial instruction should be given to increase the probability that respondents will give a personal answer to each item.

In addition, the specificity of the definition of the attitude being focused upon should not be ignored, as the following excerpt from Weigel and Newman makes clear:

> Attitude measures should be expected to predict only behaviours that are appropriate to the attitude under consideration. It would follow, then, that measures assessing attitudes towards a highly specific object or behaviour should predict behavioral responsiveness to that particular object or the likelihood that the individual will engage in the behaviour specified. As previously noted, this specificity hypothesis has received empirical support in a number of studies. On the other hand, when the object is a general or comprehensive one (e.g. black people, the environment, the government), then the behavioural criterion should be equally general or comprehensive. An adequate test of attitude–behaviour consistency under these circumstances would demand the use of several independent measures of behaviour designed to adequately sample the universe of action implications engaged by the attitude measure. (Weigel and Newman, 1976:795)

If one wanted to predict, for instance, whether or not respondents would be late for classes in 'Survey Methodology', one should not ask the respondents to rate how much they enjoy their university classes or even to rate how much they enjoy their classes in 'Survey Methodology', but rather one should ask them to rate how they think they would feel about being late for classes in that subject.

The specification of the standards of comparison that should be used

The meaning of the ordered response options that constitute the heart of any attitudinal rating scale must be shared if a researcher is to be able to properly interpret and compare respondents' answers. But this is not likely to be the case because the categories used to rate affect (e.g. 'Strongly Agree, Agree, Neutral, Disagree, Strongly disagree') lack empirical referents. Different respondents can, and do, interpret these categories in different ways. When respondents are asked to indicate whether they 'Strongly agree' — 'Strongly disagree', etc., with the item, the researcher can neither be sure that the same answers from different respondents have the same weights nor that similar answers to different items given by the same respondent carry equal weights. Thus, there is no guarantee that when one respondent says she 'Agrees' with something she is not making as strong a statement as another respondent who says he 'Strongly agrees'. In addition, the use of the response categories are likely to interact with the nature of the topic being rated, so that 'Strongly agree' to one item may not carry the same weight as 'Strongly agree' to another item. All of these problems arise because the evaluative standards are not specified, let alone defined in terms of empirical referents that can be shared by respondents.

One attempt to get respondents to define for the researcher the extremes of their perceptions, goals, and values is the ladder device used by Cantril (1965 — see figure 11.2 — 6, page 157). But even procedures like that have the drawback that each respondent may think in terms of different extremes.

There is another problem, too, that must be confronted. The researcher cannot be sure that the response options that make up a rating scale function as if they are of equal width. There are, in fact, at least two factors that make it almost inevitable that they will not.

When the two poles of a rating scale that has been designed to measure affect are not defined properly, each pole may be given a different weight. This problem is additional to any variation in the importance of the items themselves. Jordan (1965), for example, reports that the subjective strengths of positive and negative poles are not equal. The strength of the negative pole generally far outweighs the strength of the positive pole. This explains the well-documented tendency for respondents to be more willing to endorse strongly positive categories than strongly negative ones (i.e. the endorsement of a strongly positive category does not mean as much as the endorsement of a strongly negative category).

A second complication with respondents' evaluations has been raised by Schwarz and Clore (1988). These authors cite a number of studies supporting the hypothesis that respondents sometimes refer to their feelings to simplify evaluative tasks. They claim that the tendency for respondents to do this is directly related to the complexity of the topic they have been asked to evaluate. For example, respondents are more likely to be affected by their current feelings when evaluating their satisfaction with 'life as a whole' than when evaluating their satisfaction with their 'levels of income'. Moreover, respondents' feelings appear to fluctuate with their moods which, in turn, fluctuate with changes in their environments which are not always the focus of the respondents' attention (e.g. the weather). This additional complication means that evaluations of complex topics are not as stable as evaluations of simple ones.

Again, many of the problems that have just been identified arise because the standards of comparison that respondents have to employ are poorly defined. A lack of attention to the specification of the comparison standards that respondents should use when rating items has been a major feature of all the commonly employed rating scales that have been used to date. In the absence of specified evaluative standards, respondents have been forced to provide their own standards and different respondents may or may not have used the same ones. Confusion has arisen because the standards could have been either internal or external to the respondent and implicitly or explicitly invoked by the questions.

A hypothetical example of judgements that invoke implicit internal standards is discussed by Kahn and Cannell (1957:115). They suggest that a New Yorker and a rural Arkansan are likely to disagree on whether Little Rock is a big city and that an Alaskan and a Texan will have different ideas of what constitutes a hot summer. It should also be noted that the problem of implicit, internal standards underlies one of the main criticisms that have been made of Thurstone scales. It has been found that the judges do not all sort the initial statements into eleven piles in the same way because their judgements tend to reflect their social backgrounds or demographic attributes (see Selltiz et al. 1965).

Standards can also be external to the respondent in that they are built into the scale itself. Like internal standards, these can be either implicit or explicit. An example of the use of an explicit, external standard is a foot ruler which relates to the length of a standard metal bar kept in a central bank vault. All foot rulers are defined by reference to the length of this standard bar. Subsequently, when respondents answer questions about their height in feet and inches, they are, in essence, reporting their heights relative to the length of the standard bar. Unlike the foot ruler, the response categories for summated rating scales do not involve explicit comparison standards. They are not empirically defined. They do, however, often involve implicit standards that are built either into the statements or the accompanying response categories. In chapter 5, pages 54–8, we saw how questions (statements here) can reflect the assumptions the researcher holds, and how a lack of balance in the response options, the way the options are labelled, and the range the options cover can all suggest what views or behaviours the researcher thinks are normative. Additional examples that demonstrate the unpredictable effects that implicit standards can have on responses, are discussed in the next section of this chapter.

The consequence of the failure to properly specify comparison standards

Because attitude rating scales focus on a concept that has been poorly defined, pay scant regard to the relevance of the statements to the respondents, and involve implicit, ill-defined comparison standards, they must inevitably fail to work properly. Many of the failures have been attributed to what have been called 'format effects'. Format effects have been classified into two groups. The largest group has been referred to as 'stimulus centred' effects. The most important stimulus centred effects are response effects associated with the number and range of response categories, and response effects related to the anchoring effects of category labels. A smaller number of format effects concern respondent characteristics rather than characteristics of the rating scales themselves. These have been called 'respondent centred' effects. Both groups of effects are explicated below.

Stimulus-centred effects

The number of categories that should be included in rating scales

Sooner or later every researcher confronts the issue of how many response categories should be included in a rating scale. Molenaar (1982:74–75) reviews a number of studies that have looked at the relationship between the number of response categories and the reliability of respondents' ratings. While acknowledging that this relationship is complex, he concludes that the 'critical, if not optimal, number of categories would appear to be seven plus or minus two'. This conclusion is mainly based on the results of psychological investigations into the number of items between which humans can reliably discriminate (although a close look at the papers Molenaar cites [Miller, 1956; Hulbert, 1975] leads one to question it. The issue of how many distinctions respondents can reliably make proves to be a complex matter. Miller (1956), in his very widely cited article titled 'The Magical Number 7, Plus or Minus Two', reports that it is not possible to select more than six tones — regardless of the width of the auditory range looked at — that respondents can reliably recognise. Thus, if a listener can reliably distinguish between six high-pitched tones in one series of tones and six pitched tones in another series, when the two series are put together and the tones presented in random order, the listener is still able to reliably classify the tones into only six categories. But Miller goes on to draw attention to a number of factors that seem to increase or decrease the possible number of reliable distinctions. The sensory modality involved is important: in the case of taste, the maximum number of categories seems to be about four; in the case of vision (measured by the respondent's ability to reliably locate a point between two markers) the maximum number is between ten and fifteen intervals. The number is also greater for multidimensional stimuli than for unidimensional stimuli. And it is greater when respondents are making relative as opposed to absolute judgements.

The last point raises the possibility that Miller's 'magic number 7' may not be relevant to the problem of how many categories should be used in social psychological rating scales. The capacity to recognise objectively presented members of a stimulus class reliably (as is done in a psychological laboratory) may be very different from the ability to assign ill-defined social stimuli to ill-defined categories.

The fact that the possible maximum number of categories is greater when the respondents are making relative judgements rather than absolute ones raises the question of the extent to which a rating scale works in the same manner as a foot ruler. Humans are able to make a huge number of relative length discriminations if they are provided with a foot ruler that has been marked with the appropriate intervals. In the case of the ruler, the scale divisions have been objectively defined; in the case of the typical rating scale, they have not. It is this fact that makes it hard to make sense of the results of the various studies directed at determining the number of categories that rating scales should include. Many of these studies have been done by psychologists who have had subjects use category rating scales to rate objectively defined, physical stimuli. Others have been conducted by social researchers who have had survey respondents use category rating scales to rate ill-defined social stimuli. It does not make sense to lump the results of the two kinds of studies together.

Not forgetting the observations that have just been made, if one examines a number of related studies carried out by social scientists as opposed to behavioural scientists, the picture can be somewhat simplified. First, it is clear that two to five categories are not enough. Schuman and Duncan (1973/74) report that the response distribution for a four-point scale (e.g. 'Strongly agree, Agree, Disagree , Strongly disagree') does not reduce to the response distribution for a two-point scale (i.e., 'Agree, Disagree'). They found that when a four-point scale is collapsed into a two-point scale, some 18 per cent of the respondents who would answer on the positive side of the four-point scale answer on the negative side of the two-point scale. Similarly, Matell and Jacoby (1972) report that the percentage of 'Uncertain' responses goes down as the number of categories goes up. With two to five categories, an average of 20 per cent of the respondents used the middle 'Uncertain' category. When respondents used scales with seven to nineteen categories the average per cent of 'Uncertain' response dropped to around 7 per cent.

Second, studies of the reliability of ratings made with rating scales with different numbers of categories throw some light on the question of how many categories should be used. Bendig (1953) found that respondents could use up to nine-point scales reliably to rate their knowledge of twelve countries. And Finn (1972), comparing respondents' use of three-, five-, seven-, and nine-point scales to rate the complexity of different jobs, report that seven-point scales were best. Again, Andrews (1984), who investigated the validity of the data produced by rating scales ranging from two to 20+ categories in a number of large-scale surveys, concludes that the 'construct validity' of rating data goes up as the number of categories goes up (which is not to say that it goes up to high levels).

Thus the results of relevant reliability and validity studies conducted by social scientists suggest that one should use at least seven categories. There is also a more practical reason for using at least seven categories. Green and Rao (1970) have demonstrated that many of the multivariate, statistical procedures which researchers like to employ when analysing their data only work properly on data that have been generated by rating scales with six or more categories.

The conclusion that emerges from all these considerations, then, is that rating scales should have, at least, seven categories. This conclusion, however, should not obscure the importance of both properly defining the topic(s) to be rated and properly defining the categories that are to be used to make the ratings.

The anchoring effects of category labels

Labels are often used to define categories: sometimes all the categories are labelled; sometimes only the end and middle categories; and sometimes just the end categories. Whichever is the case, a minimum requirement must be that the labels should affect the respondents in an even-handed way. Evidence that this requirement is not always met is provided by the finding that responses to rating scales are usually biased toward the largest numeric anchors (e.g. Tversky and Kahneman, 1974; Frisbie and Brandenburg, 1979) and toward the most positive verbal anchors. Hippler and Schwarz (1987:112), for instance, report that respondents who were required to rank items from the 'Most important' to the 'Least important' assigned higher ratings to the items than respondents who had been required to rank the items from the 'Least important' to the 'Most important'. A similar contextual effect is reported by Levin *et al.* (1988), who found that respondents who had been told that a medical procedure had a 50 per cent *success* rate evaluated it more positively than respondents who had been told that it had a 50 per cent *failure* rate.

Besides the effects mentioned above, it appears that respondents are less influenced by intermediate or middle labels than they are by the labels in the end positions (e.g. Wildt and Mazis, 1978; Frisbie and Brandenburg, 1979).

In view of these observations, it could have been expected that Andrews (1984), after investigating the validity of data produced in a number of large scale surveys, would report that the labelling of all categories produces data of poorer quality than labelling only the end categories. If poorly defined categories generate confusions, the more poorly defined categories there are, the greater the number of confusions that will occur.

One solution to the biasing effects associated with rating scale category labels would be to eliminate the labels altogether. This solution has, in fact, been proposed by Wilson and Nias (1972), who note that the typical rating scale is made up of three components: the topic, an evaluative statement about the topic, and the response categories. They argue that, although the aim is to get at respondents' reactions to the topic, the response categories 'get in the way' by creating a double evaluative bias. Recognition of this problem prompts them to suggest dropping the rating categories altogether so that respondents merely have to tick 'Yes' or 'No' to a catchphrase representation of each topic. Wilson and Nias are able to show that this tack does reduce the typical 'acquiescent bias' from which rating scales suffer. Unfortunately, their solution to one problem raises other measurement issues. For example, if the intention is to assign total scores to respondents based on the number of items for which they have ticked 'Yes', one has to assume that each item carries equal weight. Further, the lack of variability in the responses to the items limits the kinds of statistical procedures that can be subsequently applied to analyse the data.

Respondent-centred effects

Rating scales suffer from a number of respondent-centred biases, such as the tendency for some respondents to choose central response options rather than extreme ones, to agree rather than to disagree, and to be positive rather than negative. Using a 'Guess the right answer' procedure, Berg and Rapaport (1954) found that the category series: 1,2,3,4 and A,B,C,D are prone to the central tendency effect. The series: 'Yes, Uncertain, No' and 'Agree, Indifferent, Disagree' were found to be prone to a 'yea saying' or an 'acquiescent' effect. And the two series: 'Very satisfied, Satisfied, Dissatisfied, Very dissatisfied' and 'True, False' were found to be susceptible to a positivity bias. Another experimental program designed to investigate the same effects was undertaken by

Bardo and his colleagues (Bardo *et al.*, 1982a, 1982b, 1982c), who conducted a number of experiments in which subjects were asked to respond randomly to a variety of contentless formats (i.e. formats without substantive statements attached to them). Bardo *et al.* report that the five-category and seven-category verbal and numeric Likert formats (the most commonly used formats in survey research) were subject to a substantial degree of central tendency error but not a significant level of leniency error. Line formats generated moderate levels of both central tendency error and leniency error. Face formats generated high levels of central tendency error and leniency error. They also found that central tendency error increased as the number of categories increased.

In general, it seems reasonable to deduce that respondent-centred response biases are inversely dependent upon the degree to which the topic and the categories have been properly defined, and directly influenced by the number of categories (i.e. the amount of room in which the biases can operate).

Problems associated with batteries of rating scales (i.e. summated scales)

It is a common practice to formulate several rating scales that are all designed to measure respondents' attitudes toward a specified topic and to administer them as one instrument (i.e. a summated or Likert scale). Scores for all the items are then combined into single scores. Although a common practice in the past, this practice does run into a number of major problems:

(a)   It must be kept in mind that the meanings attached to response categories can vary from one topic to the next. For example, whereas cleaning one's teeth once a week may be rated as 'Bad', going to the theatre once a week might be rated as 'Good'. Likewise 'Strongly agreeing' with a weak attitude statement might be the same as 'Agreeing' with a strong statement. In other words, the practice of totalling the responses elicited by a battery of rating scales is fraught with danger because the response categories are not fixed in their meanings (i.e.'likes' are mixed with 'unlikes').

(b)   Respondents are required to use the same set of rating categories (e.g. 'Strongly agree, Agree, Undecided, Disagree, Strongly disagree') to rate each item in a long list of items without knowing in advance the full range that the items cover. The logical consequence of this is that the meaning of the end categories will sometimes be distorted. This will happen when respondents use the extreme categories for early items and then run into more extreme items further down the list, at which point they have no alternative but to place the more extreme items in the same categories that they have already used for less extreme items. In Lodge and Tursky's words:

When a small number of categories is provided for evaluating a broad range of stimuli or for expressing strong opinions, most of the distortion appears in the end categories — the overall effect being to vitiate the expression of strong opinions. Because the variance found in the endmost categories is typically large, a researcher cannot be confident that a respondent choosing a polar category is expressing a moderate or intense opinion. This is particularly serious because most theories of behaviour posit a relationship between strength of opinion and the likelihood of a congruent behaviour: those expressing the strongest beliefs and preferences are most likely to behave in accord with their opinion, while those less strongly engaged are less likely to act on behalf of their opinions. As a result, attempts to predict behaviour as a function of categorical expressions of opinion are jeopardized. (Lodge and Tursky, 1981:415)

It might be assumed that the severity of this problem is inversely related to the number of rating categories used and directly related to the variation in the normative weights for these items. Relevant to this possibility is the fact that, on the basis of his in-depth statistical analysis of the effects of the number of rating categories used on the validity of survey data, Andrews (1984) reports that the validity of data was greater as the number of rating categories increased.

The severity of the distortion of judgements problem might also be lessened if respondents were allowed to look over the full range of items before responding to each one. Alternatively, the most extreme positive item and the most extreme negative item could be explicitly placed at the top of the list.

(c) As was pointed out in the section in which the properties of single ratings scales were discussed, ratings scales typically suffer from a fundamental ambiguity of focus in that ratings may either be 'stimulus centred' (i.e. reflect the respondent's evaluations of the statements themselves) or be 'respondent-centred' (i.e. reflect the respondent's judgements about how she or he stands in regard to each statement). This, in turn, means that the meaning of summated scale scores must be similarly ambiguous. One way around this problem might be explicitly to instruct respondents as to the kinds of judgements they should make.

Reviewing the situation, then, summated rating scales at least in their traditional form, run into a number of quite serious problems most of which can be attributed to the facts that: the concept being measured is poorly defined, individual statements may have different weights, the response categories lack explicit, empirical referents, and, the rating task itself is ambiguous. These defects are enough to ensure that meanings of summated scale scores are typically far from clear. In turn it is hard to reject the suspicion that, although researchers are often tempted to treat summated rating scale scores as interval data, they have probably — at least in the past — failed to meet even the requirements of nominal or ordinal measurement, let alone interval measurement. Since summated rating scales have been used much more often in the past than any other kind of scale this does not say a lot for much contemporary social research.

The practical solutions to the problems that have been suggested have been aimed at: (a) properly defining topics and response categories so that they are understood in the same way by all of the respondents; and (b) clearly indicating to respondents what kinds of responses they should give. For convenience the various solutions that have been suggested to improve summated scales have been listed together below.

Suggestions for improving summated rating scales

(a) An appropriate filter should be appended to establish the relevance of each item to the respondent (e.g. 'Have not had a chance to find out much about this topic' or 'Don't know anything about this topic').

(b) The rating scale should:

  1 Include, at least, 6 substantive rating categories — not counting middle and filter categories.

  2 Either: Include labels for the end categories and include, as middle categories, both a 'neutral' category and either an 'undecided' or an 'ambivalent' category:

Strongly Agree	Neutral —	Strongly Disagree	Either Don't know —
— — — — — — —	Undecided or Ambivalent		or Have not had a chance to form an opinion about this topic

Or, include labelled end categories and an appended measure either of the 'importance' of the topic or of the respondent's 'sureness' as a substitute for the middle categories.

  3 Be attached to statements that are of the same level of generality as the behaviour that is to be predicted.

(c) Make responses meaningfully comparable by:

  1 Explicitly instructing respondents that they are to make 'respondent centred' responses.

  2 Allowing respondents to look over the whole range of items before responding to each one.

A possible alternative to summated scales

For some, the problems associated with summated scales may appear too great to warrant their continued use. Because of this possibility, it is worth looking at an alternative measuring procedure to the use of summated scales. This alternative is called *magnitude scaling*. While magnitude scaling is not without its drawbacks — it is, for example more complex and takes much longer to administer than summated scales take — it should be considered because the difficulties that are encountered by traditional summated rating scales are so severe.

A brief description of magnitude scaling

The account given here is aimed only at explaining the main ideas underlying magnitude scaling procedures. For a fuller account, and for practical details of how these procedures can actually be used in social research, see Lodge and Tursky (1981).

Magnitude scaling procedures are based on developments in the theory and practice of psychophysics which 'make it feasible to scale the intensity of social judgments with the accuracy and power hitherto reserved for the scaling of sensory judgments' (Lodge and Tursky, 1981:376).

To understand the magnitude scaling of social psychological stimuli (such as respondents' perceptions of the severity of different types of crimes or their perceptions of the social standing of various occupations), we must start by looking at the basic paradigm for the psychophysical scaling of sensory stimuli. The standard procedure for the magnitude scaling of objectively definable physical stimuli is to randomly present a stimulus series to subjects and have them estimate the magnitude of each stimulus relative to the perceived magnitude of the first stimulus presented. Thus, the first stimulus that is presented acts as a 'reference'. The reference is typically a middle-level stimulus. Respondents estimate how each stimulus in the series compares with the reference — for example twice as heavy, half as heavy, ten times as heavy, one quarter as heavy, and so on. In this way all judgements are explicitly related to an explicit, empirical reference. Moreover all respondents use the same comparison standard or reference.

A great deal of past research has established the fact that human observers are able to make such magnitude judgements for any stimulus series that impinges on one of the five senses — touch, sight, hearing, smell and taste. Furthermore, it has been found that, when the perceived magnitude judgements of the strength of each stimulus in a stimulus series are converted to logarithmic values and the average log values for a sample of subjects are plotted against the logs of their objective values, a straight line graph typically results.

'The principle underlying this linear relationship in ratio ruled coordinates is simple and lawful — equal stimulus ratios produce equal subjective ratios' (Lodge and Tursky, 1981:379). This general relationship between objective and subjective stimulus values is called the 'power law' of psychophysics. The power law is normally represented by the following formula:

$$\psi = kS^b$$

Where:

ψ is the magnitude of response (i.e. the subjective estimate);
S   is the objective stimulus value;
b   is an exponent characteristic of the particular stimulus series;
k   is a constant determined by the choice of units used for making the measurements.

When the power law is transformed into logarithms, the general equation becomes:

$$\log \psi = b \log S + \log k$$

In this form the general equation defines a linear relationship. That is, when $\log \psi$ is plotted against $\log S + \log k$, the resultant graph is a straight line.

Early on in the development of magnitude scaling, it was found that the exponent relating magnitude estimates to the sensory stimuli (i.e., the 'b' in the power law equation) varied systematically from one sensory modality to another. For example, numeric estimation of the length of lines was found to have a characteristic exponent of 1.0; heaviness of weights an exponent of 1.45; and the brightness of lights an exponent of 0.5.

In the case of a stimulus series that can be objectively measured (e.g. length, weight, brightness), it is a simple matter to see if the power law holds. The investigator only needs to plot the objective values against the perceived values to see whether or not the resulting graph follows a straight line. The question is: how can one know if it holds for a stimulus series for which there is no objective measure of each stimulus in the series (as would be the case, if subjects were asked to estimate the subjective magnitudes of severity of different types of crimes)?

The solution to this problem is to check to see if the set of social psychological stimuli behave as lawfully as physical stimuli do. This can be done by adapting a cross-modality matching procedure that was first developed for validating magnitude scales involving physical stimuli. The cross matching procedure rests on the argument that if the same set of physical stimuli are evaluated in terms of two sensory modalities, the magnitudes of the sensory responses in terms of the first modality will be functionally equivalent to the magnitudes of the sensory responses in terms of the second modality. This can be schematically represented in the following way:

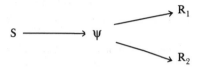

Where:

S   is the physical stimulus (e.g. a weight)

ψ is the magnitude of the subjective response (i.e. the perceived heaviness of the weight)

R_1 is the magnitude of the subjective response in terms of the first modality e.g. a line which respondents perceive as standing in the same relationship to a 'reference' line as the stimulus is perceived as standing to the subjective magnitude of the stimulus that was paired with the 'reference line'.

R_2 is the magnitude of subjective response in terms of the second modality e.g. the number which respondents perceive stands in the same relationship to a 'reference' number as the stimulus is perceived as standing to the subjective magnitude of the stimulus that was paired with the 'reference' number.

It has already been noted that when the log values of the subjective estimates of each stimulus in a stimulus series made in terms of one sensory modality are plotted against the log values of the objective values for the same stimulus series, a straight line graph results. If it is true that the magnitudes of the sensory responses in one modality are functional equivalents to the magnitudes of the sensory responses in another modality, then, when the first set of sensory responses are plotted against the second set of sensory responses, a straight line graph will result. Moreover, the slope (i.e. exponent) of this straight line graph should equal the ratio of the established exponents for each of the sensory modalities (see figure 11.3, p. 174). Of course, both of these outcomes will occur only if the power law holds for both modalities. Looked at another way, the occurrence of both of these outcomes can be taken as proof that both sets of subjective magnitude estimates have been produced in accordance with the power law — in other words, as proof that the sensory estimations and the objective stimulus series they represent constitute internally consistent scales.

Notice that this criterion for establishing whether or not a set of physical stimuli form a scale does not directly involve the objective magnitudes. It is because of this that the cross matching paradigm can be used to validate the hypothesis that a series of social psychological stimuli for which objective values are not available do, in fact, form a scale. The hypothesis that the social standing of occupations forms a scale, for example, can be checked by plotting the subjective magnitude estimates made in terms of one modality against the subjective magnitude estimates made in terms of another modality to see if the resulting graph coincides with the expected straight line with a slope equal to the ratio of the exponents for the two sensory modalities. If the stimuli in question do not scale, the resulting graph will not coincide with the predicted straight line.

Once a scale has been established, it can be used as any scale would be used. For example, individuals might be ordered in terms of the items to which they are personally 'closest' (e.g. ordered in terms of their occupation, or ordered in terms of the worst crime that each has committed).

Before concluding this short account of magnitude scaling, it should be stressed that the procedure that has just been described avoids two of the principal problems that dog Likert scales.

First, Lodge and Tursky (1981) suggest using line production (i.e. estimating the relative magnitude of each stimulus by drawing a line relative to the length

Figure 11.3 *A straight line graph that is the result of plotting the subjective estimates of a stimulus series made in terms of one modality against the subjective estimates made in terms of another modality*

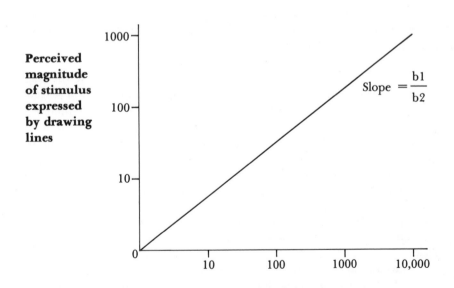

Perceived magnitude of stimulus expressed numerically

of a 'reference line' associated with the first stimulus presented) and numeric estimation (i.e. estimating the relative magnitude of each stimulus in terms of numbers that are relative to a 'reference number' that is paired with the first stimulus presented) in social research. Neither of these sensory modalities requires special equipment and both are easily understood by most respondents. More importantly, both allow open-ended estimates — that is, a line response can be as long or as short as the respondent wants to make it, and a numeric estimation can be any multiple or fraction of the 'reference' number. Thus respondents' estimates are not constrained in the way that they are when a limited set of rating categories is employed. For this reason the magnitude scaling procedure avoids the 'jamming' effects associated with the extreme categories from which Likert scales suffer.

Second, because each of the stimulus items in a magnitude scale are related to 'reference' responses, each has a clear empirical meaning and, further, each can be meaningfully related to other items. In comparison, Likert scales are based on the rather dubious assumptions that items are equally significant (i.e. functionally equivalent) and that respondents ascribe the same meaning to each of the rating categories.

A demonstration of the use of magnitude scaling procedures for measuring attitudes

The example of the use of magnitude scaling that is discussed below has been drawn from the results of a national survey done in the United States in 1975 by the Michigan Survey Research Center (see Lodge, 1981:41–58 for additional details). The part of this study that we will look at was designed to test the general utility of magnitude scaling procedures for social research in a survey situation for measuring the political support for a number of political institutions, policies and leaders. To simplify matters, attention will be limited to three of the specific research goals. The first goal was to ensure that respondents were able to make magnitude estimations using different sensory modalities. The second was to assess the relative strength of approval, or disapproval, normatively associated with each of the following thirteen response categories: Absolutely perfect, Terrific, Excellent, Very good, Good, Satisfactory, So-so, Not adequate, Not-so-bad, Bad, Very bad, Terrible, and Disgusting. The third goal was to use the thirteen scaled response categories to order respondents in terms of their support for a United States Supreme Court decision on abortion. In essence, each of these goals involved a separate step.

Step 1

Respondents were taught to make proportional, psychophysical judgements of items in two stimulus series. The stimulus series used were a set of lines and a set of numbers. Respondents began by estimating the magnitude of each line in terms of numeric estimates relative to a 'reference' number which had been paired with a middle length line. Next, they had to estimate the magnitude of each number in a series of numbers by drawing lines relative to the length of a 'reference' line which had been paired with a middle sized number. The researchers chose the response modalities that were employed (numeric estimation and line production) on the grounds of convenience. The instructions, which are set out below, indicate the way respondents were taught to make the required magnitude judgements for the series of lines:

> This booklet contains a series of line lengths. Please leaf through the booklet and notice that some of the lines are longer than the first line and some of the lines are shorter than the first line. Your task is to tell how much longer or shorter they are compared to the first line. The first line is your reference. We have given it the number 50.

---

[50]

> The number 50 is your reference. All you need to do is write a number in the box for each line. The longer a line appears to be compared to your reference line, the bigger the number you will write in compared to 50. For example, if one of the lines seems about two times longer than the reference line, you would write in the number 100. If a line were ten times longer, you would write in 500. On the other hand, some of the lines are shorter than the reference. If a line were about one half as long, you would write in a number about one half of 50, about 25. Another line about one tenth as long would be given the number one tenth of 50, 5. Give each line a number, whatever number seems appropriate, to express how the line compares to your reference line. The longer the line, the bigger your number compared to 50. The shorter the line, the smaller your number compared to 50. Once you begin, please do not turn back to check your numbers or to look at the reference line. We are only interested in your general impressions. (Lodge, 1981:44–45)

As soon as the respondents had completed this task, they were given a similar booklet with a numeric stimulus printed on each page and asked to draw a line for each stimulus relative to a 50 mm reference line that had been printed on the first page. Use of the two sets of physical stimuli at this stage allowed the researchers to do two things. One, they were able to objectively validate the respondents' ability to make proportional judgements. Two, they could estimate the extent of any response biases exhibited by respondents. In fact only 6.4 per cent of the respondents failed to grasp the idea of making proportional judgements. We will return to the second issue below.

Step 2

Subjects were told that, now they had practised using lines and numbers to make evaluative judgements, the interviewer would like them to use numbers and lines to express the different degrees of approval or disapproval implied by each of the thirteen categories (Absolutely perfect, through to Disgusting). Starting with the numeric estimation task, they were asked to equate the reference category 'So-So' with the reference number 50. After a few examples and practice trials, they were asked to work through a booklet expressing their evaluations of the category printed on each page in terms of relative numeric estimations. As soon as they had completed this task, they were asked to repeat the whole process again by drawing lines relative to a 50 mm reference line to express their evaluations of the categories. Respondents were asked to complete both tasks so that the cross-matching paradigm that was described earlier could be used to confirm that respondents were able to make consistent psychophysical evaluations of the adjectival modifiers under investigation. The result of this validity check is set out in figure 11.4 (p. 178). It can be seen that the resulting graph was very close to the predicted straight line after a slight adjustment had to be made to allow for the tendency — disclosed by step 1 — for respondents to draw lines that are slightly too short if the stimulus is greater than the reference stimulus and slightly too long if it is less than the reference stimulus. The magnitude weights that are displayed in figure 11.4 (p. 178) are the combined geometric means for each scale item (see Lodge, 1981:54, for the formula that was used).

Step 3

Each respondent was asked to indicate which of the thirteen response categories best expressed his or her own opinion of the Supreme Court decision concerning abortion. This allowed the ordering of the respondents themselves in terms of their support for the Court's decision, according to the results of step 2. Reading across from the vertical axis of figure 10.4, it can be seen, for instance, the distances between 'Terrible', 'So-So', 'Good' 'Very good' and 'Excellent' are roughly equal (i.e roughly 40 units each). Because the magnitude weight for 'Terrible' is roughly 10, the response 'So-So' would be some four times as

Figure 11.4   *Cross-modality matching of line production responses (Y axis) and number production responses (X axis) to 13 adjectival modifiers of support*

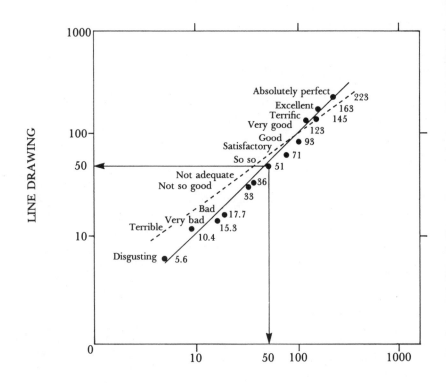

1. Solid line = graph after correction has been made for regressive nature of line drawing responses. Original graph lies along broken line.
2. Each point represents the pooled estimates of 12 respondents sampled from the Murphy-Tannehaus CPS/SRC survey. The magnitude weights are the combined geometric means for each scale item. Because the magnitude values reflect ratio relationships between the stimulus values, one can legitimately infer the degree of support implied by each adjectival modifier. Hence, on average for these respondents: 'Absolutely Perfect' (ψ = 223) expressed some 40 times the support/implied by 'Disgusting' (ψ = 5.6); 'Good' (ψ = 93) about 2 times the support implied by 'So-So' (ψ = 50); and, 'Bad' (ψ = 18) and 1/3 of the support implied by 'So-So'.

Source: Lodge and Tursky, 1981:399, figure 3. Modified by the author. Title and footnotes by the author.

supportive as 'Terrible' while the response 'Good' would be some eight times as supportive as that category.

Generalising results to achieve greater efficiency in the collection of data

In the same way that the magnitude-scale categories were used to order respondents in terms of their support for the Supreme Court's decision on abortion, they could be used to order individuals in terms of their support on other, similar topics — for example, the president's defence strategy, the president's handling of the economy, etc. Thus, although the procedure discussed above may appear to be very time consuming, it is less so if the researcher can use the results of the first two steps conducted on a limited sample as the basis for ordering respondents in terms of other similar issues.

Alternatively, some of the effort involved in the procedure described above can be eliminated by having respondents make direct magnitude estimations of support for the item in which the researcher is interested. In the case of the Supreme Court's decision on abortion, for instance, respondents could first be asked to directly express the level of their support by selecting a number relative to a reference number associated with middle-level support and then be asked to directly express the level of their support by drawing a line relative to a reference line associated with middle level support.

Lodge *et al.* refer to the first approach that was described is a 'stimulus centred' approach because the stimuli themselves are scaled and the respondents later ordered in terms of the stimulus to which they are personally closest. And they refer to the approach mentioned in the last paragraph as 'response centred' because the respondents are ordered directly in terms of the strength of their responses. Both approaches are shown to be superior to the traditional category rating methods. They do have, however, strengths and weaknesses when compared with one another. The principal advantages of the 'stimulus centred' approach are:

(a)   the scale values are average values for a sample of respondents and, for this reason, are less variable than values based on individual data; and

(b)   the response categories can be used over and over again to order individuals in terms of any number of similar issues.

The principal disadvantages are:

(a)   it squeezes respondents into a limited number of categories so that some information is necessarily lost; and,

(b)   the scale values assigned to the categories are specific to the type of issue (and maybe even the particular issue) that the respondent makes judgements about in the first two steps.

Summary

Summated rating scales have been used more often than any other rating device for measuring attitudes. Yet they have a number of serious defects. Researchers have rarely focused upon a clearly defined dimension but have typically confused several dimensions at once (e.g. affect, salience, intensity). In addition, problems arise because respondents have been required to express their answers using categories that are both limited in number and undefined in terms of explicit comparison standards. The first of these problems could be cured by a sharper definition of the topic for respondents. The second problem could be mitigated by using rating scales with a larger number of categories than is usual — for example, seven, nine or more categories. A number of suggestions were made to get around the third problem. For convenience, the suggestions that have been made have been listed together on page 170.

For those for whom the problems associated with summated scales are too great, the alternative procedure of magnitude scaling was discussed. While magnitude scales do avoid most of the problems associated with summated rating scales, it was acknowledged that they, too, have a number of shortcomings. In the main, these shortcomings stem from the fact that magnitude scales are more difficult for both the researcher and the respondents to understand and from the fact that they take longer to administer.

Chapter 12

CHECKS TO ENSURE
THAT QUESTIONS WORK AS INTENDED

Numerous examples of questions which have not worked as they were intended to work have been presented throughout the previous chapters. Reference has also been made to a number of studies in which questions that had supposedly been piloted in order to iron out any faults were misunderstood by large percentages of respondents. We will take another look at these studies, now, because they set the stage for the rest of this chapter.

Nuckols (1953) took nine questions from 'The Quarters Polls' that varied in difficulty and presented them to forty-eight randomly chosen, middle-income respondents. The respondents were asked to restate the questions 'in their own words'. One in six of the interpretations given was either partly or completely wrong. An unexpected finding was that there was little, if any, relationship between the error rate and the difficulty ratings for the questions.

Belson (1981) advances similar findings. He and his colleagues analysed over 2000 questions that had been designed by twenty-four different market researchers over a two-year period and identified questions that might be expected to cause respondents some difficulty. They then selected for in-depth study four examples of each of the six most frequently occurring kinds of problem questions. The kinds of questions selected for investigation were questions that required more than one answer; contained too many meaningful words; included qualifying clauses or phrases; included reference to two or more subjects; included difficult vocabulary; or included instructions. An initial administration of these questions disclosed few signs of difficulty or uncertainty on the part of the respondents. Yet in-depth testing disclosed a great deal of mis-understanding:

> For all the questions tested, the proportion ... [of interpretations that could be accepted as reflecting the intended meanings] ... was, on average, only 29 per cent. Moreover, going behind this average, we find that for 8 of the test questions, the percentage within permissible limits was less than 16 per cent and for one of them not a single respondent out of the 59 persons tested on it came within those limits. Moreover, the highest score for any of the questions tested was only 58 per cent. (Belson, 1981:350–51)

Belson (1981:356–9) analyses the ways in which many of the key words used in the questions (e.g. 'your', 'usually', 'weekday', 'children', 'household', 'gen-erally', 'regularly', 'impartial', 'proportion') were understood. In the case of one question, the word 'usually' was meant to be interpreted as, 'ordinarily', 'com-monly', 'as a rule', 'generally', 'normally', or 'habitually', but only 60 per cent of 445 interpretations of the word fitted this intention. Many respondents over-looked the word altogether or weakened it to mean, 'regularly', 'more often than not', 'at least sometimes', and so on.

Hunt *et al.* (1982) report the results of another investigation into the effec-tiveness of pre-testing (by which they mean piloting) questions as a means of detecting five common faults identified by Payne (1951). The five common faults were: leading questions, double questions, ambiguous wording, the use of inappropriate response options, and missing response options. They presented questions that embodied these faults to samples of respondents who were told to be critical. On average, only 12.8 per cent of the respondents made a com-ment about each of the test questions that indicated that they thought there was something wrong with it. The highest fault-detection rate was for questions with missing alternatives. But even for this problem, the detection rate was only 52 per cent.

The results reported by both Belson (1981) and Hunt *et al.* (1982) strongly suggest that one should not rely upon respondents' reactions to indicate when there are problems with questions. In fact, Belson (1981:5) and others (e.g. Fowler and Mangione, 1990) have been led to contend that, although piloting questions might be a useful procedure for discovering potential interviewer problems, it is not a reliable method for discovering if respondents interpret questions as the researcher intended.

It seems that respondents do their level best to answer all questions put to them. They even modify questions, in their minds, if they have to, so that they can answer them. In line with this view, Belson (1981:370) hypothesises: 'When a respondent finds it difficult to answer a question, he is likely to modify it in such a way as to be able to answer it more easily.'

The sorts of questions that are particularly vulnerable to modification, according to Belson, are questions that call for mental calculations (e.g. 'how much X does the respondent use each month?'), questions that do not apply to the respondent (e.g. that ask respondents about behaviours they don't engage in themselves, or about issues about which they do not have any experience), very general questions and questions with conflicting parts which are prone to being partially answered.

The lesson inherent in the studies just discussed is clear. The researcher should always expect some respondents to fail to interpret questions as they are intended to interpret them. Moreover, since each of the studies looked at questions that had already been used in actual surveys, it is also clear that conventional piloting procedures are not, in themselves, foolproof ways of checking the validity of questions.

This leaves us with the problem of what can be done to ensure that questions will work as intended. Besides the traditional use of 'editing' rules and 'piloting' procedures, there are a number of courses of action that the researcher can adopt. These procedures include having respondents rephrase questions in their own words, directly questioning respondents about their interpretations of key words, and having respondents 'think aloud' as they formulate answers. In the next section, we will review each of these procedures — including the traditional procedures of using 'editing rules' and pilot surveys.

Editing rules

Few would dispute that a basic aim of everyone who formulates questions for use in social research is to have their questions understood by respondents as intended. Standard methodological advice in the past has been to formulate questions in accordance with a list of principles of 'good practice' which have been codified from past experience, and then to pilot or trial these questions on a small sample of respondents (i.e. twenty to thirty) drawn from the target population. A list of editing rules is set out below. This list is an amalgamation of a number of the lists that have been advanced by other methodologists, together with a few additions which are necessitated by the conclusions reached in chapters 3 to 8 of this text. There can be little doubt that questions which satisfy all of the principles listed below would be more likely to work as the researcher intends them to work than would questions that fail to meet them. Nevertheless, it must be acknowledged that reliance upon these principles alone will not be enough to protect the researcher from formulating questions that fail to work as intended.

Editing rules to aid the formulation of questions
The following list is an amalgamation of lists prepared by: Cantril and Fried

(1944); Selltiz *et al.* (1965); Hunt *et al.* (1982) and, Belson (1986); plus the conclusions set out in chapters 3 to 8 of this text.

In the case of each question, the researcher should:

(a)   Make sure that the topic has been clearly defined.

(b)   Be clear both about the information that is required about the topic and the reason for wanting this information.

(c)   Make sure that the topic has been defined properly for the respondents by:
   — avoiding the use of 'blab' words (i.e. words that are so abstract or general that they lack specific empirical referents),
   — avoiding words that are unlikely to be understood by all respondents either because they are rarely used in everyday life, or are specialist (i.e. jargon) words.

(d)   Make sure that the question is relevant to respondents by:
   — using an appropriate filter,
   — avoiding asking for information respondents are likely to have forgotten,
   — avoiding hypothetical issues.

(e)   Make sure that the question is not biased by:
   — ensuring balance in the introduction to the question (e.g. some people like X, and some people dislike X. — Do you like X or dislike X?),
   — ensuring that sets of response options are complete,
   — ensuring that sets of response options are balanced,
   — avoiding using words that are likely to invoke stereotypical reactions.

(f)   Eliminate complexities that prevent respondents from easily assimilating the meaning of the question by:
   — avoiding asking 2 or more questions at once,
   — avoiding the use of words that have several meanings,
   — checking whether the question has been worded as simply as possible,
   — avoiding the use of too many 'meaningful' words in the one question,
   — avoiding the use of qualifying clauses and phrases and the addition of complicating instructions which cause respondents to start to answer, before they have been exposed to the whole question — if qualifying clauses and phrases have to be used, they should be placed at the beginning rather than at the end of the question,
   — making sure that the question is as short as possible,
   — avoiding the use of both negatives and double negatives.

(g)   Ensure that respondents understand what *kind* of answer is required by:
   — setting the question in context,

— informing respondents why the question is being asked,
— informing respondents what will be done with the information they give,
— specifying the perspective that respondents should adopt.

Piloting questions

There is an emerging consensus among survey methodologists that piloting questions on a small sample of respondents drawn from the target population is more useful for uncovering aspects of questions that will cause interviewers to have difficulty than for discovering whether or not the respondents interpret the questions as intended. Even so, interviewers' impressions are an indirect source of information about how the respondents 'see' questions and several suggestions have been made to improve this channel of information to the researcher.

In the past, researchers have been content to instruct interviewers to note those questions that respondents have difficulty with — that is, 'hesitate over', 'laugh at', 'ask for clarification', etc. This is really asking a lot from interviewers, who have more than enough to concentrate upon when interviewing respondents. In response to this problem, DeMario (1983:101) has proposed that interviewers work in pairs when piloting questions, so that one of them is free to concentrate fully on conducting the interview while the other is free to listen to and observe both the interviewer's and the respondent's behaviour. The idea is that this procedure will lessen the chance that interviewer 'overload' will cause the researcher to miss any evidence of respondent difficulty.

Concerned over the same issue, Converse and Presser (1986) suggest that interviewers who carry out pilot surveys should be encouraged to make copious notes in the margins of the questionnaires while they are doing the interviews and that they should take part in group discussions once they have completed them, to help identify problem questions. They also recommend that interviewers should be systematically asked:

(a)   Did any of the questions seem to make respondents uncomfortable?
(b)   Did you have to repeat any questions?
(c)   Did the respondents misinterpret any questions?
(d)   Which questions were the most difficult or awkward for you to read? Have you come to dislike any specific questions? Why?
(e)   Did any sections seem to drag?
(f)   Were there any sections in which you felt that the respondents would have liked the opportunity to say more?

And Fowler and Mangione (1990:93) suggest that pilot interviews should be tape-recorded so that a check can later be made of the number of times each question is read exactly as written, the number of times respondents ask for clarification and the number of times 'probing' was required before respondents gave adequate answers. Fowler and Mangione (1990:91) state that:

> We think identifying questions that generate a high rate of probing and improving them before finalizing the questionnaire is one of the most fruitful ways to reduce interviewer-related error in surveys.

Question testing

Three techniques have been developed that fit under the general rubric 'question testing procedures'. Unlike piloting, which usually involves trialling the whole questionnaire or interview schedule, these procedures usually limit attention to the in-depth testing of no more than six or seven questions at a time.

Asking respondents to rephrase questions in their own words

This procedure was first used by Nuckols (1953) who presented nine selected questions from 'The Quarters Polls' to a small sample of respondents. After each question had been presented and answered in the normal way, the respondents were asked to state, in their own words, the meaning of the questions as precisely as they could. The respondents' interpretations were recorded verbatim and later coded into one of the following four categories:

(a) fully correct — leaving out no vital parts;
(b) generally correct — no more than one part altered or omitted;
(c) partially wrong — but indicating that the respondent knew the general subject of the question;
(d) completely wrong and no response.

Nuckols admits that the ability of a person to paraphrase a question does not necessarily entail comprehension of its meaning. On the other hand, Nuckols argues that if respondents give faulty interpretations, it seems fairly safe to conclude that they have misinterpreted it. Not all methodologists would accept this argument. Belson (1981:14), for instance, puts forward the view that having to repeat a question in one's own words is a separate task from understanding the question. While the first might be within the capacities of some respondents, the second may not. If Belson is correct, Nuckols' procedure is likely to underestimate the extent to which respondents fail to understand a question.

The double interview

This procedure basically entails presenting each question that has been selected for testing to respondents in the normal way, and then, after it has been answered, to ask a series of questions designed to uncover the respondent's interpretations of the key concepts (see Cantril and Fried, 1944; Gordon, 1963 — cited by Belson, 1981:20; Belson 1981:390–395, 1986:29–32).

Belson and his colleagues have put a lot of effort into developing the double interview procedure. They begin (1986:30–31) with a standard pilot interview after which the interviewer continues the interview to test three to four questions. For each question to be tested, the interviewer starts by reading the question to the respondent again along with the respondent's original answer. The interviewer then asks the respondent to explain how he or she arrived at that answer. If necessary, the interviewer probes extensively for a full explanation in the respondent's own words:

'Now I want you to think back and tell me exactly how you arrived at that answer...'
e.g. 'What led you to answer...'

In this way, the interviewer asks a set of specific questions that the researcher has designed to find out how respondents interpret the key concepts. For a question such as, 'How many people are there in your household?', check questions might be:

When you answered that question were you giving a rough count or an exact count?
Did you include yourself in the count?
What period of time were you referring to — right now, a week ago...?
Did you exclude anyone — e.g., babies, family members who were away, lodgers, parents living with the family, etc.?

Asking respondents to think aloud as they answer each question

This approach rests on the principle of having respondents think aloud as they are formulating answers to the questions selected for in-depth investigation (see, Hunt *et al.* 1982; and Jabine *et al.*, 1984 — discussed by Fowler and Mangione, 1990:92). The interviewer either records the respondents' verbalisations or asks the respondents to write them down. Later, independent coders classify this material according to the kinds of difficulties experienced by the respondents.

Hunt *et al.* (1982) used both the 'double interview' and 'think aloud' procedures to test the same set of questions on two accidental store samples. They also used the think aloud method to test the same questions in a random sample of telephone respondents. The two methods produced very similar results with the store samples. And the 'think aloud' procedure produced better results when used with the telephone sample than when used with the store sample. Unfortunately, Hunt and his colleagues did not use the 'double interview' procedure with a telephone sample so we do not know if the 'double interview' method would have also worked better with the telephone sample. It is possible that people who had gone to the store to shop were too preoccupied to attend carefully to questions. If this were the case, the 'double interview' procedure would show the same improvement as the 'think aloud' method did when used with a telephone sample. This is one of those issues that calls for further investigation.

Summary

All too often, survey questions fail to work as they are intended to. Although the use of editing rules may reduce the number of problematic questions that are used, their use should not be seen as a guarantee that all potential problems will be avoided. And while no one would argue against piloting questions before they are put to serious use, it does appear that piloting questions is more useful for identifying interviewer difficulties than it is for identifying problems relating to respondent comprehension. The in-depth testing of both key concepts and problematic questions is an indispensable addition to social research. To date, three question testing procedures have been developed. These are: having respondents rephrase questions in their own words; the 'double interview' procedure, in which respondents first answer a question and are then asked how they arrived at their answer; and having respondents think aloud as they answer questions. There is as yet little evidence to hold that any one of these procedures is better than the others. In the absence of such evidence, the soundest recommendation would be to employ at least two of them whenever possible.

Chapter 13

*C*ONCLUDING COMMENTS

Over the years, social researchers have become more and more reliant upon verbal data and this trend does not seem to be in any danger of reversing. Although the procedures that have been used to collect verbal data are probably no worse than the procedures that have been used to collect other kinds of data (e.g. observational procedures, unobtrusive measures of physical phenomena) it is still worth our while to make every effort to improve both their validity and their reliability. The position that has been taken, in this text, is that the best way to improve the quality of the verbal data we collect is through a better understanding of the nature of question-answer behaviour.

It has been a basic contention that factors which affect the way questions work cannot be understood in isolation from the context in which they are employed. This position has been adopted because human communication is seen to be reflexive in character. Human beings take one another's viewpoint into account when interpreting each other's verbal behaviour. Respondents' answers reflect what they assume the researcher wants to know as well as what they assume the researcher will do with the information they give. Among other things, these principles imply that respondents should be seen as constantly formulating interpretations of the researcher's behaviour which, in turn, constantly influence their own behaviour toward the researcher. They also imply that it is wrong to treat respondents as if they are passive players reacting only to the researcher's demands. It is more fruitful to see respondents as active agents engaged in the task of trying to make sense of the questions that are put to them. They should also be seen as active agents who are constantly trying to exercise some control over the situations in which they find themselves.

The model of question–answer behaviour that was first presented in chapter 2 represents an attempt to integrate these insights. In the subsequent exploration of this model (chapters 3–6), three issues were stressed as being especially important if answers are to be interpretable and comparable. First, it is clearly important that all respondents have the same idea of what a question is about — in other words, they should define the topic in the same way. Second, it is important to establish that respondents are likely to actually have the required information — that is, that a question is relevant to them. And, third, it is important that the researcher specify the perspective that respondents should adopt when framing their answers. Even though these issues have been stressed many times, they are emphasised again here for two reasons: first, because they are so important, and second to reinforce their links with the symbolic interaction theoretical framework that has been employed.

The requirement that all respondents define the topic in the same way demands that a number of concerns have to be addressed. In chapter 3 it was noted that all topics are multidimensional. This means, in the case of any particular topic, that unless the researcher both stipulates and defines the dimension(s) upon which they should focus, different respondents can (a) focus on different dimensions or combinations of dimensions, and (b) define the different dimensions quite differently.

When a topic has been poorly defined (which usually means defined in 'general' or 'abstract' terms without empirical referents), respondents are likely both to look for contextual clues to help them interpret the question and to modify the question to make it more relevant to themselves. They are also more likely to be influenced by format characteristics. Thus Payne (1951, chapter 8) concludes that difficult and abstract closed questions are prone to 'recency' effects (i.e. the tendency for respondents to endorse the last response option they hear). And Schwarz and Hippler (1987) make the point that the severity of response biases is likely to be positively related to how clearly the topic has been defined for the respondents. Likewise, the 'specific-to-general' question effects discussed by Strack and Martin (1987) and McClendon and O'Brien (1988 — see chapter 5, section IIIi), can be seen as arising because respondents use the content of the specific questions to help them interpret the general questions. Similarly, the tendency for respondents to be influenced by the range covered by a set of response categories is another example of how respondents seize upon tangential cues to help them interpret poorly defined topics (Schwarz *et al.*, 1985; Schwarz and Hippler, 1987). The tendency for answers to open questions to be much more diverse than answers to corresponding closed questions is also likely to be the result of the difficulty that respondents have when trying to interpret open questions (Campbell, 1945; Schuman and Presser, 1979a).

Just as important as whether respondents have defined a topic the same way is whether or not the researcher has any reason to believe that respondents do, in fact, have the information being sought by the researcher. Many of the problems discussed in the preceding chapters arose because respondents were simply not likely to have the information which was relevant to the topic and consequently were likely to have a very poor understanding of it. Response effects, for example, are more likely to occur when responses do not reflect well-based attitudes and beliefs. Respondents should be encouraged to admit that they do not have the information being sought when this is the case.

Almost all of the problems that result when respondents do not understand a question properly lessen in severity when we take care to make sure that there are grounds for believing the respondents are likely to have the information we want.

It must be accepted that memory traces and cues fade over time so that eventually most, if not all, events will be forgotten. This applies to all events — even though the time it takes for the memory traces associated with some events to fade may be longer than the time it takes for other events. Although, there are several techniques that can be used to help respondents recall information from their memories (see chapter 7), the researcher should avoid asking respondents for information that they can have little hope of remembering.

It should also be recognised that respondents will only give information to the researcher if they want to. But again, the researcher is not entirely at the mercy of fate. For example, Dillman's (1978) advice to maximise respondent rewards and minimise respondent costs is useful. In addition, a number of techniques that can be employed to lessen fears of social, political or economic sanctions have been discussed in chapter 9.

No matter how clearly the researcher defines a topic, and how carefully the researcher establishes whether it is reasonable to assume that the respondents have the information required and are willing to give the researcher honest answers, communication between respondents and the researcher will collapse if the researcher is unable to properly interpret the respondents' answers. Further, if the researcher cannot properly interpret the respondents' answers, different respondents' answers will not be meaningfully comparable with one another.

Many researchers seem to believe respondents naturally define a topic in the same way and employ the same perspective to frame an answer to a question if they are allowed to do these things for themselves (perhaps because they assume that their respondents have all been socialised in the same culture and have all had similar life experiences). The evidence suggests, however, that respondents typically adopt both a variety of definitions of the topic and a variety of perspectives when the topic is not properly defined and a response framework has not been explicitly specified. This is not very surprising since both topics and response frameworks are multidimensional and respondents inevitably have a large number (perhaps an infinite number) of degrees of freedom when left to their own devices. The solution to this problem is for the researcher to clearly define the topic for the respondents and to clearly stipulate the response framework which should be used (i.e. the kinds of answers that they should give). Obviously, the way the topic is defined and the response framework that is stipulated should relate to the researcher's reason for asking the question in the first place.

Some researchers may have trouble accepting the conclusion that they should both define the topic for respondents and tell them what kinds of answers are required — especially researchers who operate on the assumption that there are 'real' facts out there waiting to be discovered. Yet the assumption that we ever discover 'real' facts, that the data speak for themselves, has never been sound. Even in the case of an open question, interviewers need to have a good idea of why a question is being asked so that they can both recognise inadequate or irrelevant answers and be able to 'probe' to correct any deficiencies (Campbell, 1945; Schuman and Presser, 1979a). If open questions are used, and if the respondents are not told what kinds of answers to give, the researcher will have to invent codes after the responses have been given. This raises the problem of how the researcher can be certain that the 'correct' response categories have been identified or abstracted. It makes no sense for a researcher to ask respondents which categories should be employed. Such a course would merely introduce the likelihood of an infinite regression as the researcher confronts the problem of coding the respondents' second lot of answers.

The heart of the matter is that we must accept that *we do impose either our own view of reality, or our guesses about our respondents' views of reality, upon our respondents' answers* whether we admit it or not. The only issue is how self-conscious are we when we do this. Some might happily impose their own response options upon their respondents and force their respondents to answer their questions in terms of these response options, regardless of whether or not their respondents feel comfortable with them. Others might choose to act as if they are discovering (in an absolute way) their respondents' truth. This text has taken a middle course. It recommends that the researcher specify the perspective that should be employed and then complement this by setting up conditions that would encourage respondents to indicate when they think that the kind of answers they have been asked to give are inappropriate to their situations as they see them. In this, the symbolic interactionist tenet that human communication is systemic and reflexive in character is taken seriously.

In conclusion, the core task that has been confronted in this text has been that of increasing the validity of the questions used in social research. The aim has been to improve our ability to collect data that are relevant to our purposes, can be properly interpreted, and can be sensibly compared.

THE 'TAP' PARADIGM FOR CONSTRUCTING QUESTIONS

The key principles explicated in this text can be summarised under the acronym: 'TAP'. Since 'Tapping' valid, reliable, respondent information is the primary aim underlying the use of questions in social research, the 'TAP' acronym is a useful reminder of the three issues that researchers should keep in mind when they are constructing questions for interviews and question-naires.

Topic
The topic should be properly defined so that each respondent clearly understands what is being talked about.

Applicability
The applicability of the question to each respondent should be established: respondents should not be asked to give information that they do not have.

Perspective
The perspective that respondents should adopt, when answering the question, should be specified so that each respondent gives the same kind of answer.

References

Akiyama, M.M., W.F. Brewer and E.J. Shoben (1979), 'The Yes-No Question Answering System and Statement Verification', *Journal of Verbal Learning and Verbal Behaviour* 18: 365–380.

Alexander, C.S. and H.J. Becker (1978), 'The Use of Vignettes in Survey Research', *Public Opinion Quarterly* 42: 93–104.

Allport, G. (1935), 'Attitudes', in C. Murchison (ed.), *Handbook of Social Psychology*, Clark University Press, pp. 798–844, reissued 1966, NY: Russell and Russell.

Alwin, D.F. and J.A. Krosnick (1985), 'The Measurement of Values in Surveys: A Comparison of Ratings and Rankings', *Public Opinion Quarterly* 49: 535–552.

Andrews, F.M. (1984), 'Construct Validity and Error Components of Survey Measures: A Structural Modelling Approach', *Public Opinion Quarterly* 48: 409–442.

Arkin, R.M. and E.A. Lake (1983), 'Plumbing the Depths of the Bogus Pipeline: A Reprise', *Journal of Research in Personality* 17: 81–88.

Bachman, J.G. and P.M. O'Malley (1981), 'When Four Months Equal a Year: Inconsistencies in Student Reports of Drug Use', *Public Opinion Quarterly* 45: 536–548.

Baddeley, A. (1979), 'The Limitations of Human Memory: Implications for the Design of Retrospective Surveys', in L. Moss and H. Goldstein (eds), *The Recall Method in Social Surveys*, Studies in Education 9, University of London, Institute of Education.

Barath, A. and C.F. Cannell (1976), 'Effect of Interviewer's Voice Intonation', *Public Opinion Quarterly* 40: 470–473.

Bardo, J.W., S.R. Stelber and D.J. Bardo (1976), *Probing a Collective Unconsciousness: How Sociologists Measure Attitudes*, Paper presented at the Annual Meeting of the North Central Sociological Association.

Bardo, J.W., S.J. Yeager and M.J. Klingsporn (1982a), 'Preliminary Assessment of Format-specific Central Tendency and Leniency Error in Summated Rating Scales', *Perceptual and Motor Skills* 54: 227–234.

Bardo, J.W. and S.J. Yeager (1982b), 'Note on Reliability of Fixed-response Formats', *Perceptual and Motor Skills* 54: 1163–1166.

Bardo, J.W. and S.J. Yeager (1982c), 'Consistency of Response Style Across Types of Response Formats', *Perceptual and Motor Skills* 55: 307–310.

Barton, A.H. (1958), 'Asking the Embarrassing Question', *Public Opinion Quarterly* 22: 67–68.

Beighley, K.C. (1952), 'Experimental Study of the Effects of Four Speech Variables on Listening Comprehension', *Speech Monographs* XIX: 249–258.

Belson, W. and J.A. Duncan (1962), 'A Comparison of the Check-list and Open Response Questioning systems', *Applied Statistics* 11: 120–132.

Belson, W.A. (1981), *The Design and Understanding of Survey Questions*, Aldershot: Gower.

Belson, W. (1986), *Validity in Social Research*, Aldershot: Gower.

Bem, D.J. (1978), 'Self-perception Theory', pp. 221–282 in Leonard Berkowitz (ed.), *Cognitive Theories in Social Psychology*, New York: Academic Press.

Bendig, A.W. (1953), 'The Reliability of Self-ratings as a Function of the Amount of Verbal Anchoring and the Number of Categories on the Scale', *The Journal of Applied Psychology* 37: 38–41.

Benney, M., D. Riesman and S.A. Star (1956), 'Age and Sex in the Interview', *American Journal of Sociology* LXII: 143–152.

Benson, L.E. (1941), 'Studies in Secret-ballot Technique', *Public Opinion Quarterly* 5: 79–82.

Berg, I.A. and G.M. Rapaport (1954), 'Response Bias in an Unstructured Questionnaire', *Journal of Psychology* 38: 475–481.

Bilmes, J. (1975), 'Misinformation in Verbal Accounts: Some Fundamental Considerations', *Man* 10: 60–71.

Bishop, G.F. (1987a), 'Experiments with the Middle Response Alternative in Survey Questions', *Public Opinion Quarterly* 51: 220–232.

Bishop, G.F. (1987b), 'Context Effects on Self-perceptions of Interest in Government and Public affairs, chapter 10 in H. Hippler, N. Schwarz and S. Sudman (eds), *Social Information Processing and Survey Methodology*, NY: Springer-Verlag.

Bishop, G.F., R.W. Oldendick and A.J. Tuchfarber (1978), 'Effects of Question Wording and Format on Political Attitude Consistency', *Public Opinion Quarterly* 42: 81–92.

Bishop, G.F., R.W. Oldendick, A.J. Tuchfarber and S.E. Bennett (1980), 'Pseudo-opinions on Public Affairs', *Public Opinion Quarterly* 44: 198–209.

Bishop, G.F., R.W. Oldendick and A.J. Tuchfarber (1983), 'Effects of Filter Questions in Public Opinion Surveys', *Public Opinion Quarterly* 47: 528–546.

Bishop, G.F., R.W. Oldendick and A.J. Tuchfarber (1984), 'What Must My Interest in Politics be if I Just Told You "I Don't Know"?' *Public Opinion Quarterly* 48: 510–519.

Bishop, G.F., A.J. Tuchfarber and R.W. Oldendick (1986), 'Opinions on Fictitious Issues: The Pressure to Answer Survey Questions', *Public Opinion Quarterly* 50: 240–250.

Bittner, E. (1983), 'Realism in Field Research', in R.M. Emerson (ed.), *Contemporary Field Research*, Illinois: Waveland Press.

Blair, E., S. Sudman, N.M. Bradburn and C. Stocking (1977), 'How to Ask Questions About Drinking and Sex: Response Effects in Measuring Consumer Behaviour', *Journal of Marketing Research* XIV: 316–321.

Blankenship, A.B. (1940), 'Does the Question Form Influence Public Opinion Poll Results?' *Journal of Applied Psychology* 24: 27–30.

Bloor, M.J. (1983), 'Notes on Member Validation', in R.M. Emerson (ed.), *Contemporary Field Research*, Illinois: Waveland Press.

Blum, G.S., J.R. Graef, L.S. Hauenstein and F.T. Passini (1971), 'Distinctive Mental Contexts in Long-term Memory', *The International Journal of Clinical and Experimental Hypothesis* XIX(3): 117–133.

Blumer, H. (1965/66), 'Sociological Implications of the Thought of George Herbert Mead', *American Journal of Sociology* 71: 535–548.

Blumer, H. (1967), 'Society as Symbolic Interaction', in J. Manis and B. Meltzer (eds), *Symbolic Interaction: A Reader in Social Psychology*, Boston; Allyn and Bacon, 1st edition.

Blumer, H. (1969), *Symbolic Interactionism: Perspective and Method*, Englewood Cliffs Prentice-Hall.

Bogart, L. (1967), 'No Opinion, Don't Know and Maybe No Answer', *Public Opinion Quarterly* 31: 332–345.

Bradburn, N.M. (1982), 'Question-wording Effects in Surveys', in R. Hogarth (ed.), *New Directions for Methodology of Social and Behavioural Science: Question Framing and Response Consistency*, No. 11, San Francisco: Jossey-Bass.

Bradburn, N.M. and S. Sudman (1979), *Improving Interview Method and Questionnaire Design: Response Effects to Threatening Questions in Survey Research*, San Francisco: Jossey-Bass.

Bradburn, N.M., S. Sudman, E. Blair and C. Stocking (1978), 'Question Threat and Response Bias', *Public Opinion Quarterly* 42: 221–234.

Brenner, M. (1985), 'Survey Interviewing', chapter 2 in M. Brenner, J. Brown and D. Canter (eds), *The Research Interview: Uses and Approaches*, New York: Academic Press.

Briggs, C.L. (1986), *Learning How to Ask: A Sociological Appraisal of the Interview in*

Social Science Research, 'Studies in Social and Cultural Foundations in Language'#1, Cambridge: Cambridge University Press.

Brown, J. and B.G. Gilmartin (1969), 'Sociology Today: Lacunae, Emphases, and Surfeits,' *American Sociologist* 4: 283–291.

Butler, D. and U. Kitzinger (1976), *The 1975 Referendum*, London: Macmillan.

Campbell, A.A. (1945), 'Two Problems in the Use of the Open Question', *Journal of Abnormal and Social Psychology* 40: 340–343.

Cannell, C.F. (1977), *A Summary of Research Studies of Interviewing Methodology, 1959–1970*, Data Evaluation and Methods Research Series 2, Number 69, US Department of Health, Education and Welfare, Public Health Service, Health Resources Administration National Centre for Health Statistics, Rockville, Md.

Cannell, C.F., P.V. Miller and L. Oksenberg (1981), 'Research on Interviewing Techniques', chapter 11 in Samuel Leinhardt (ed.), *Sociological Methodology*, San Francisco: Jossey-Bass.

Cantril, H. (1965), *The Pattern of Human Concern*, New Brunswick, N.J.: Rutgers University Press.

Cantril, H. and E. Fried (1944), 'The Meaning of Questions', chapter 1 in Cantril *et al.*, *Gauging Public Opinion*, Princeton: Princeton University Press.

Cantril, H. and research associates in the Office of Public Opinion Research (1944), *Gauging Public Opinion*, Princeton: Princeton University Press.

Carver, M.E. (1935), 'Listening vs Reading', chapter IX in H. Cantril and G.W. Allport (eds), *The Psychology of Radio*, Harper Bros.

Chaikin, S. and A.H. Eagly (1976), 'Communication Modality as a Determinant of Message Persuasiveness and Message Comprehensibility', *Journal of Personality and Social Psychology* 34: 605–614.

Charters, W.W. Jr. and T.M. Newcomb (1968), 'Some Attitudinal Effects of Experimentally Increased Salience of a Membership Group', in H. Hyman and E. Singer (eds), *Readings in Reference Group Theory and Research*, NY: Free Press.

Cicourel, A.V. (1964), *Method and Measurement in Sociology*, NY: Free Press.

Cicourel, A.V. (1982), 'Interviews, Surveys and the Problem of Ecological Validity', *American Sociologist* 17: 11–20.

Clark, H.H. (1985), 'Language Use and Language Users', chapter 18 in G. Lindzey and E. Aronson (eds), *Handbook of Social Psychology*, vol. II, Random House. 3rd edition.

Cloud, J. and G.M. Vaughan (1970), 'Using Balanced Scales to Control Acquiescence', *Sociometry* 33: 193–202.

Collins, H.M. (1983), 'The Meaning of Lies: Accounts of Action and Participatory Research', chapter 3 in G.N. Gilbert and P. Abel (eds), *Survey Conference on Sociological Theory and Method*, Aldershot: Gower.

Converse, J.M. (1976), 'Predicting No Opinion in the Polls', *Public Opinion Quarterly* 40: 515–530.

Converse, J.M. (1984) 'Strong Arguments and Weak Evidence: The Open/Closed Questioning Controversy of the 1940s', *Public Opinion Quarterly* 48: 267–282.

Converse, J.M. and S. Presser (1986), *Survey Questions: Handcrafting the Standardized Questionnaire*, Sage University Papers, Series on Quantitative Applications in the Social Sciences, Series No. 07–063, Newbury Park, Cal: Sage.

Converse, J.M. and H. Schuman (1984), 'The Manner of Inquiry: An Analysis of Survey Question Form Across Organizations and Over Time', chapter 10 in C.F. Turner and E. Martin (eds), *Surveying Subjective Phenomena* (vol. 2), New York: Russell Sage Foundation.

Converse, P.E. (1964), 'The Nature of Belief Systems in Mass Politics', in D.E. Apter (ed.), *Ideology and Discontent*, Glencoe: Free Press.

Coombs, C.H. and L.C. Coombs (1976), ' "Don't Know": Item Ambiguity or Respondent Uncertainty', *Public Opinion Quarterly* 40: 497–514.

Corey, S.M. (1934), 'Learning from Lectures vs Learning from Readings', *Journal of Educational Psychology* 25: 459–470.

Cox, E.P. (1980), 'The Optimal Number of Response Alternatives for a Scale: A Review', *Journal of Marketing Research* XVII: 407–422.

Crutchfield, R.S. and D.A. Gordon (1947), 'Variations in Respondents' Interpretations of an Opinion-poll Question', *International Journal of Opinion and Attitude Research* 1: 1–12.

Davies, B. (1982), 'Talk in Conversational Interviews from the Point of View of the Participants', Paper presented at the 12th Annual Meeting of the Australian Social Psychologists Institute of Administration, University of New South Wales, Sydney, 1983.

Dawes, R.M. and T.L. Smith (1985), 'Attitude and Opinion Measurement', chapter 10 in G. Lindzey and E. Aronson (eds), *Handbook of Social Psychology*, Vol. II, NY: Random House, 3rd edition.

DeFleur, M. and F.R. Westie (1963/4), 'Attitude as a Scientific Concept', *Social Forces* 42: 17–31.

DeLamater, J. (1973), 'Methodological Issues in the Study of Premarital Sexuality', *Sociological Methods and Research* 2: 30–61.

DeLamater, J. (1982), 'Response-effects of Question Content', chapter 2 in W. Dijkstra and J. Van der Zouwen (eds), *Response Behaviour and the Survey Interview*, New York: Academic Press.

DeMaio, T.J. (ed.) (1983), 'Approaches to Developing Questionnaires', Statistical Policy Working Paper 10, Washington DC: Office of Management and Budget.

Deming, W.E. (1944), 'On Errors in Surveys', *American Sociological Review* 9: 359–369.

Denitch, B. (1972), 'Elite Interviewing and Social Structure: An Example from Yugoslavia', *Public Opinion Quarterly* 36: 143–158.

Deutscher, I. (1966), 'Words and Deeds: Social Science and Social Policy', *Social Problems* 13: 235-254.

Deutscher, I. (1973), *What We Say/What We Do: Sentiments and Acts*, Glenview Ill.: Scott Foresman and Co.

Dijkstra, W. and J. Van der Zouwen (1977), 'Testing Auxiliary Hypotheses Behind the Interview', *Annals of Systems Research* 6: 49-63.

Dillman, D. (1978), *Mail and Telephone Surveys: The Total Design Method*, NY: Wiley.

Dillon, J.T. (1982), 'The Multidisciplinary Study of Questioning', *Journal of Educational Psychology* 74: 147-165.

Dohrenwend, B.S. (1965), 'Some Effects of Open and Closed Questions on Respondents' Answers', *Human Organization* 24: 175-184.

Dohrenwend, B.S. (1970), 'An Experimental Study of Directive Interviewing', *Public Opinion Quarterly* 34: 117-125.

Dohrenwend, B.S., J. Colombotos and B.P. Dohrenwend (1968), 'Social Distance and Interview Effects', *Public Opinion Quarterly* 32: 410-422.

Dohrenwend, B.S. and S. Richardson (1963), 'Directiveness and Nondirectiveness in Research Interviewing', *Psychological Bulletin* 60: 475-485.

Doob, L.W. (1947), 'The Behaviour of Attitudes', *Psychological Review* 54: 135-156.

Douglas, J.D. (1985), *Creative Interviewing*, vol. 159, Sage Library of Social Research, London: Sage Publications.

Duffy, J.C. and J.J. Waterton (1984), 'Underreporting of Alcohol Consumption in Sample Surveys: The Effect of Computer Interviewing in Fieldwork', *British Journal of Addiction* 79: 303-308.

Dunnette, M.D., W.H. Uphoff and M. Aylward (1956), 'The Effect of Lack of Information on the Undecided Response in Attitude Surveys', *Journal of Applied Psychology* 40: 150-153.

Edwards, A.L. (1942), 'The Retention of Affective Experiences — A Criticism and Restatement of the Problem', *Psychological Review* 49: 43-54.

Emerson, R.M. (ed.) (1983), *Contemporary Field Research*, Illinois: Waveland Press.

Fee, J.F. (1981), 'Symbols in Survey Questions: Solving the Problems of Multiple Word Meanings', *Political Methodology* 7: 71-95.

Feldman, S. (1966), *Cognitive Consistency: Motivational Antecedents and Behavioural Consequents*, New York: Academic Press.

Ferber, R. (1956), 'The Effect of Respondent Ignorance on Survey Results', *Journal of American Statistical Association* 51: 576-587.

Festinger, L. (1954), 'A Theory of Social Comparison Processes', *Human Relations* 7: 117-140.

Fidler, D.S. and R.E. Kleinknecht (1977), 'Randomized Response Versus Direct Questioning: Two Data-collection Methods for Sensitive Information', *Psychological Bulletin* 84: 1045-1049.

Finn, R.H. (1972), 'Effects of Some Variations in Rating Scale Characteristics on the Means and Reliabilities of Ratings', *Educational and Psychological Measurement* 32: 255–265.

Fishbein, M. (ed.) (1967), *Readings in Attitude Theory and Measurement*, New York: Wiley.

Foddy, M. (1978), 'Role-taking in a Communication Task', *Personality and Social Psychology Bulletin* 4: 388–391.

Fowler, F.J. (1966), 'Education, Interaction and Interview Performance', Ph.D. dissertation, University of Michigan.

Fowler, F.J. Jr and T.W. Mangione (1990), *Standardized Survey Interviewing: Minimizing Interviewer-Related Error*, Newbury Park Cal.: Sage: Applied Social Research Methods Series #18.

Francis, J.D. and L. Busch (1966), 'What We Now Know About "I Don't Knows" ', *Public Opinion Quarterly* 30: 399–415.

Freed, M.N. (1964), 'In Quest of Better Questionnaires', *Personnel and Guidance Journal*: 187–188.

Frisbie, D.A. and D.C. Brandenburg (1979), 'Equivalence of Questionnaire Items with Varying Response Formats', *Journal of Educational Measurement* 16: 43–48.

Gallup, G. (1947), 'The Quintamensional Plan of Question Design', *Public Opinion Quarterly* 11: 385–393.

Gallup, G.H. (1978), *The Gallup Poll: Public Opinion, 1972–1977*, Wilmington, Del.: Scholarly Resources.

Garfinkel, H. (1967), *Studies in Ethnomethodology*, Englewood Cliffs, NJ: Prentice-Hall.

Gilbert, G.N. and P. Abel (eds) (1983), *Accounts and Action*, Aldershot: Gower.

Gilbert, G.N. and M. Mulkay (1983), 'In Search of the Action', chapter 1 in G.N. Gilbert and P. Abel (eds), *Accounts and Actions: Survey Conference on Sociological Theory and Method*, Aldershot: Gower.

Glass. A.L. and K.J. Holyoak (1986), *Cognition*, Random House.

Godden, D.R. and A.D. Baddeley (1975), 'Context-dependent Memory in Two Natural Environments: On Land and underwater', *British Journal of Psychology* 66: 325–331.

Goode, W.J. and P.K. Hatt (1952), *Methods in Social Research*, NY: McGraw-Hill.

Goody, E.N. (1978), 'Towards a Theory of Questions', in E.N. Goody (ed.), *Questions and Politeness: Strategies in Social Interaction*, Cambridge Papers in Social Anthropology, No. 8, Cambridge: Cambridge University Press.

Gordon, R.L. (1956), 'Dimensions of the Depth Interview', *American Journal of Sociology* LXII: 158–164.

Gordon, V.V. (1984) 'Life History Interviewing', Didactic Seminar, American

Sociological Association, 79th Annual Meeting, San Antonio, August 27th-31st.

Gordon, W.D. (1963), 'Double Interview', in *New Developments in Research*, London: Market Research Society with Oakwood Press.

Green, P.E. and V.R. Rao (1970), 'Rating Scales and Information Recovery — How Many Scales and Response Categories to Use?' *Journal of Marketing Research* 34: 33–39.

Grice, H.P. (1975), Logic and Conversation, in P. Cole and J. Morgan (eds), *Syntax and Semantics Vol. 3: Speech Acts*, New York: Academic Press.

Gritching, W. (1986), Public Opinion Versus Policy Advice, *Australian Psychologist* 21: 45–58.

Gross, E.J. (1964), 'The Effects of Question Sequence on Measures of Buying Interest', *Journal of Advertising Research* 4: 40–41.

Guest, L. (1962), 'A Comparison of Two-choice and Four-choice Questions', *Journal of Advertising Research* 2: 32–34.

Guttman, L. and E.A. Suchman (1947), 'Intensity and a Zero Point for Attitude Analysis', *American Sociological Review* 12: 57–67.

Hall, O. (1944), 'The Informal Organization of Medical Practice', unpub. PhD Dissertation, University of Chicago. Quoted in Buford Junker (ed.) (1960), *Field Work*, Chicago: University of Chicago Press: 5.

Hampleman, R.S. (1958), 'Comparison of Listening and Reading Ability of Fourth and Sixth Grade Pupils', *Elementary English* 35: 49–53.

Hartley, E. (1946), *Problems in Prejudice*, New York: King's Crown Press.

Haugh, O.M. (1951/2), 'The Relative Effectiveness of Reading and Listening to Radio Drama as Ways of Imparting Information and Shifting Attitudes', *Journal of Educational Research* 45: 489–498.

Helmstadter, G.C. (1970), *Research Concepts in Human Behaviour: Education, Psychology, Sociology*, NY: Appleton-Century-Crofts.

Henry, H. (1971), We Cannot Ask "Why", chapter 6.2 in H. Henry (ed.), *Perspectives in Management and Marketing Research*, London: Crossby Lockwood.

Hiller, P. (1973), 'The Subjective Dimension of Social Stratification: The Case of the Self-identification Question', *Australian and New Zealand Journal of Sociology* 9: 14–21.

Hippler, H.J. and G. Hippler (1986), 'Reducing Refusal Rates in the Case of Threatening Questions: The "Door-in-the-Face" Technique', *Journal of Official Statistics* 2: 25–33.

Hippler, H.J. and N. Schwarz (1986), 'Not Forbidding Isn't Allowing: The Cognitive Basis of the Forbid-allow Asymmetry', *Public Opinion Quarterly* 50: 87–96.

Hippler, H.J. and N. Schwarz (1987), 'Response Effects in Surveys', chapter 6 in H. Hippler, N. Schwarz and S. Sudman (eds), *Social Information Processing and Survey Methodology*, NY: Springer-Verlag.

Hippler, H.J. and N. Schwarz (1989), ' "No Opinion" Filters: A Cognitive Perspective,' *International Journal of Public Opinion Research* 1: 77–87.

Hitlin, R. (1976), 'Research Note: On Question Wording and Stability of Response', *Social Science Research* 5: 39–41.

Hobbs, J.R. and J.J. Robinson (1979), 'Why Ask?', *Discourse Processes* 2: 311–318.

Holdaway, E.A. (1971), 'Different Response Categories and Questionnaire Response Patterns', *Journal of Experimental Education* 40: 57–60.

Hovde, H.T. (1936), 'Recent Trends in the Development of Market Research', *American Marketing Journal* 3: 3.

Hovland, C.I. and Rosenberg, M.J. (ed) (1960), *Attitude Organization and Change*, New Haven NJ.: Yale University Press.

Hulbert, J. (1975), 'Information Processing Capacity and Attitude Measurement', *Journal of Marketing Research* 12: 104–106.

Hund, J.M. (1959), 'Changing Role in the Interview Situation', *Public Opinion Quarterly* 23: 236–246.

Hunt, S.D., R.D. Sparkman Jr. and J.B. Wilcox (1982), 'The Pretest in Survey Research: Issues and Preliminary Findings', *Journal of Marketing Research* XIX: 269–273.

Hunt, W.H., W.W. Crane and J.C. Wahlke (1964), 'Interviewing Political Elites in Cross-cultural Comparative Research', *American Journal of Sociology* 70: 59–68.

Hyman, H.H. et al. (1954), *Interviewing in Social Research*, Chicago: University of Chicago Press.

Hyman, H.H. and P.B. Sheatsley (1950), 'The Current Status of American Public Opinion', in J.C. Payne (ed.), *The Teaching of Contemporary Affairs*, Twenty-first Yearbook of the National Council of Social Studies, pp 11–34.

Jabine, T.B., M.L. Straf, J.M. Tanor and R. Tourangeau (eds) (1984), *Cognitive Aspects of Survey Methodology: Building a Bridge Between Disciplines*, Washington DC: National Academic Press.

Johnson, J.M. (1983), 'Trust and Personal Involvements in Fieldwork', in R.M. Emerson (ed.), *Contemporary Field Research*, Illinois: Waveland Press.

Jones, E.E. and H. Sigall (1971), 'The Bogus Pipeline: A New Paradigm for Measuring Affect and Attitude', *Psychological Bulletin* 76: 349–364.

Jordan, N. (1965), 'The "Asymmetry" of "Liking" and "Disliking": A Phenomenon Meriting Further Reflection and Research', *Public Opinion Quarterly* 29: 315–322.

Joshi, A.K. (1983), 'Varieties of Cooperative Responses in Question–Answer Systems', pp. 229–240 in F. Kiefer (ed.), *Questions and Answers*, Boston: Reidel Pub. Co.

Kahn, R.L. and C.F. Cannell (1957), *The Dynamics of Interviewing: Theory Technique and Cases*, New York: Wiley.

Kalton, G., M. Collins and L. Brook (1978), 'Experiments in Wording Opinion Questions', *Applied Statistics* 27: 149–161.

Kalton, G., J. Roberts and D. Holt (1980), 'The Effects of Offering a Middle Response Option with Opinion Questions', *The Statistician* 29: 65–78.

Katz, D. (1942), 'Do Interviews Bias Poll Results?' *Public Opinion Quarterly* 6: 248–268.

Katz, D. (1944), 'The Measurement of Intensity', chapter 3 in H. Cantril (ed.), *Gauging Public Opinion*, Princeton: Princeton University Press.

Katz, D. (1945/6), 'The Interpretation of Survey Findings', *Journal of Social Issues* 1/2: 32–43.

Katz, D. and H. Cantril (1937), 'Public Opinion Polls', *Sociometry* 1: 155–179.

Katz, J. (1983), 'A Theory of Qualitative Methodology: The Social System of Analytic Fieldwork', in R.M. Emerson (ed.), *Contemporary Field Research*, Illinois: Waveland Press.

Kearsley, G.P. (1976), 'Questions and Question Asking in Verbal Discourse: A Cross-Disciplinary Review', *Journal of Psycholinguistic Research* 5: 355–375.

Kibler, R.J. (1962), 'The Impact of Message Style and Channel in Communication', PhD Thesis, Ohio State University, University Microfilms Inc., Ann Arbor, Michigan. P 90 K 46.

Kidder, L.H. (1981), *Selltiz, Wrightsman and Cook's Research Methods in Social Relations*, NY: Holt Rinehart and Winston, 4th edn.

Kidder, L.H. and C.M. Judd (1986), *Research Methods in Social Relations*, NY: CBS Publishing Japan Ltd, 5th edn.

Kornhauser, A. and P.B. Sheatsley (1965), 'Appendix C: Questionnaire Construction and Interview Procedure', in C. Selltiz, M. Johoda, M. Deutsch and S. W. Cook, *Research Methods in Social Relations*, Rev. edn, London: Methuen.

Kraut, R.E. and E.T. Higgins (1984), 'Communication and Social Cognition', chapter 3 in R.S. Wyer Jr and T.K. Srull (eds), *Handbook of Social Cognition*, Hillsdale NJ: Laurence Erlbaum.

Krosnick, J.A. (1989), 'Question Wording and Reports of Survey Results: The Case of Louis Harris and Associates and Aetna Life and Casualty', *Public Opinion Quarterly* 53: 107–113.

Krosnick, J.A. and D.F. Alwin (1987), 'An Evaluation of a Cognitive Theory of Response-order Effects in Survey Measurement', *Public Opinion Quarterly* 51: 201–219.

Laing, A.M. (ed.) (1957), *Louder and Funnier: Anecdotes for Speakers*, London: Allen and Unwin.

LaPiere, R.T. (1934/5), 'Attitudes vs Actions', *Social Forces* 13: 230–237.

Laird, D.A. (1932), 'How the Consumer Estimates Quality by Subconscious Sensory Impressions', *Journal of Applied Psychology* 16: 241–246.

Lau, R.R., D.O. Sears and R. Centers (1979), 'The "Positivity Bias" in Evaluations of Public Figures: Evidence Against Instrument Artifacts', *Public Opinion Quarterly* 43: 347–358.

Laurent, A. (1972), 'Effects of Question Length on Reporting Behaviour in the Survey Interview', *Journal of the American Statistical Association* 67: 298–305.

Lazarsfeld, P.F. (1944), 'The Controversy Over Detailed Interviews — An Offer for Negotiation', *Public Opinion Quarterly* 8: 38–60.

Lazarsfeld, P.F. (1972a), 'The Art of Asking Why', chapter 8 in *Qualitative Analysis: Historical and Critical Essays*, Boston: Allyn and Bacon.

Lazarsfeld, P.F. (1972b), 'Some Principles of Classification in Social Research', chapter 10 in *Qualitative Analysis: Historical and Critical Essays*, Boston: Allyn and Bacon.

Lazarsfeld, P.F. and A.H. Barton (1962), 'Some General Principles of Questionnaire Classification', in P.F. Lazarsfeld and Morris Rosenberg (eds), *The Language of Social Research*, Ill.: Glencoe.

Lee, R.M. and C.M. Renzetti (1990), 'The Problems of Researching Sensitive Topics', *American Behavioural Scientist* 33: 510–528.

Lehman, D.R. and J. Hulbert (1972), 'Are Three-point Scales Always Good Enough?' *Journal of Marketing Research* IX: 444–446.

Lehnert, W.G. (1978), *The Process of Question Answering: A Computer Simulation*, Hillsdale, NJ: Erlbaum.

Lemkau, P.V. and G.M. Crocetti (1962), 'An Urban Population's Opinion and Knowledge About Mental Illness', *American Journal of Psychiatry* 118: 692–700.

Lenski, G. (1963), *The Religious Factor*, NY: Anchor.

Levin, I.P., S.K. Schnittjer and S.L. Thee (1988), 'Information Framing Effects in Social and Personal Decisions', *Journal of Experimental Social Psychology* 24: 520–529.

Link, H.C. (1943), 'An Experiment in Depth Interviewing on the Issue of Internationalism vs Isolationism', *Public Opinion Quarterly* 7: 267–279.

Locander, W.B. and J.P. Burton (1976), 'The Effect of Question Form on Gathering Income Data by Telephone', *Journal of Marketing Research* XIII: 189–192.

Lodge, M. (1981), *Magnitude Scaling: Quantitative Measurement of Opinions*, Sage University Paper, Series on Quantitative Application in the Social Sciences 07–025, Beverly Hills and London: Sage Publications.

Lodge, M. and B. Tursky (1981), 'The Workshop on the Magnitude Scaling of Political Opinion in Survey Research', *American Journal of Political Science* 25: 376–419.

Loftus, E.F. (1982), 'Interrogating Eyewitnesses — Good Questions and Bad', in R.M. Hogarth (ed.), *New Directions for Methodology of Social Science No. 11. Question Framing and Response Consistency*, San-Francisco Jossey-Bass.

Loftus, E.F., S.E. Fienberg and J.M. Tanur (1985), 'Cognitive Psychology Meets the National Survey', *American Psychologist* 40: 175–180.

Loftus, E.F., M.R. Klinger, K.D. Smith and J. Fiedler (1990), A Tale of Two Questions: Benefits of Asking More than One Question, *Public Opinion Quarterley* 54: 330–345.

Loftus, E.F., and W. Marburger (1983), Since the Eruption of Mt St Helens, Has Anyone Beat You Up? Improving the Accuracy of Retrospective Reports with Landmark Events, *Memory and Cognition* 11: 114–120.

Lyn, J. and A. Jay (1986), *Yes Prime Minister*, vol. 1, chapter 3, The Prime Ministerial Broadcast, London: BBC Publications.

McClendon, M.J. (1984), The Effects of No Opinion Filters on Don't Know Responses, Substantive Responses and Attitude Strength, Paper presented at 79th Annual Meeting, American Sociological Association, San Antonio, August 27th–31st.

McClendon, M.J. and D.J. O'Brien (1988), Question Order Effects on the Determinants of Subjective Well-Being, *Public Opinion Quarterly* 52: 351–364.

McFarland, S.G. (1981), Effects of Question Order on Survey Responses, *Public Opinion Quarterly* 45: 208–215.

McGuire, W.J. (1960), 'A Syllogistic Analysis of Cognitive Relationships' in Hovland, C.I. and M. Rosenberg (eds) *op. cit.*

McGuire, W.J. and C.V. McGuire (1982), Significant Others in Self-Space: Sex Differences and Developmental Trends in the Social Self, chapter 3 in J. Suls (ed.), *Psychological Perspectives on the Self*, Hillsdale NJ: Erlbaum.

McGuire, W.J. and A. Padawer-Singer (1976), 'Trait Salience in the Spontaneous Self-concept', *Journal of Personality and Social Psychology* 33: 743–754.

Manning, P.K. (1966), 'Occupational Types and Organized Medicine: Physicians Attitudes Toward the American Medical Association', unpub. PhD Thesis, Duke University.

Manning, P.K. (1966/7), 'Problems in Interpreting Interview Data', *Sociology and Social Research* 51: 302–316.

Marquis, K.H. (1970), 'Effects of Social Reinforcement on Health Reporting in the Household Interview', *Sociometry* 33: 203–215.

Marquis, K.H., J. Marshall and S. Oskamp (1972), 'Testimony Validity as a Function of Question Form, Atmosphere and Item Difficulty', *Journal of Applied Social Psychology* 2: 167–186.

Martin, E. (1986), *Report on the Development of Alternative Screening Processes for the National Crime Survey*, Washington, DC: Bureau of Social Science Research.

Matell, M.S. and J. Jacoby (1972), 'Is There an Optimal Number of Alternatives for Likert-scale Items?' *Journal of Applied Psychology* 56: 506–509.

The Melbourne *Age* (1985), 'P.M.'s Popularity Sinks While Peacock's Rises', Saturday, 6th July: 3.

Mellinger, G.D., C.L. Huffine and M.B. Balter (1982), 'Assessing Comprehension in a Survey of Public Reactions to Complex Issues', *Public Opinion Quarterly* 46: 97–109.

Menzel, H. (1978), 'Meaning — Who Needs It?' in Michael Brenner, P. Marsh and M. Brenner (eds), *The Social Contexts of Method*, London: Broom Helm.

Merton, R.K. (1957), *Social Theory and Social Structure*, NY: Free Press of Glencoe, rev. edn.

Miller, G.A. (1956), 'The Magical Number Seven, Plus or Minus Two: Some Limits on Our Capacity for Processing Information', *Psychological Review* 63: 81–97.

Mishler, E.G. (1986), *Research Interviewing: Context and Narrative*, Cambridge, Mass.: Harvard University Press.

Molenaar, N.J. (1982), 'Response-effects of "Formal" Characteristics of Questions', chapter 3 in W. Dijkstra and J. Van der Zouwen (eds), *Response Behaviour and the Survey Interview*, New York: Academic Press.

Monson, T.C. and M. Snyder (1977), 'Actors, Observers, and the Attribution Process: Toward a Reconceptualization', *Journal of Experimental Social Psychology* 13: 89–111.

Montgomery, A.C. and K.S. Crittenden (1977), 'Improving Coding Reliability for Open-ended Questions', *Public Opinion Quarterly* 41: 235–243.

Moore, J.C. Jr (1969), 'Social Status and Social Influence: Process Considerations', *Sociometry* 32: 145–158.

Morris, P. (1981), 'The Cognitive Psychology of Self Reports', chapter 8 in C. Antaki, *The Psychology of Ordinary Explanations of Social Behaviour*, New York: Academic Press.

Mostyn, B. (1985), 'The Content Analysis of Qualitative Research Data: A Dynamic Approach', chapter 6 in M. Brenner, J. Brown and D. Canter (eds), *The Research Interview: Uses and Approaches*, New York: Academic Press.

Murray J. and others (1974), *The Impact of the 1973–1974 Oil Embargo on the American Household*, Report No. 126, Chicago: National Opinion Research Center.

Nachman, S.R. (1984), 'Lies My Informants Told Me', *Journal of Anthropological Research* 40: 536–555.

Newstead, S.E. and J. Arnold (1989), 'The Effect of Response Format on Ratings of Teaching', *Educational and Psychological Measurement* 49: 33–43.

Nisbett, R.E. and T. D. Wilson (1977), 'Telling More Than We Can Know: Verbal Reports on Mental Processes', *Psychological Review* 84: 231–259.

Noelle-Neumann, E. (1970), 'Wanted: Rules for Wording Structured Questionnaires', *Public Opinion Quarterly* 34: 191–201.

Norman, D.A. (1973), 'Memory, Knowledge and the Answering of Questions', in R.L. Solso (ed.), *Contemporary Issues in Cognitive Psychology: The Layola Symposium*, Washington, DC: Winston (distributed by Halsted Press, Wiley).

Nowakowska, M. (1973), 'Perception of Questions and Variability of Answers', *Behavioural Science* 18: 99–108.

Nuckols, R.C. (1949/50), 'Verbi!' *International Journal of Opinion and Attitude Research* 3: 575–586.

Nuckols, R.C. (1953), 'A Note on Pre-Testing Public Opinion Questions', *Journal of Applied Psychology* 37: 119–120.

Oakley, A. (1979), *Becoming a Mother*, Oxford: Martin Robertson.

Oakley, A. (1981), 'Interviewing Women: A Contradiction in Term', chapter 2 in H. Roberts (ed.), *Doing Feminist Research*, Routledge and Kegan Paul.

Ottati, V.G., E.J. Riggle, R.S. Wyer Jr, N. Schwarz and J. Kuklinski (1989), 'Cognitive and Affective Bases of Opinion Survey Responses', *Journal of Personality and Social Psychology* 57: 404–415.

Palmer, G.L. (1943), 'Factors in the Variability of Response in Enumerative Studies', *Journal of the American Statistical Association* 38: 143–152.

Parry, H.J. and H.M. Crossley (1950), 'Validity of Responses to Survey Questions', *Public Opinion Quarterly* 14: 61–80.

Pawson, R. (1989), *A Measure for Measures: A Manifesto for Empirical Sociology*, London: Routledge.

Payne, S.L. (1949/50), 'Case Study in Question Complexity', *Public Opinion Quarterly* 13: 653–657.

Payne, S.L. (1951), *The Art of Asking Questions*, Princeton: Princeton University Press.

Petersen, K.K. and J.E. Dutton (1975), 'Centrality, Extremity, Intensity: Neglected Variables in Research on Attitude-behaviour Consistency', *Social Forces* 54: 393–414.

Peterson, R.A. (1984), 'Asking the Age Question: A Research Note', *Public Opinion Quarterly* 48: 379–383.

Phillips, D.L. (1971), *Knowledge From What: Theories and Methods in Social Research*, Chicago Rand McNally.

Platt, J. (1981), 'On Interviewing One's Peers', *British Journal of Sociology* 32: 75–91.

Potter, J. and M. Mulkay (1985), 'Scientists' Interview Talk: Interviews as a Techniques for Revealing Participants' Interpretative Practices', chapter 11 in M. Brenner, J. Brown and D. Canter (eds), *The Research Interview: Uses and Approaches*, New York: Academic Press.

Prendergast, S. and A. Prout (1980), 'What Will I Do . . .? Teenage Girls and the Construction of Motherhood', *Sociological Review* 28: 517–535.

Presser, S. (1984), 'Is Inaccuracy on Factual Survey Items Item-specific or Respondent-specific?' *Public Opinion Quarterly* 48: 344–355.

Ray, J.J. (1971), 'The Questionnaire Measurement of Social Class', *Australian and New Zealand Journal of Sociology* 7: 58–64.

Rich, M.C. (1979), 'Verbal Reports on Mental Processes: Issues of Accuracy and Awareness', *Journal of the Theory of Social Behaviour* 9: 29–37.

Riesman, D. and N. Glazer (1948/49), 'The Meaning of Opinion', *Public Opinion Quarterly* 12: 633–648.

Richardson, S.A. (1960), 'The Use of Leading Questions in Non-schedule Interviews', *Human Organization* 19: 86–89.

Robertson, S.P., J.B. Black and W.G. Lehnert (1985), 'Misleading Question Effects as Evidence for Integrated Question Understanding and Memory Search', chapter 6 in A.C. Graesser and J.B. Black (eds), *The Psychology of Questions*, Hillsdale NJ: Lawrence Erlbaum Ass.

Robinson, J.A. (1976), 'Sampling Autobiographical Memory', *Cognitive Psychology* 8: 578–595.

Roslow, S. and A.B. Blankenship (1939), 'Phrasing the Question in Consumer Research', *Journal of Applied Psychology* 23: 612–622.

Roslow, S., W.H. Wulfeck and P.G. Corby (1940), 'Consumer and Opinion Research: Experimental Studies on the Form of the Question', *Journal of Applied Psychology* 24: 334–346.

Rugg, D. (1941), 'Experiments in Wording Questions: II', *Public Opinion Quarterly* 5: 91–92.

Rugg, D. and H. Cantril (1944), 'The Wording of Questions', chapter II in H. Cantril (ed.), *Gauging Public Opinion*, Princeton: Princeton University Press.

Schuman, H. (1982), 'Artifacts are in the Mind of the Beholder', *American Sociologist* 17: 21–28.

Schuman, H. (1984), 'Question Forms, Wording and Context: Effects on Survey Responses', Didactic Seminar, American Sociological Association, 79th Annual Meeting, San Antonio, August 27th–31st.

Schuman, H. and J.M. Converse (1971/2), 'The Effects of Black and White Interviewers on Black Responses', *Public Opinion Quarterly* 35: 44–68.

Schuman, H. and O. D. Duncan (1973/4), 'Questions About Attitude Survey Questions', chapter 9 in H.L. Costner (ed.), *Sociological Methodology*, San Francisco: Jossey-Bass.

Schuman, H. and M.P. Johnson (1976), 'Attitudes and Behaviour', *Annual Review of Sociology* 2: 161–207.

Schuman, H., G. Kalton and J. Ludwig (1983), 'Context and Contiguity in Survey Questionnaires', *Public Opinion Quarterly* 47: 112–115.

Schuman, H. and J. Ludwig (1983), 'The Norm of Even Handedness in Surveys as in Life', *American Sociological Review* 48: 112–120.

Schuman, H. and S. Presser (1977), 'Question Wording as an Independent Variable in Survey Analysis, Special Issue: *Sociological Methods and Research* 6: 27–46 and reprinted in D.F. Alwin (ed.) (1977), *Survey Design and Analysis: Current Issues*, Sage Contemporary Social Science Issues No. 46 Beverley Hills: Sage.

Schuman, H. and S. Presser (1979a), 'The Open and Closed Question', *American Sociological Review* 44: 692–712.

Schuman, H. and S. Presser (1979b), 'The Assessment of "No Opinion" in Attitude Surveys', chapter 10 in Karl F. Schuessler (ed.), *Sociological Methodology*, San Francisco Jossey-Bass.

Schuman, H. and S. Presser (1980), 'Public Opinion and Public Ignorance: The Fine Line Between Attitudes and Non-attitudes', *American Journal of Sociology* 85: 1214–1225.

Schuman, H. and S. Presser (1981), *Questions and Answers in Attitude Surveys: Experiments on Question Form, Wording and Context*, New York: Academic Press.

Schuman, H., S. Presser and J. Ludwig (1981), 'Context Effects on Survey Responses to Questions About Abortion', *Public Opinion Quarterly* 45: 216–223.

Schuman, H. and J. Scott (1987), 'Problems in the Use of Survey Questions to Measure Public Opinion', *Science* 236: 957–959.

Schwarz, N. and G.L. Clore (1988), 'How Do I Feel About It?: The Informative Function of Affective States', chapter 3 in K. Fiedler and J. Forgas (eds), *Affect, Cognition and Social Behaviour*, Gottingen: C.J. Hogrete.

Schwarz, N. and H.J. Hippler (1987), 'What Response Scales May Tell Your Respondents: Informative Functions of Response Alternatives', chapter 9 in H.J. Hippler, N. Schwarz and S. Sudman (eds), *Social Information Processing and Survey Methodology*, NY: Springer-Verlag.

Schwarz, N., H.J. Hippler, B. Deutsch and F. Strack (1985), 'Response Scales: Effects of Category Range on Reported Behaviour and Comparative Judgments', *Public Opinion Quarterly* 49: 388–395.

Sears, D.O. and R.R. Lau (1983), 'Inducing Apparently Self-interested Political Preferences', *American Journal of Political Science* 27: 223–252.

Selltiz, C., M. Jahoda, M. Deutsch and S.W. Cook (1965), *Research Methods in Social Relations*, rev. edn., London: Methuen.

Sigelman, L. (1981), 'Question-order Effects on Presidential Popularity', *Public Opinion Quarterly* 45: 199–207.

Silvey, J. (1975), *Deciphering Data: The Analysis of Social Surveys*, London: Longman.

Simpson, R.H. (1944), 'The Specific Meaning of Certain Terms Indicating Differing Degrees of Frequency', *Quarterly Journal of Speech* 30: 328–330.

Skelton, V.C. (1963), 'Patterns Behind "Income Refusals" ', *Journal of Marketing* 27: 38–41.

Smith, E.R. and Miller, F.D. (1978), 'Limits on Perception of Cognitive Processes: A Reply to Nisbett and Wilson', *Psychological Review* 85: 355–362.

Smith, E.R.A.N. and P. Squire (1990), 'The Effects of Prestige Names in Question Wording', *Public Opinion Quarterly* 54: 97–116.

Smith, H.L. and H. Hyman (1950), 'The Biasing Effect of Interviewer Expectations on Survey Results', *Public Opinion Quarterly* 14: 491–506.

Smith, T.W. (1981), 'Qualifications to Generalized Absolutes: "Approval of Hitting" Questions on the GSS', *Public Opinion Quarterly* 45: 224–230.

Smith, T.W. (1984a), 'Nonattitudes: A Review and Evaluation', chapter 8 in C.F. Turner and E. Martin (eds), *Surveying Subjective Phenomena* (Vol. 2), New York: Russell Sage Foundation.

Smith, T.W. (1984b), 'Book Review: Questions and Answers in Attitude Surveys: Experiments on Question Form, Wording, and Context', by Howard Schuman and Stanley Presser, Academic Press, *American Journal of Sociology*: 228–230.

Smith, T.W. (1989), 'Random Probes of GSS Questions', *International Journal of Public Opinion Research* 1: 305–325.

Sorensen, R.C. (1972), *Adolescent Sexuality in Contemporary America*, NY: World Pub.

Sorensen, A.B. (1976), 'Estimating Rates from Retrospective Questions', chapter 6 in David R. Heise (ed.), *Sociological Methodology*, San Francisco: Jossey-Bass.

Spector, P.E. (1976), 'Choosing Response Categories for Summated Scales', *Journal of Applied Psychology* 61: 374–375.

Strack, F. and L.L. Martin (1987), 'Thinking, Judging and Communicating: A Process Account of Context Effects on Attitude Surveys', chapter 7 in H. Hippler, N. Schwarz and S. Sudman, *Social Information Processing and Survey Methodology*, NY: Springer-Verlag.

Strube, G. (1987), 'Answering Survey Questions: The Role of Memory', chapter 5 in H. Hippler, N. Schwarz and S. Sudman (eds), *Social Information Processing and Survey Methodology*, NY: Springer-Verlag.

Sudman, S. and N.M. Bradburn (1974), *Response Effects in Surveys: A Review and Synthesis*, NORC Monographs in Social Research, Chicago Adline.

Sudman, S. and N.M. Bradburn (1982), *Asking Questions: A Practical Guide to Questionnaire Design*, San Francisco: Jossey-Bass.

Sudman, S., N.M. Bradburn, E. Blair and C. Stocking (1977), Modest Expectations, Special Issue: *Sociological Methods and Research* 6; and reprinted in D.F. Alwin (ed.), *Survey Design and Analysis: Current Issues*, Sage Contemporary Social Science Issues No. 46 Beverley Hills: Sage.

Sudman, S., A. Finn and L. Lannom (1984), 'The Use of Bounded Recall Procedures in Single Interviews', *Public Opinion Quarterly* 48: 520–524.

The Melbourne *Age* (1988), 'The Tertiary Tax Debate: Dawkins Answers 'Age' Education Tax Questions', 18th May: 16.

Thomas, D.L., D.D. Franks and J.M. Calonico (1972), 'Role-taking and Power in Social Psychology', *American Sociological Review* 37: 605–614.

Thompson, D.M. and E. Tulving (1970), 'Associative Encoding and Retrieval: Weak and Strong Cues', *Journal of Experimental Psychology* 86: 255–262.

Tittle, C.R. and R.T. Hill (1967), 'Attitude Measurement and Prediction of

Behaviour: An Evaluation of Conditions and Measurement Techniques', *Sociometry* 30: 199-213.

Tourangeau, R. (1987), 'Attitude Measurement: A Cognitive Perspective', chapter 8 in H. Hippler, N. Schwarz and S. Sudman (eds), *Social Information Processing and Survey Methodology*, Springer-Verlag.

Tourangeau, R. and K.A. Rasinski (1988), 'Cognitive Processes Underlying Context Effects in Attitude Measurement', *Psychological Bulletin* 103: 299-314.

Tulving, E. (1974), 'Cue-dependent Forgetting', *American Scientist* 62: 74-82.

Turnbull, W. (1944), 'Secret vs. Non Secret Ballots', chapter V in H. Cantril (ed.), *Gauging Public Opinion*, Princeton: Princeton University Press.

Turner, C.F. (1984), 'Why Do Surveys Disagree? Some Preliminary Hypotheses and Disagreeable Examples', chapter 7 in C.F. Turner and E. Martin (eds), *Surveying Subjective Phenomena* (Vol. 2), New York: Russell Sage Foundation.

Tversky, A. and D. Kahneman (1974), 'Judgment Under Uncertainty: Heuristics and Biases', *Science* 185: 1124-1131.

Van der Zouwen, J. (1982), 'Hypotheses Behind the Sociological Interview: Test and Reformulation', chapter 8 in R. Cavallo (ed.), *Systems Methodology in Social Sciences Research: Vol. II*, Boston: Kluwer Nijhoff Publishing.

Van der Zouwen, J. and W. Dijkstra (1982), 'Conclusions', chapter 8 in W. Dijkstra and J. Van der Zouwen (eds), *Response Behaviour and the Survey Interview*, NY: Academic Press.

Ward, C.D. (1970), *Laboratory Manual in Experimental Social Psychology*, NY: Holt Rinehart and Winston Inc.

Warner, L.G. and M.L. DeFleur (1969), 'Attitude as an Interactional Concept: Social Constraint and Social Distance as Intervening Variables Between Attitudes and Action', *American Sociological Review* 34: 153-171.

Wax, R.H. (1979), 'Gender and Age in Fieldwork and Fieldwork Education: No Good Thing is Done by Any Man Alone', *Social Problems* 26: 508-522.

Weigel, R.H. and L.S. Newman (1976), 'Increasing Attitude-Behaviour Correspondence by Broadening the Scope of the Behavioural Measure', *Journal of Personality and Social Psychology* 33: 793-802.

Weiss, C.H. (1968), 'Validity of Welfare Mothers' Interview Responses', *Public Opinion Quarterly* 32: 622-633.

White, P. (1980), 'Limitations on Verbal Reports of Internal Events: A Refutation of Nisbett and Wilson and of Bem', *Psychological Review* 87: 105-112.

Whitten II, W.B. and J.M. Leonard (1981), 'Directed Search Through Autobiographical Memory', *Memory and Cognition* 9: 566-579.

Wieder, D. L. (1983), 'Telling the Convict Code', in R.M. Emerson (ed), *Contemporary Field Research*, Illinois: Waveland Press.

Wildt, A.R. and M.B. Mazis (1978), Determinants of Scale Response: Label Versus Position, *Journal of Marketing Research* 15: 261-267.

Williams, D.C., J. Paul and J.C. Ogilvie (1957), Mass Media, Learning and Retention, *Canadian Journal of Psychology* 11: 157–163.

Williams, J.A. (1964), Interviewer-Respondent Interaction: A Study of Bias in the Information Interview, *Sociometry* 27: 338–352.

Wilson, G.D. and D.K.B. Nias (1972), Measurement of Social Attitudes: A New Approach, *Perpetual and Motor Skills* 35: 827–834.

Wilson, T. D. and R.E. Nisbett (1978), The Accuracy of Verbal Reports About the Effects of Stimuli on Evaluations and Behaviour, *Social Psychology* 41: 118–131.

Woods, K.M. and J.R. McNamara (1980), Confidentiality: Its Effect on Interviewee Behaviour, *Professional Psychology* 5: 714–721.

Woolgar, S. (1976), Writing an Intellectual History of Scientific Development: The Use of Discovery Accounts, *Social Studies of Science* 6: 395–422.

Yeager, S.J. and J.W. Bardo (1983), 'The Impact of Format-specific Response Bias on Faces Scales', *Journal of Psychology* 114: 235–242.

Zdep, S.M. and I.N. Rhodes (1976), 'Making the Randomized Response Technique Work', *Public Opinion Quarterly* 40: 531–537.

Zeisel, H. (1958), *Say It With Figures*, London: Routledge and Kegan Paul.

Zeisel, H. (1985), *Say It With Figures*, Harper and Row, 6th edn.

Zetterberg, H.L. (1965), *On Theory and Verification in Sociology*, New Jersey: Bedminister Press, 3rd edn.

Zuckerman, H. (1972), *Interviewing an Ultra-elite*, *Public Opinion Quarterly* 36: 159–175.

Zurcher, L.A. (1977), *The Mutable Self: A Self Concept for Social Change*, 59 Sage Library of Social Research Beverley Hills: Sage.

Index

Acknowledgements

Any text is the product of the work of many people. The present text is no exception. I owe a great deal to a great many people. First there are the host of methodological writers who stimulated my interest in the problems associated with the use of verbal data in the social sciences: Lazarsfeld, Cannell, Cicourel, Deutscher, Phillips . . . the list is too long reproduce here. Second there are the hundreds of respondents who have been a challenge to every questionnaire and interview schedule I have constructed. Third there have been my colleagues, students and friends who have been willing to debate the different issues with me. And then there have been the editors at Cambridge University Press and their reviewers who have made numerous suggestions, almost all of which I have taken.